THE
ACTIVE
FILTER
HANDBOOK

Other TAB books by the author:

THE
ACTIVE
FILTER
HANDBOOK

TAB BOOKS
BLUE RIDGE SUMMIT, PA. 17214

FIRST EDITION

FIRST PRINTING—JUNE 1979

Copyright © 1979 by TAB BOOKS

Printed in the United States of America

Library of Congress Cataloging in Publication Data

Tedeschi, Frank P.
    The active filter handbook.

    Bibliography: p.
    Includes index.
    1. Electric filters, Active. I. title.
TK7872.F5T43   621.3815′32   79-12530
ISBN 0-8306-9788-8
ISBN 0-8306-1133-9 pbk.

Preface

This book is intended for electronics buffs who want to understand the theory, design, and application of active filter circuits. Active filters employ high gain amplifiers (usually linear ICs) with two passive components, resistors, and capacitors. Hence, active filters become low cost, miniature circuits that replace expensive, bulky circuit filters using inductors and capacitors.

Two basic active filter types are used throughout the book: Butterworth and Chebyshev. Those two types of filters are implemented with the Sallen Key and Infinite Gain Multiple Feedback operational amplifier circuits that yield low-pass, high-pass, and band-pass active filter circuits. Other types of active filters discussed throughout the book are the all-pass and notch filter.

Many examples of low-pass, high-pass, band-pass, and notch active filters are illustrated in complete detail, including frequency normalizing and de-normalizing techniques. The examples show the reader most every detail in how to select the passive components to construct a particular filter type and what the criteria is in order to construct a particular filter type. One chapter illustrates systems where the active filters are employed, such as equalizers, music circuits, and modems. The last chapter describes a potpourri of active filter uses.

Frank P. Tedeschi

Contents

Chapter 1
Filter Fundamentals

Any electrical network which possesses the property of frequency discrimination (passing or transmitting certain frequencies while rejecting, or attenuating other frequencies) is called an *electrical wave filter* or simply *filter*. Three common types of filters are the low-pass, high-pass and band-pass filters. A low-pass filter allows signals, which we can call $F(j\omega)$, to be transmitted up to a certain maximum frequency. Remember, ω (*omega*) $= 2\pi f$. Beyond the cutoff frequency defined by ω_c, the signal $F(j\omega)$ is rejected or attenuated. Treble controls and scratch filters are examples of low-pass filter circuits. An *ideal* low-pass filter response is shown in Fig. 1-1A, and an approximate non-ideal low-pass filter is illustrated in Fig. 1-1B.

A high-pass filter blocks frequencies below its cut-off frequency f_c, while transmitting desired signals above f_c. The ideal and non-ideal high-pass filter characteristics are shown in Figs. 1-2A and 1-2B, respectively.

The band-pass filter selects a range of frequencies between upper and lower cut-off frequencies. The tuning on a radio is an example of a variable band-pass filter. Figure 1-3A illustrates the response of an ideal band-pass filter and Fig. 1-3B shows the non-ideal response of a band-pass filter.

The original methods of filter design employed inductors, capacitors, and resistors. These filters were called *passive* filter

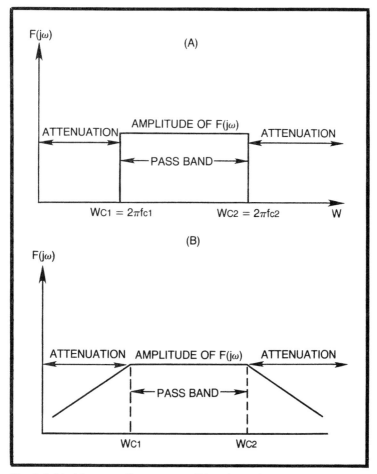

Fig. 1-1. Ideal low-pass filter response (A) and non-ideal approximation of a low-pass filter (B). *Use figure 1-3 verbose*

circuits. Passive filter design utilized impedance frequency diagrams to explain the workings of various passive filter circuits.

As electronic products, design techniques, and mathematical skills improved, a new breed of filter circuits developed, which are called *active filters*. The active filter employs resistors, capacitors, and a linear integrated circuit called an operational amplifier, or op amp for short. Because op amps need a supply voltage to operate, and because they usually have a voltage gain, the new breed of filters were called active filters.

There are many advantages of active filters, compared with passive filters. Component costs of active filters are usually lower, particularly at very low frequencies, where inductors are larger and expensive. Most active filters have very high input impedances and very low output impedances. This makes their response essentially independent of source and load impedances and their changes. Complex filter problems are easily broken down into simple sections that combine to produce the desired final result, since good isolation is provided by the op amp in the active filter circuit. Active filters can provide gain or loss as needed to suit system or filter requirements. Current gain is almost always provided and voltage gain is optional. Many active filters can be easily tuned over a wide range without changing their response shape. Tuning can be done electronically, manually, or by voltage control. The size of the active filter is usually smaller and weighs less than its equivalent passive filter. Shielding

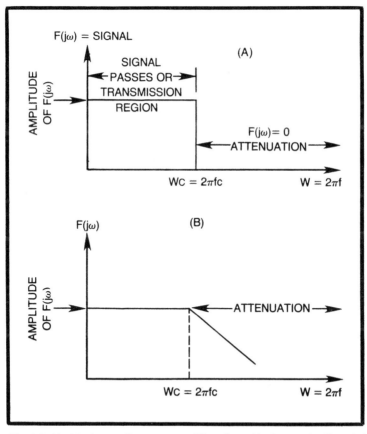

Fig. 1-2. Ideal high-pass filter response (A) and non-ideal approximation of a high-pass filter (B).

13

and coupling problems are essentially nonexistent in active filters. Compared with design methods of passive filters, the methods of active filter design are extremely easy.

However, active filters do have their limitations. A power supply is needed to operate the linear integrated circuit in the active filter. The operational amplifier employed sets definite signal limits, based on its input noise, its dynamic range, its bandwidth, and its ability to handle large signals. The filter designer also has to understand a different mathematical approach to active filter design. The new mathematical approach to active filter design utilizes the *voltage amplification transfer function*, which requires an understanding of the *operational approach to circuit analysis*. The remainder of this chapter outlines the mathematical approach used in active filter design.

DEFINITIONS AND CONCEPTS

Some of the important terms used in the mathematics of active filters are listed below.

asymptote: A line on the frequency response curve of the active filter that approximates the actual frequency response.

break frequency: The point on the frequency response curve where the active filter drops 3 dB, or 0.707 of its largest value on the way out of the passband. (This definition considers the active filter frequency response to roll off to a smaller value out of the passband. It is entirely possible for a break frequency to occur when the active filter will experience a rise in the response curve. Remember that the active filter contains an op amp which can generate gain in the active filter system.)

cascade: In active filters, the RC sections that are placed one after another.

cut-off frequency: See break frequency.

damping: An index (number) of the tendency of an active filter toward oscillation. Practical damping values range from 2 to 0, with zero damping as the value for an oscillation. Highly damped filter sections combine to produce smooth filters with good overshoot and transient response. Slightly damped filters combine to produce filters with sharp rejection characteristics.

decade: A 10 to 1 frequency interval.

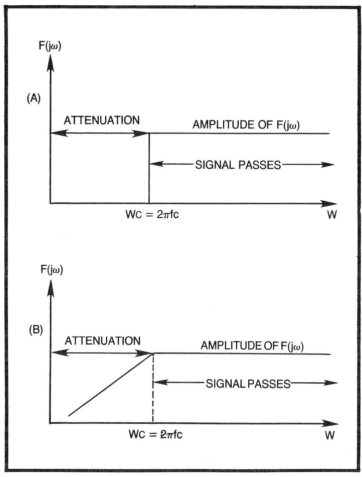

Fig. 1-3. Ideal band-pass filter response (A) and non-ideal approximation of a high-pass filter (B). *Use figure 1-2 verbage*

decibel or dB: Decibels are a logarithmic way of measuring gain or loss. Decibels are defined as $20 \log_{10}$ of a voltage ratio. In active filter design, dBs refer to only a voltage ratio.

gain: The ratio of output voltage to input voltage. Often, gain will be expressed by the symbol $N(j\omega)$ which refers to a straight voltage ratio. Also, the symbol $N_{dB}(j\omega)$ may be used, which means the voltage ratio has been changed to decibels. The symbol $N(j\omega)$ is read "N as a function of j omega."

normalization: The adjustment of component values and frequency response curve of a filter to a convenient frequency.

octave: A 2:1 frequency interval.

omega (ω): The symbol that defines angular velocity, which is associated with sinusoidal functions. Remember, $\omega = 2\pi f$.

order: The strength of the fall off of a filter with frequency. For example, a third-order low-pass filter falls off as the *cube* of frequency, which means at a 3 times 6 dB/octave = 18 dB/octave, or 3 times 20 dB/decade = 60 dB/decade. The number of energy storage capacitors in most active filters determines their order, so a third-order usually has three capacitors.

Q: The inverse of the damping value. In other words, $Q = 1/d$. The value of Q is used to measure the bandwidth of a second order bandpass section. Practical Q values range from less than one to several hundred.

scaling: Denormalizing a filter by changing its frequency or component values. Impedance level scaling is increased by multiplying all resistors and dividing all capacitors by a desired factor. To double the frequency, decrease all capacitor values by 2, or cut resistor values by 2. If you decrease by 2 both the resistor and capacitor values, the frequency will be quadrupled.

sensitivity: A measure of how accurate the component and operational amplifier tolerances must be to get a response within certain limits of what is desired. The sensitivities of the active filters illustrated throughout this book are quite good.

transfer function: The output of a filter compared to the input. The transfer function is usually expressed as the ratio of V_{OUT}/V_{IN}. The transfer function could include both the amplitude and phase information. The phase information refers to the phase shift from the input to the output.

TRANSFORMED IMPEDANCE

The operational approach of circuit analysis (which includes filters) requires little past knowledge of AC or DC circuit methods and requires some knowledge of algebra. The operational approach to dealing with resistors, inductors, and capacitors is to define the transformed impedance of R, L, and C, which is respectively R, sL, and $1/sC$. The transformed admittances of the components are the reciprocals of the transformed impedances, which are $1/R$, $1/sL$, and sC. Figure 1-4 shows the schematic representation of R, L, and C, and their transformed impedance.

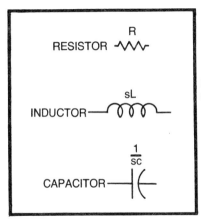

Fig. 1-4. Transform impedance of a resistor, inductor, and capacitor.

The quantity "s" is called the complex variable, and has a real part, σ (sigma), and an imaginary part, $j\omega$. Usually in active filter design the real part is omitted, and $j\omega$ is used in place of the complex variable s.

The circuit in Fig. 1-5 is a simple RC high-pass filter circuit of the first order (notice it has only one capacitor). The transformed impedance $Z(s)$ of the circuit is found by adding the transformed impedance of R and the transformed impedance of C, since the resistor and capacitor are in series with each other. Hence, the equation for the transformed impedance of the circuit in Fig. 1-5 is:

$$Z(s) = R + \frac{1}{sC} \qquad \textbf{Equation 1-1}$$

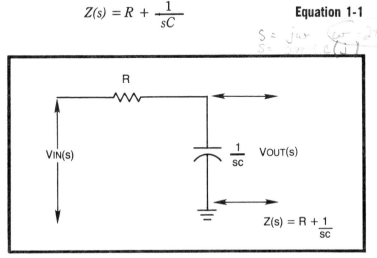

Fig. 1-5. High-pass filter circuit.

17

Examples of finding transformed impedances of other circuits are shown in Fig. 1-6. The simple series and parallel circuit principles of finding equivalent impedances is carried over into finding transformed impedance as illustrated in Fig. 1-6.

TRANSFER FUNCTION

Looking at Fig. 1-5, we can write an expression for the high-pass filter called a transfer function $T(s)$ defined as follows:

[1] $\quad T(s) = \dfrac{V_{OUT}(s)}{V_{IN}(s)}$

[2] $V_{OUT}(s) = I(s)\dfrac{1}{sC}$ *(resistor + C)*

$V_{IN} = \text{total voltage}$ [3] $V_{IN}(s) = I(s)\,Z(s) = I(s)\left(R + \dfrac{1}{sC}\right)$ *(R + C)*

[4] $T(s) = \dfrac{I(s)\left(\dfrac{1}{sC}\right)}{I(s)\left(R + \dfrac{1}{sC}\right)} = \dfrac{V_{OUT}(s)\;[2]}{V_{IN}(s)\;[3]}$

[5] $= \dfrac{\dfrac{1}{sC}}{\dfrac{sRC + 1}{sC}}$ ✓ *simplify*

simplify

[6] $= \dfrac{1}{1 + sRC}$

[7] $= \dfrac{\dfrac{1}{RC}}{\dfrac{1}{RC} + \dfrac{sRC}{RC}}$ *Divide by RC*

[8] $= \dfrac{\dfrac{1}{RC}}{s + \dfrac{1}{RC}}$

Equation 1-2

18

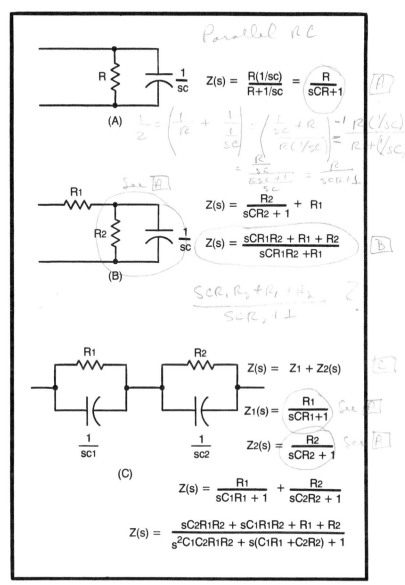

Fig. 1-6. Other transformed circuits.

Equation 1-2 represents the transfer function of the high-pass filter circuit in Fig. 1-5. The approach to active filters in this book will be to state or find the transfer function of an active filter, and from the transfer function determine the phase and amplitude characteristics of the active filter.

19

BODE DIAGRAMS

Once the transfer function for an active filter is determined, we next plot the amplitude and phase characteristic of the active filter. A very useful technique for obtaining a close approximation of the amplitude and phase curve from the transfer function is called the *Bode diagram*. Consider as a first exmaple the transfer function for a pure differentiating device:

$$G(s) = s \qquad \text{Equation 1-3}$$

The frequency response of this device is obtained by substituting $j\omega$ for s in the transfer function. The amplitude and phase shift are as follows:

$$N(\omega) = |G(j\omega)| = \omega \qquad \text{Equation 1-4A}$$

$$\phi(\omega) = G(j\omega) \; = +90° \qquad \text{Equation 1-4B}$$

where $|\;\;|$ indicates absolute value, and $<$ indicates angle in degrees. In Fig. 1-7, a table lists the values for $N(\omega)$, $N_{dB}(\omega)$. and $\phi(\omega)$ for various values of v. Following the table in Fig. 1-7 is a sample calculation of the data in the table for the value of $\omega = 10$.

□ SAMPLE CALCULATION:

$\omega = 10$ in the table of Fig. 1-7, find N(ω), N$_{dB}$(ω), and $\phi(\omega)$.

$N(\omega) = |G(j\omega)| = |10| = + 10$

$N_{dB}(\omega) = 20 \log_{10}(+10) = 20(1) = 20$ dB

$\phi(\omega) = \underline{|G(j\omega)} = \underline{/}$ phase angle associated with a differentiator

$\phi(\omega) = +90°$

At this time we can say only that the phase angle associated with a differentiating device is constant for all frequencies and has a value of +90°. Hence, the phase shift curve for a differentiating device is simply a flat line curve for all input frequencies, and its value is +90°.

The results in Table 1-1 are plotted on semilog graph paper. The quantity $N_{dB}(\omega)$ plotted against the frequency variable ω is a straight line as illustrated in Fig. 1-8. The slope of the straight line is measured as the change in dB level between two frequency points which are separated by a given distance along the horizontal axis. This distance cannot be measured in radians per second because a given distance at the low frequency end of the scale will represent a change of very few radians per second, while the same distance at the high frequency end will represent a change of very many radians per second. However, a given distance along the horizontal axis will

Table 1-1. Frequency response data for the transfer function G(s) = s.

ω RADS/SEC.	$N(\omega)$	$N_{dB}(\omega)$ IN dB	$\phi(\omega)$ DEGREES
0.0	0.0	-00	$+90$
0.1	0.1	-20	$+90$
0.5	0.5	-6.02	$+90$
1.0	1.0	0	$+90$
2.0	2.0	$+6.02$	$+90$
5.0	5.0	$+13.94$	$+90$
10.0	10.0	$+20$	$+90$
100.0	100.0	$+40$	$+90$
∞	∞	∞	$+90$

represent the same percentage change in frequency, no matter where that distance is taken along the frequency scale. Therefore, the slope of the $N_{dB}(\omega)$ curve is expressed in dB per the percentage change in frequency. A change in frequency of 100 percent from say $\omega = 1$ to $\omega = 2$ is called an octave, so for this curve the amplitude

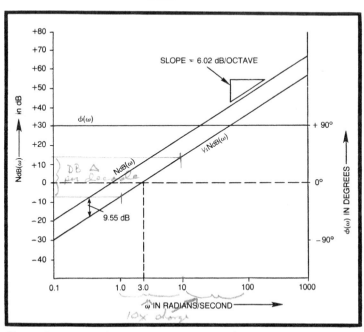

Fig. 1-7. Bode plot of $G_1(j\omega) = j\omega$ and $G_2(j\omega) = 1/3j\omega$.

$N_{dB}(\omega)$ changes at a rate of 6.02 dB/octave. However, for a very close approximation we refer to a 6 dB/octave change.

A change in frequency by a factor of 10 (from $\omega = 1$ to $\omega = 10$) is called a decade, so in this system the curve $N_{dB}(\omega)$ has a slope of 20 dB/decade. Remember 6 dB/octave is the same slope as 20 dB/decade.

The plot of $N_{dB}(\omega)$ is called a *Bode plot*, for the person who developed the diagram. Let us analyze the Bode plot and phase diagram of the function shown below:

$$G(s) = Ks \qquad \textbf{Equation 1-5}$$

This equation is the transfer function of the differentiating device multiplied by a constant K. The amplitude and phase shift are as follows:

$$N(\omega) = G(j\omega) = K\omega \qquad \textbf{Equation 1-6A}$$
$$\phi(\omega) = G(j\omega) = +90° \qquad \textbf{Equation 1-6B}$$

A table of frequency response data for this system would be the same as that shown in Fig. 1-7, except that the numbers in the $N(\omega)$ column would be K times those shown, and the numbers in the $N_{dB}(\omega)$ column would be those in Table 1-1 plus $20 \log_{10} K$. From this we conclude that if a transfer function is multiplied by a constant, the phase shift of the system is *unaffected*, but the amplitude ratio is increased (or decreased) by the constant factor. On the Bode diagram this increase (or decrease) shows up in the amplitude curve as a vertical shift by the number of decibels corresponding to the constant multiplier. For example, if $K = 1/3$, the amplitude curve would be shifted downward 9.55 dB, since $20 \log_{10}(1/3) = -9.55$ dB. The Bode plot of this system is shown on the graph in Fig. 1-7. However, note the slope of the response has not changed from the first example when $K = 1$, to the second example when $K = 1/3$.

As another example of the straight line Bode plot, consider the transfer function shown below:

$$G(s) = \frac{K}{s} \qquad \textbf{Equation 1-7A}$$

Equation 1-7A is the transfer function of an integrator device. The amplitude and phase shift of the integrator are found by substituting $j\omega$ for s in the transfer function. Hence, the transfer function becomes:

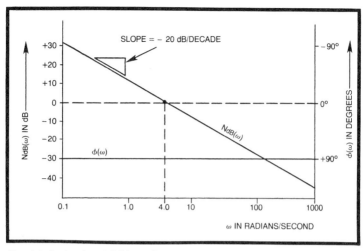

Fig. 1-8. Bode plot of G(jv) = 4/jω.

$$G(j\omega) = \frac{K}{j\omega} \qquad \textbf{Equation 1-7B}$$

Next, we find the amplitude and phase shift of this equation.

$$N(\omega) = |G(j\omega)| = \frac{K}{\omega} \qquad \textbf{Equation 1-8A}$$

$$\phi(\omega) = \angle G(j\omega) = -90° \qquad \textbf{Equation 1-8B}$$

The amplitude ratio is inversely proportional to ω, so that at $\omega = K$, then $N(\omega) = 1$, which is equal to 0 dB. The slope of the $N_{dB}(\omega)$ curve will be -6.02 dB/octave or -20 dB/decade, as shown on the curve of Fig. 1-8. The Bode diagram has been drawn for $K = 4$. At this time we can only say that the phase angle associated with the integrator device is constant for all frequencies and has a value of $-90°$, which is plotted on the graph of Fig. 1-8.

Let us find the frequency response (amplitude response) and phase shift of a double integrator. The transfer function of a double integrator is given in Equation 1-9.

$$G(s) = \frac{K}{s^2} \qquad \textbf{Equation 1-9}$$

We substitute $s = j\omega$ in the equation.

$$G(j\omega) = \frac{K}{(j\omega)^2} = \frac{K}{j^2\omega^2} = \frac{K}{-\omega^2}$$

23

For this transfer function the frequency response and phase shift are given by the following equations.

$$N(\omega) = |G(j\omega)| = \frac{K}{\omega^2} \qquad \textbf{Equation 1-10A}$$

$$\phi(\omega) = G(j\omega) = -180° \qquad \textbf{Equation 1-10B}$$

Again, the Bode plot for $N_{dB}(\omega)$ is a straight line having a negative slope, since $N(\omega)$ decreases with an increase in ω, but the slope will be -40 dB/decade, or -12 dB/octave, since an increase of one decade in ω causes $N(\omega)$ to change by a factor of 100. The amplitude and phase curves are drawn for $K = 4$ in Fig. 1-9. At this time we can only say that the phase angle associated with the integrator device is constant for all frequencies and has a value of $-80°$, which is plotted on the graph of Fig. 1-9.

A comparison of the curves in Fig. 1-7, 1-8, and 1-9 indicates that the Bode plot for a transfer function of the form:

$$G(s) = Ks^n \qquad \textbf{Equation 1-11}$$

In the above equation the value of n can be positive or negative. The quantity n has the following properties:

- [ ] $N_{dB}(\omega)$ will be a straight line having a slope of 20n dB/decade. Of course, if n is negative the slope of $N_{dB}(\omega)$ will be negative.
- [ ] $N_{dB}(\omega)$ will cross the zero dB line at the frequency $\omega = K^{-1}/n$.
- [ ] $\phi(\omega)$ will be constant at $90n°$.

Bode Diagrams of First Order Transfer Functions

We now consider transfer functions having Bode plots which are not straight lines, but which can be approximated by straight lines. We will accomplish this by considering the *asymptotic behavior* of transfer functions of the first order, at extremely low and extremely high frequencies.

Let us consider the transfer function with the first order form shown below.

$$G(s) = K(s + a) \qquad \textbf{Equation 1-12}$$

The order of the transfer function is determined by the highest power of s. In Equation 1-11, the quantity s has the power of 1, hence we have a first order transfer function. If the highest power of s would be 2, then we would have a second order transfer function, and so on.

To obtain the frequency (amplitude) response and phase characteristics, we let $s = j\omega$, and substitute this value for s in the first order transfer function of Equation 1-11. The result is shown below:

$$G(j\omega) = K(j\omega + a) \qquad \text{Equation 1-13}$$

Next, we find the absolute value (magnitude) of Equation 1-13.

$$N(\omega) = G(j\omega) = K(\omega^2 + a^2)^{1/2} \qquad \text{Equation 1-14A}$$

The absolute value or magnitude of Equation 1-13 is a vector since the quantity a represents a real number, and the quantity $j\omega$ is a complex number situated at an angle of 90° from a. Figure 1-11A illustrates how the magnitude of the first order transfer function is obtained.

The phase shift of the first order transfer function is also illustrated in Fig. 1-11A. The phase shift angle has a tangent which is equal to ω/a. In other words, $\tan \phi =$ the side opposite the angle ϕ in Fig. 1-11A divided by the side adjacent the angle ϕ in Fig. 1-10A,

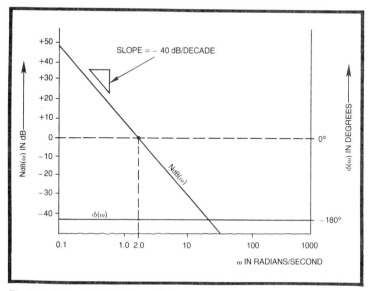

Fig. 1-9. Bode plot of $G(j\omega) = 4/(j\omega)^2$.

or in equation form $\tan \phi = \omega/a$. To express the angle $\phi(\omega)$ we must find the inverse tangent function, which is called the arc tan or written $\tan^{-1}$. This function can be expressed as shown below:

$$\phi(\omega) = \underline{/G(j\omega)} = \tan^{-1} \omega/a = \text{arc tan } \omega/a \qquad \textbf{Equation 1-14B}$$

Now, consider how we can graph the behavior of $N(\omega)$. First consider when the frequencies are very low; that is when ω is much smaller than a. At these low frequencies, $N(\omega)$ will be approximately equal to the product of K times a. In equation form we can write this approximation as:

$$N(\omega) \cong Ka \text{ when } \omega << a \qquad \textbf{Equation 1-15}$$

This equation is a straight line of zero slope with a dB value of 20 $\log_{10} (Ka)$, as shown in the Bode diagram of Fig. 1-10B.

Next, we consider when the frequencies are very high, that is when ω is much larger than a. At these high frequencies $N(\omega)$ will be approximately equal to the product of K times ω. In equation form we can write this approximation as:

$$N(\omega) \cong K\omega \text{ when } \omega >> a \qquad \textbf{Equation 1-16}$$

The above is a straight line having a slope of 20 dB/decade and passing through the 20 $\log_{10} (Ka)$ point at $\omega = a$, as illustrated in Fig. 1-10B. Thus, the two straight lines, shown as dotted lines in Fig. 1-10B, intersect at $\omega = a$ and comprise a very close approximation to the amplitude response curve $N_{dB} (\omega)$, which is shown as a solid curve in Fig. 1-10B.

We have seen that the approximation of the overall frequency response is very good at very low and at very high frequencies, but let us now investigate the error at frequencies in the neighborhood of $\omega = a$. In Fig. 1-10B this occurs at the intersection of the two dotted lines. At $\omega = a$, we have

$$N(\omega)|_{\omega = a} = K(a^2 + a^2)^{\frac{1}{2}} = \sqrt{2} \, Ka$$

In terms of dB we have the value:

$$N_{dB}(\omega)|_{\omega = a} = 20 \log_{10}(Ka) + 20 \log_{10}\sqrt{2}$$

Finding the value of the second term in the above equation will tell us how many dB the actual curve is above the intersection of the two straight line approximations.

$$20 \log_{10}\sqrt{2} = 3.01 \text{ dB}$$

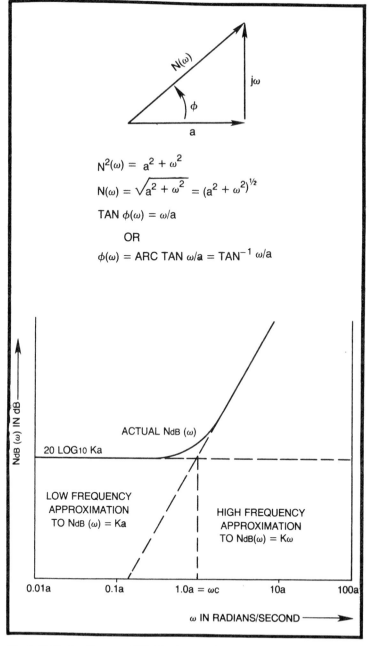

$$N^2(\omega) = a^2 + \omega^2$$

$$N(\omega) = \sqrt{a^2 + \omega^2} = (a^2 + \omega^2)^{\frac{1}{2}}$$

$$\text{TAN } \phi(\omega) = \omega/a$$

OR

$$\phi(\omega) = \text{ARC TAN } \omega/a = \text{TAN}^{-1} \omega/a$$

Fig. 1-10. Vector diagram of N(ω) for the transfer function G(s) = s + in (A) and straight line approximations to N$_{dB}$ (ω) on the Bode chart for the transfer function G(s) = K(s + a) in (B).

Hence, the Bode plot of the frequency response actually passes through a point which is 3.01 dB above the intersection of the two straight lines. The quantity $\omega_C = a$ is called the *break frequency* or the *corner frequency* of this transfer function.

At a frequency one octave below the break frequency, that is at $\omega = a/2$, the amplitude ratio is

$$N(\omega)|_{\omega=a/2} = K \left(\frac{a^2}{4} + a^2 \right)^{\frac{1}{4}} = (\sqrt{5/4})Ka$$

which, expressed in decibels, is

$$N_{dB}(\omega)_{\omega = a/2} = 20 \log_{10}(Ka) + 20 \log_{10}\sqrt{5/4}$$

But the value of $20 \log_{10}\sqrt{5/4} = 0.969$.

Hence, the Bode plot passes through a point which lies 0.969 dB above the straight line asymptote at $\omega = a/2$.

Similarly, at a frequency one octave above the break frequency at $\omega = 2a$, the Bode plot will pass through a point which is 6.99 dB above the low frequency asymptote or 0.97 dB above the high frequency asymptote. When the asymptotes are drawn on the graph as shown in Fig. 1-10B, and the three points $\omega_1 = a/2$, $\omega_2 = a$, and $v_3 = 2a$ are spotted on the graph, it is possible with the aid of a French curve to draw the graph for the actual function $N_{dB}(\omega)$. The actual graph of $N_{dB}(\omega)$ is shown by the solid line curve in Fig. 1-10B. In many problems it is not necessary to have an extremely accurate graph, and the deviations of the straight line asymtotes from the actual $N_{dB}(\omega)$ curve may be taken as 1, 3, and 1 dB instead of the more accurate 0.969, 3.01 and 0.97 dB at the three frequencies considered above.

A plot of the phase shift curve given by Equation 1-14 is an arc tangent curve as shown in Fig. 1-11. At the break frequency the phase shift is exactly 45°. At $\omega = a/2$ the phase shift is about 26.57°, and at $\omega = 2a$ the phase shift is about 63.43°. A straight line may be drawn through these three points on the phase shift curve of Fig. 1-11. The straight line, which is shown broken, will intersect the $\phi(v) = 0$ line (which may be considered to be the low frequency asymptote) at $\omega = 0.184a$, and it will intersect the $\phi(\omega) = 90°$ line (the high frequency asymptote) at $\omega = 5.43a$. These two frequencies, 0.184a and 5.43 a, may be considered to be break frequencies on the $\phi(\omega)$ curve. A simple calculation will show that the phase shifts at these two frequencies are 10.435° and 79.565°. These

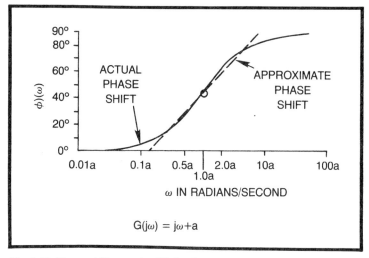

Fig. 1-11. Phase shift curve for $G(j\omega) = j\omega + a$.

figures form a basis for making a straight line approximation to the phase shift curve. Using Equation 1-14B, we could derive other straight line approximations to the phase shift curve. For example, the tangent to the $\phi(\omega)$ curve at $\omega = a$ could be used to approximate the mid-frequency phase shift curve.

POLE AND ZERO VALUES FOR THE TRANSFER FUNCTION

As a further example of the straight line approximation technique, consider the transfer function:

$$G(s) = \frac{K(s + a)}{s + b} \qquad \textbf{Equation 1-17A}$$

The transfer function defined by Equation 1-17A may be decomposed as the product of three transfer functions as follows:

$$G(s) = \left(\frac{Ka}{b}\right)\left(\frac{s + a}{a}\right)\left(\frac{b}{s + b}\right) \qquad \textbf{Equation 1-17B}$$

The *poles* of the above transfer function are found by equating the denominator of Equation 1-17B to zero, and solving for s as follows:

$$s + b = 0$$

and $s = -b$, pole of Equation 1-17B.

29

The *zeros* of the transfer function in Equation 1-17B are found by equating the numerator of Equation 1-17B to zero, and solving for s as follows:

$$s + a = 0$$

and $s = -a$, a zero of Equation 1-17B.

If a transfer function is composed of several first order poles and zeros, the composite frequency response curve may be drawn by considering the individual transfer functions containing the poles and zeros, drawing their frequency response curves as discussed in the preceding sections, and combining their results to obtain the overall frequency response. Every pole and zero defines a break frequency, which is numerically equal to the pole or zero value. Now the task at hand is to draw the frequency response curve for the transfer function of Equation 1-14B.

First we must draw a straight line approximation to the amplitude ratio for each of the three simple transfer functions in Equation 1-14B. This is illustrated in Fig. 1-13. It is assumed that a is greater than b, and that Ka/b is greater than 1. Also, it is convenient to factor the transfer function so that each of the fre-

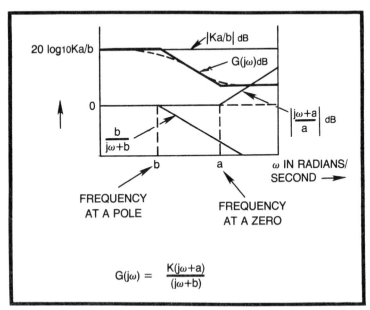

Fig. 1-12. Asymptotic approximation to $|G(j\omega)| = |K(j\omega +a)/(j\omega + b)|$.

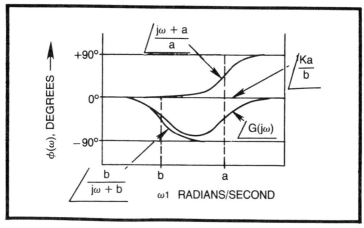

Fig. 1-13. Phase shift curve for $G/j\omega) = K(j\omega + a)/(j\omega + b)$.

quency dependent terms has a zero frequency gain of unit (0 dB). The asymptotes for the $(s + a)/a$ term are drawn in exactly the same manner as in the previous sections, which is illustrated in Fig. 1-11B. Hence, the zero of a transfer function, will break from the 0 dB line at a frequency of $\omega = a$, with a slope of +20 dB/decade. This is illustrated in Fig. 1-12.

The low frequency asymptote for the $b/(s + b)$ term is also the 0dB until the break frequency $\omega = b$ is reached, which is the pole of the transfer function. The low frequency asymptote breaks at a slope of -20 dB. Finally, the constant term Ka/b is plotted as a constant of $20 \log_{10} Ka/b$, as illustrated in the graph of Fig. 1-12. A composite curve is drawn in a heavier line, by simply adding the three component approximations. The actual magnitude curve will lie close to this composite straight line approximation, as indicated by the dotted lines in Fig. 1-12.

In summary, if a transfer function is composed of poles and zeros, the composite frequency response curve may be drawn by adding the response curves of each pole term, zero term, and constant term of the original transfer function. One straight line approximation is required for each of the individual components at the break frequency corresponding to that component. The break frequency is numerically equal to the pole or zero value, and high frequency asymptote breaks *up* for the component contributed by a zero of the transfer function, and it breaks *down* for the component contributed by a pole of the transfer function.

31

The phase shift curves for the individual transfer functions are sketched in Fig. 1-13. Notice that the phase shift for the $b/(s + b)$ term is negative or *lagging,* and the phase shift for the $(s + a)/a$ term is positive or *leading.* The phase shift for the constant term is zero, of course. The composite phase shift curve is formed by adding the three individual curves in the same manner as the composite amplitude curve was formed in Fig. 1-12.

PLOTTING APPROXIMATE AMPLITUDE RESPONSE

As a final example of approximating the amplitude characteristic, consider the transfer function:

$$G(s) = \frac{40(s + 1) (s + 24)}{(s + 2) (s + 6) (s + 40)} \qquad \textbf{Equation 1-18}$$

The zeros of the transfer function in Equation 1-18 occur at s = − 1 and s = − 24. Remember, the zeros of the transfer function define break frequencies at $\omega = 1$ and $\omega = 24$ as shown on the graph of Fig. 1-14. The straight line approximation of the zero break frequencies break up at a +20 dB/decade slope. The poles of the transfer function in Equation 1-18 occur at s = − 2, s =− 6, and s =−40. Remember, the poles of the transfer function define break frequencies at $\omega = 2$, $\omega = 6$, and $\omega = 40$ as shown on the graph of Fig. 1-14. The straight line approximation of the pole break frequencies break down at a −20 dB/decade slope.

The initial value of 6 dB was found through the arrangement of the transfer function as follows:

$$G(s) = \frac{(40) (1) (24)}{(2) (6) (40)} \frac{(s + 1)}{1} \frac{(s + 24)}{24} \frac{2}{(s + 2)} \frac{6}{(s + 6)} \frac{40}{(s + 40)}$$

Then the value of $20 \log_{10} \frac{(40) (1) (24)}{(2) (6) (40)} = 6$ dB

is the beginning of the amplitude response of the curve in Fig. 1-15. The dotted line shows approximately where the actual magnitude curve would lie.

FREQUENCY AND IMPEDANCE SCALING OR NORMALIZING

The frequency response of a given active filter can be shifted, scaled, or normalized to a different region of the frequency axis by

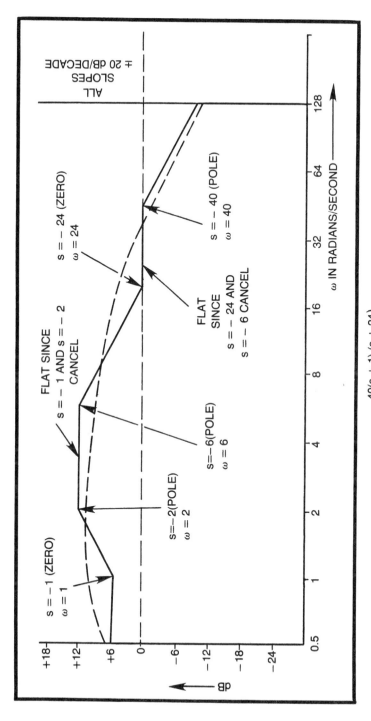

Fig. 1-14. Amplitude ratio curve (approximation) for $G(s) = \dfrac{40(s+1)(s+24)}{(s+2)(s+6)(s+40)}$.

33

dividing *either* the resistor *or* capacitor values by a frequency normalizing factor u. The quantity u is expressed as follows:

$$u = \frac{\text{Desired frequency}}{\text{Existing frequency}}$$ **Equation 1-19**

Both the numerator and denominator must be expressed in the same units. In other words, either frequency (f) must be used in both numerator and denominator, or frequency (ω) must be used in both numerator and denominator. Usually, 3 dB points (break frequency locations) are selected as reference frequency for low-pass or high-pass filters, and the center frequency is selected for a band-pass filter. The following example will illustrate the use of the frequency normalizing factor u.

For the normalized low-pass filter and associated frequency response shown in Fig. 1-15, find the denormalized low-pass filter circuit and the associated frequency response, if the break frequency occurs at 1000 Hz.

First we calculate the frequency normalizing factor u.

$$u = \frac{2\pi \ (1000) \ \text{rad/second}}{1 \ \text{rad/second}} = 6280$$

Next, we divide the capacitor values by the quantity u, which results in the denormalized filter circuit of Fig. 1-16A, and the response curve shown in Fig. 1-16B.

It is clear that the capacitor values in Fig. 1-16A are too large, and at the same time the resistor values are too small. This situation is resolved by impedance scaling. An active filter will retain its response if all the resistor values are multiplied by an impedance scaling factor ISF, and at the same time all the capacitors are divided by the ISF. In the circuit of Fig. 1-16A, if the resistors are multiplied by an ISF = 10,000 and capacitors are divided by the same ISF, the circuit of Fig. 1-17 results. The values of R and C in Fig. 1-17 are certainly practical, and these values retain the same frequency response as shown in Fig. 1-16B.

The process of frequency and impedance scaling can be combined into the following equations:

$$C_p = \frac{C_n}{(u)(\text{ISF})}$$ **Equation 1-20**

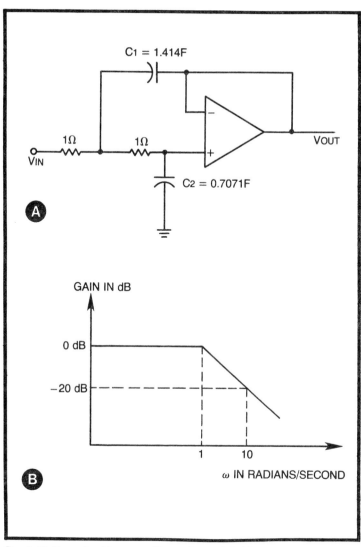

Fig. 1-15. Normalized low-pass filter and associated frequency response.

C_p = practical capacitor value
C_n = normalized capacitor value
u = frequency normalizing factor
ISF = impedance scaling factor
$R_p = R_n$ (ISF)   **Equation 1-21**
R_p = practical resistor value
R_n = normalized resistor value

SECOND ORDER TRANSFER
FUNCTION AMPLITUDE AND PHASE RESPONSE

If a transfer function should contain a term with s^2 the transfer function cannot be decomposed to a product or individual first order transfer functions. Hence, a straight line approximation to the frequency response characteristics will not be quite as simple as it is when only first order transfer functions are present.

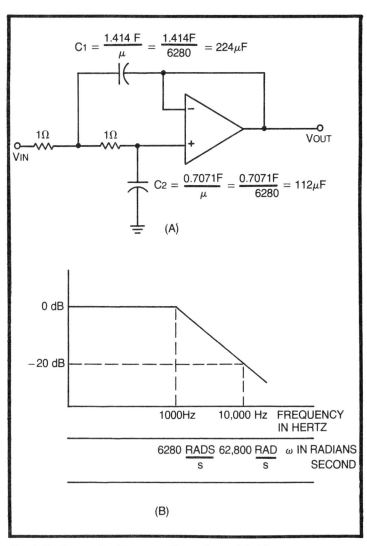

Fig. 1-16. Denormalized low-pass filter and associated frequency response.

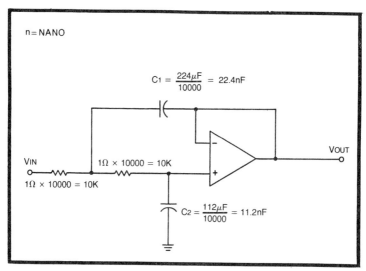

Fig. 1-17. Denormalized low-pass filter with impedance scaling.

Consider the second order transfer function:

$$G(s) = \frac{\omega_n^2}{s^2 + 2\ \zeta\omega_n^s + \omega_n^2} \qquad \textbf{Equation 1-22}$$

Both the amplitude response $N(\omega)$ and the phase shift $\phi(\omega)$ depend upon two quantities in Equation 1-22. The first quantity is called the *damping d*. The second quantity is called the *natural* frequency ω_n. It is convenient to normalize the amplitude response $N(\omega)$ and the phase shift $\phi(\omega)$ with respect to ω_n. We start with substituting $s = j\omega$ in Equation 1-19.

$$G(j\omega) = \frac{\omega_n^2}{(j\omega)^2 + 2\zeta\omega_n(j\omega) + \omega_n^2}$$

$$G(j\omega) = \frac{\omega_n^2}{(-\omega^2) + j2\zeta\ \omega_n\omega + \omega_n^2}$$

Divide numerator and denominator by ω_n^2

$$G\left(\frac{j\omega}{\omega_n}\right) = \frac{1}{-\left(\frac{\omega}{\omega_n}\right)^2 + j2\zeta\left(\frac{\omega_n}{\omega_n}\right)\left(\frac{\omega}{\omega_n}\right) + \left(\frac{\omega_n}{\omega_n}\right)^2}$$

37

Normalizing the frequency by letting $u = \omega/\omega_n$, we have:

$$G(ju) = \frac{1}{-(u)^2 + j2\zeta(1)(u) + 1^2}$$

$$= \frac{1}{(1 - u^2) + j2\zeta u}$$

Finding the magnitude of the previous equation we have:

$$|G(ju| = N(u) = \frac{1}{[(1 - u^2)^2 + (2\zeta u)^2]^{1/2}} \qquad \textbf{Equation 1-23}$$

Next, finding the phase shift we have:

$$\phi(u) = -\tan^{-1}\left(\frac{2\zeta u}{1 - u^2}\right) \qquad \textbf{Equation 1-24}$$

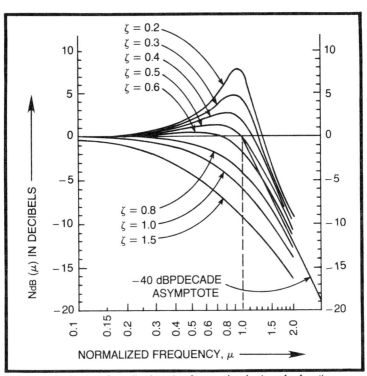

Fig. 1-18. Bode plot of amplitude ratio of second-order transfer function.

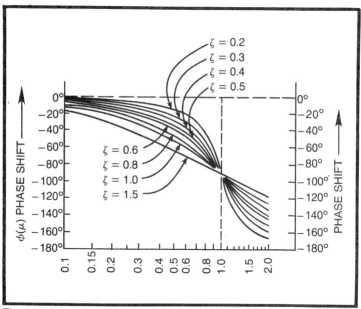

Fig. 1-19. Bode plot of phase shift for a second-order transfer function.

Now the amplitude and phase shift depend upon two variables ζ and u. The amplitude response $N(u)$ and the phase response $\phi(u)$ are accurately plotted for various values of ζ on Bode charts in Fig. 1-18 and Fig. 1-19 respectively. The high frequency asymptote for all curves in Fig. 1-18 is a straight line passing through the zero dB line at $u = 1$ and having a slope of -40dB/decade. Notice also that as the damping d is decreased the peaking of the response curve around $u = 1$ becomes flatter, but with a sacrifice of getting into the attenuation band slower. If the damping was equal to zero ($\zeta = 0$) we would get an infinite peak response or oscillation would occur.

When the normalized frequency response curves for the second order transfer function are available it is possible to make an asymptotic approximation to the frequency response characteristics of any transfer function which is the ratio of two algebraic polynomials in s, since this type of transfer function may always be factored into first and second order terms.

THIRD ORDER TRANSFER FUNCTION
AMPLITUDE AND PHASE RESPONSE

The following example will illustrate the use of the second order response curves in making a Bode plot of a transfer function

39

containing s^3 as one of its terms. Consider the following transfer function:

$$G(s) = \frac{50 \, (s + 4)}{s^3 + 4s^2 + 100 \, s}$$

Factor this equation as follows:

$$G(s) = \frac{50 \, (s + 4)}{s(s^2 + 4s + 100)}$$

$$= \frac{(50) \, (4)}{(100)} \frac{(s + 4)}{(4)} \frac{(1)}{(s)} \frac{(100)}{(s^2 + 4s + 100)}$$

The first three terms in the above equation may be sketched onto the Bode plot very quickly and easily as shown in Fig. 1-20. The quadratic term that contains a second order term is sketched using the normalized curves in Fig. 1-18. This second order term has ω_n^2 = 100 or ω_n = 10 and a damping of ζ = 0.2, whose calculation is shown.

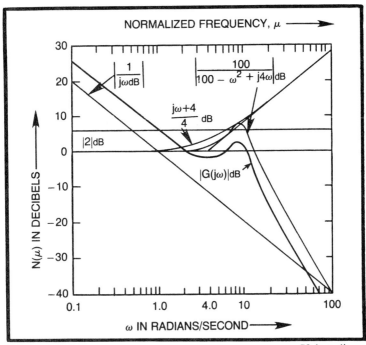

Fig. 1-20. Constructing the amplitude ratio curve for $G(s) = \dfrac{50 \, (s + 4)}{s(s^2 + 4s + 100)}$.

$$2\zeta\omega_n = 4$$
$$\zeta = 4/2\omega_n = 4/(2)(10) = 4/20$$
$$= 0.2$$

At $u = 1$ in Fig. 1-18 corresponds to $\omega = u\omega_n = (1)(10) = 10$ in Fig. 1-20. Hence, the second order is sketched on Fig. 1-20 from Fig. 1.18, when $\zeta = 0.2$. Next the composite amplitude curve is drawn as the sum of the four individual curves and is shown as the darker graph on Fig. 1-20.

It is apparent that it is possible to approximate frequency response curves for a transfer function of any order simply by decomposing it into the product of simple first and second order functions. The asymptotic approximations made on the Bode plot require much less time than any other method which might be used to compute the frequency response of active filter transfer functions.

Chapter 2
Operational Amplifier
Characteristics and Circuits

The *operational amplifier* (op amp) is a linear integrated circuit (IC), which employs several differential amplifier stages in cascade. The differential amplifiers require both positive and negative power supplies; hence, op amp circuits require two opposite polarity power supplies usually of equal value (e.g., +15 V and −15 V). The ideal op amp, shown in Fig. 2-1, offers the following characteristics:

- ☐ Infinite input impedance Z_{IN}.
- ☐ Zero output impedance Z_{OUT}.
- ☐ Infinite voltage amplification A_v.
- ☐ Infinite bandwidth.
- ☐ When the input voltage is zero, the output voltage is zero.
- ☐ Instantaneous recovery from saturation.

The ideal op amp characteristics mean that almost any low-level signal can turn it on. Practically no loading of one amplifier stage cascaded to another stage exists, and the op amp itself can drive an infinite number of other devices. However, the real world of electronics tells us that op amps have an input impedance of 100M, an output impedance of 10Ω and a voltage gain of 100,000 which drops sharply as frequency is increased.

Figure 2-2 is the schematic of a simple current amplifier. In the circuit the output voltage is equal to the product of the output current and the feedback resistor R_F. This result is accomplished through the fact that the op amp input impedance is much larger than

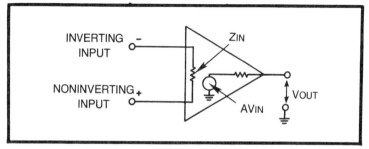

Fig. 2-1. Ideal op amp.

R_F and R_{IN} so that the op amp draws *zero* current. We can develop an expression for voltage gain A and input impedance Z_{IN}.

At the input node to the $(-)$ side of the amplifier we can write $I_{IN} = I_F + I_A$, but I_A is zero since the op amp has a very high input impedance. Thus, $I_{IN} = I_F$.

$$V_{IN} = I_{IN}R_{IN} = I_FR_{IN}$$

$$V_{OUT} = -I_FR_F$$

Equation 2-1

$$A = \frac{V_{OUT}}{V_{IN}} = \frac{-I_FR_F}{I_FR_{IN}}$$

$$= \frac{-R_F}{R_{IN}}$$

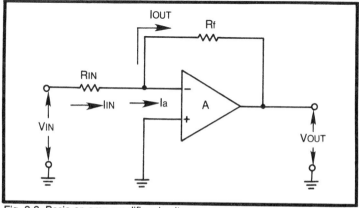

Fig. 2-2. Basic op amp amplifier circuit.

43

$$Z'_{IN} = \frac{V_{IN}}{I_{IN}}$$

$$I = \frac{V_{OUT} - V_{IN}}{R_F}$$

$$Z'_{IN} = \frac{V_{IN}R_F}{V_{IN} - V_{OUT}} = \frac{V_{IN}R_F}{V_{IN} - (-V_{IN}A)}$$

$$= \frac{R_F}{1 + A} \qquad \textbf{Equation 2-2}$$

For Equation 2-2, if the absolute magnitude of R_F approaches the absolute value of the gain of the device, we no longer have an op amp, and Equation 2-2 is no longer valid. For large values of A, Z'_{IN} is so small that the input terminal marked (−) is called virtual ground. This input becomes a null point, which means the current from an input source will flow as though the source were returned to ground.

Figure 2-3 further develops the circuit of Fig. 2-2 by adding a bias resistor R_B to minimize the offset voltage at the output of the amplifier resulting from input-bias current. The value of the bias resistor is equal to the parallel combination of R_F and R_{IN}. The circuit in Figure 2-3 is the basic op amp circuit used to calculate closed loop response.

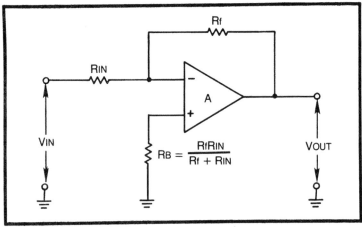

Fig. 2-3. Op amp amplifier circuit with biasing resistor.

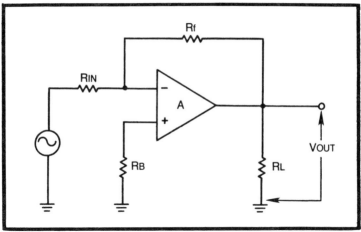

Fig. 2-4. Inverting feedback op amp.

FREQUENCY RESPONSE AND GAIN

Some of the design consideration for IC op amps are the result of trade offs between gain and frequency response, which is also called bandwidth. The open loop (no feedback) gain and frequency response are characteristics of the basic IC circuit, but these internal characteristics can be changed with external compensation networks. The closed loop (feedback) gain and frequency response are primarily dependent on the external feedback components.

The inverting and noninverting feedback op amp circuits appear in Figs. 2-4 and 2-5, respectively. Loop gain in these figures is

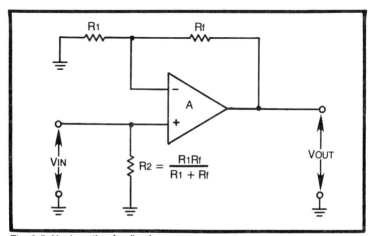

Fig. 2-5. Noninverting feedback op amp.

defined as the ratio of open loop to close loop gain as illustrated in Fig. 2-6. The open loop gain rolls off at the specified op amp characteristic, which is shown to be 6 dB/octave or 20 dB/decade. (The term 6 dB/octave means that the gain drops be 6 dB each time the frequency is doubled. Also, this is the same as a 20 dB drop in gain each time the frequency is increased by a factor of 10.)

If the open loop gain of an amplifier was given in Fig. 2-6, any stable closed loop gain could be produced by the proper selection of feedback components, provided the closed loop gain was less than the open loop gain. The main concern is a trade off between gain and frequency response. For example, if a gain of 40 dB (10^2) was desired, a feedback resistance 10^2 times higher than the input resistance would be selected. The gain would then be flat to 10^4 Hz and roll off at 20 dB/decade to unity gain at 10^6 Hz.

The open loop frequency response curve of a practical amplifier is illustrated in Fig. 2-7. The open loop gain is flat at 60 dB to about a frequency of 200 kHz, then rolls off at 6 dB/octave to 2 MHz. Further on, a roll off continues at 12 dB/octave to 20 MHz, then a third roll off of 18 dB/octave occurs.

The phase response of the amplifier is also shown on Fig. 2-7. The phase response indicates that a negative feedback (at lower frequencies) can become positive and cause the op amp to be

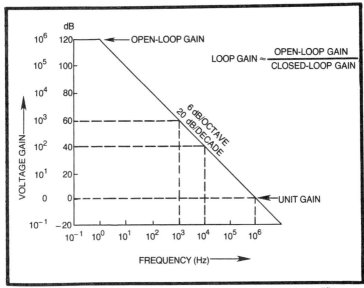

Fig. 2-6. Frequency response curve of a theoretical operational amplifier.

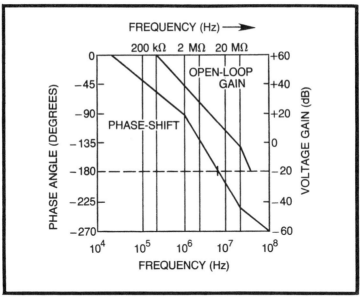

Fig. 2-7. Frequency response and phase-shift curve of a practical operational amplifier.

unstable at high frequencies (possibly oscillations). The op amp has a 180° phase shift at an open loop gain of about 20 dB.

In practice, when a selected close loop gain is equal to or less than the open loop gain at the 180° phase point, the circuit will be unstable. For example, if a closed loop gain of 20 dB or less had been selected, a circuit with the curves of Fig. 2-7 would be unstable. Therefore, the closed loop gain must be more than the open loop gain at the frequency where 180° phase shift occurs. Hence, the closed loop gain would have to be greater than 20 dB but less than 60 dB.

OP AMP SPECIFICATIONS

The terms presented are most often used in op amp specifications as a measure of amplifier performance. An *input bias current*, I_B, is defined as the average of the two currents flowing into the op amps input terminals. In equation form we can define input bias current as:

$$I_B = \frac{I_{B1} + I_{B2}}{2}$$ **Equation 2-3**

The base currents I_{B1} and I_{B2} are about equal to each other, which means that $I_B = I_{B1} = I_{B2}$. Depending on the type of op amp, the value of input bias current is usually small, generally in the range of 10 to 500 nA. Though this seems small, it can be a problem in circuits using relatively large feedback resistors.

The *input offset current* I_{OS}, is defined as the difference between I_{B1} and I_{B2}.

$$I_{OS} = I_{B1} - I_{B2}$$ **Equation 2-4**

Typical values for input offset currents range from 0.05 to 150 nA.

Input offset voltage, v_{OS}, is the voltage that must be applied between the input terminals through two equal resistances to force the output voltage to zero. When the output voltage is at zero, the op amp is said to be *nulled* or *balanced*. Typical values for input offset voltages range from 0.2 to 8 mV.

The op amp *input impedance, z_{IN}* is defined as the ratio of the change in input voltage to the change in input current. Typical values of input impedance ranges from 100K to 30M.

The op amp *output impedance, Z_{OUT}* is defined as the ratio of the change in output voltage to the change in output current. Typical values of output impedance ranges from 1 to 100 ohms.

The *common mode rejection ratio,* CMRR, is defined as the ratio of the input voltage range to the peak-to-peak change in input offset voltage over this range. Typical values of CMRR range from 60 to 120 dB.

The *slew rate* dv/dt is the rate of output voltage change caused by a step input voltage and is usually measured in volts/ microsecond. Typical values of slew rate range from 0.1 to 1000 V/μs. The slew rate specification applies to transient response. For a step function input, the slew rate tells how fast the output voltage can swing from one voltage level to another.

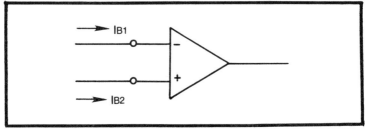

Fig. 2-8. Base bias currents for an op amp.

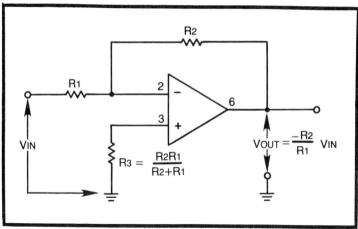

Fig. 2-9. Inverting amplifier.

WHICH OP AMP TO USE

The designer must select an op amp that meets the requirements of the job. The specifications on the op amp data sheet do not tell the whole story. Factors not readily obtainable from the data sheet which can affect the selection of an op amp include reliability, acceptability, capability to withstand environmental stresses, and of course cost. Decide which specifications are critical and which are not. For example, in building a voltage regulator with op amp ICs where there is a large differential voltage during turn-on, this must be considered to be a very critical parameter. In active filter design, a very high gain-high source impedance amplifier must be used; therefore, both offset current and offset voltage are critical parameters.

Besides selecting which specifications are needed and which are not, choices regarding safety factors may be required. Problems that will arise under fault conditions should be considered. For example, op amps come with or without protection against output short circuit and input overvoltage. Since the emitter to base junctions of input transistors are sensitive to damage by large applied voltages, some form of input protection may be desirable. Ungrounded soldering irons, excessive input signals and static discharges are all apt to challenge the input of the IC.

The op amp designer should know the roll off curve of his amplifier in order to build a circuit with adequate gain stability over the working frequency range. The manufacturer may be perfectly justified in departing from the conventional 6 dB/octave frequency compensation to achieve such desirable features as fast settling time, high slew rate, fast overload recovery, or increased gain stability over a wide range of frequencies. But obtaining these improved features generally requires fast roll off characteristics and, therefore, a tendency toward oscillation.

Another characteristic that is often overlooked is the slew rate. For the most part, slew rate is just another way of looking at the rate limiting of the circuitry of the amplifier. The slew rate specification applies to transient response, whereas full power response applies to steady state or continuous response. For a step function input, slew rate tells how fast the output voltage can swing from one voltage level to another. Fast amplifiers will slew at up to 2000 V/μs, but amplifiers designed for DC applications often slew at 0.1 V/μs.

INVERTING OP AMP

The basic inverting op amp circuit is shown in Fig. 2-10. The triangle which represents the IC op amp is assumed to depict the ideal op amp circuit. In other words, the open loop amplifier gain is infinite (practically 200,000), the amplifier input impedance is infinite (actually 2M), and the amplifier output impedance is zero (actually 100Ω).

The circuit in Fig. 2-9 gives a closed loop gain of R_2/R_1. The input impedance is equal to R_1. The closed loop bandwidth is equal to the unity gain frequency divided by the quantity, 1, plus the closed loop gain. The resistor R_3 is chosen to be equal to the parallel combination of R_1 and R_2 to minimize the offset voltage error due to bias current. Amplifier offset voltage is the predominant error for low source resistances, and offset current causes the main error for high source resistances.

NONINVERTING AMPLIFIER

The circuit in Fig. 2-10 shows a noninverting amplifier. The output voltage of the noninverting amplifier is given by the equation:

$$V_{OUT} = V_{IN} \ \frac{R_1 + R_2}{R_1}$$

The primary differences between this circuit and the inverting circuit are that the output is not inverted and that the input impe-

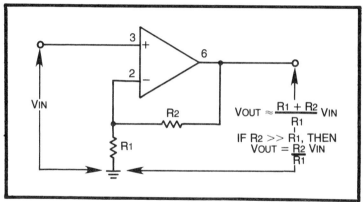

Fig. 2-10. Noninverting amplifier.

dance is very high and is equal to the differential input impedance multiplied by loop gain. In DC coupled applications, input impedance is less important than input current and its voltage drop across the source resistance.

In the equation for output voltage of the noninverting amplifier, if the resistance R_1 is much smaller than R_2 then the output voltage equation can be written as follows:

$$V_{OUT} = V_{IN} \frac{R_2}{R_1}$$

Application precautions are the same for this amplifier as for the inverting amplifier, with one exception. The amplifier output will go into saturation if the input is allowed to float. This may be important if the amplifier must be switched from source to source. The compensation trade off discussed for the inverting amplifier is also valid for this connection.

VOLTAGE FOLLOWER

The voltage follower is frequently used as a buffer amplifier to reduce voltage error caused by source loading and to isolate high impedance sources from following circuitry. Figure 2-11 shows the diagram for a *voltage follower op amp.* The gain of the circuit is unity. The output follows the input voltage; hence the name voltage follower.

The *unity gain buffer* gives the highest input impedance of any op amp circuit. Input impedance is equal to the differential input impedance multiplied by the open loop gain, in parallel with common mode input impedance. The gain error of this circuit is equal to the reciprocal of the amplifier open loop gain or to the common mode rejection, whichever is less. Bias current for the amplifier will be supplied by the source resistance and will cause an error at the amplifier input because of its voltage drop across the source resistance.

Three precautions should be observed for the unity gain buffer:

☐ The amplifier must be compensated for unity gain operation.

☐ The output swing of the amplifier must be limited by the amplifier common mode range.

☐ Some amplifiers exhibit a latchup mode when the amplifier common mode range is exceeded.

SUMMING AMPLIFIER

The summing amplifier shown in Fig. 2-12 is a special case of the inverting amplifier. The circuit gives an inverted output which is equal to the weighted algebraic sum of all three inputs. The gain of any input of this circuit is equal to the ratio of the appropriate input resistor to the feedback resistor R_4. The equation for output voltage in terms of the three input voltages can be written as follows:

$$V_{OUT} = -R_4 \left[\frac{V_1}{R_1} + \frac{V_2}{R_2} + \frac{V_3}{R_3} \right]$$

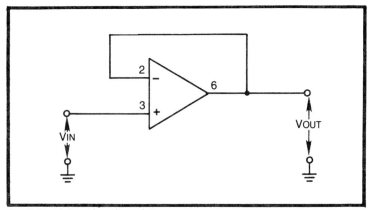

Fig. 2-11. Unity gain voltage follower.

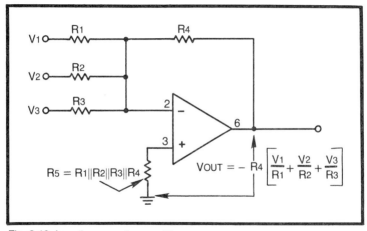

Fig. 2-12. Inverting summing amplifier.

Amplifier bandwidth may be calculated as in the inverting amplifier, by assuming the input resistor to be the parallel combination of R_1, R_2, and R_3. Application cautions are the same as for the inverting amplifier.

DIFFERENCE AMPLIFIER

The *difference amplifier* is the complement of the summing amplifier and allows the subtraction of two voltages or as a special case, the cancellation of a signal common to the two inputs. The difference amplifier is shown in Fig. 2-12, and it is useful as a

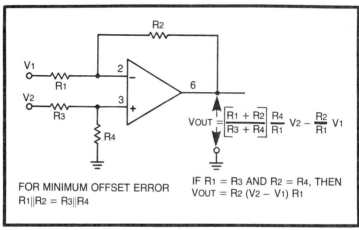

Fig. 2-13. Difference amplifier.

computational amplifier, in making a differential to single ended conversion or in rejecting a common mode signal.

Circuit bandwidth may be calculated in the same manner as for the inverting amplifier, but input impedance is somewhat more complicated. Input impedance for the two inputs is not necessarily equal; inverting input impedance is the same as for the inverting amplifier, and the noninverting input impedance is the sum of R_3 and R_4. Gain for either input is the ratio of R_1 to R_2 for the special case of a differential input single ended output where $R_1 = R_3$ and $R_2 = R_4$. The general expression for V_{OUT} is given below:

$$V_{OUT} = \left[\frac{(R_1 + R_2) \, R_4}{(R_3 + R_4) \, R_1} \right] V_2 - \left(\frac{R_2}{R_1} \right) V_1$$

When $R_1 = R_3$ and $R_2 = R_4$ the equation for V_{OUT} can be written as follows:

$$V_{OUT} = \frac{R_2}{R_1} (V_2 - V_1)$$

DIFFERENTIATOR

The *differentiator* is shown in Fig. 2-14. As the name implies the circuit performs the mathematical operation of differentiation. The circuit shown is *not* the practical differentiator. It is a true differentiator and is extremely susceptible to high frequency noise, since the gain increases at the rate of 6dB/octave. In addition, the feedback network of the differentiator, R_2C_1, is an RC low-pass filter

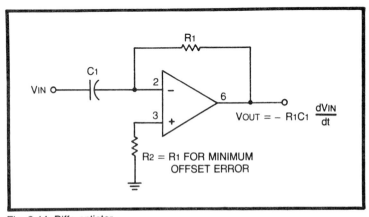

Fig. 2-14. Differentiator.

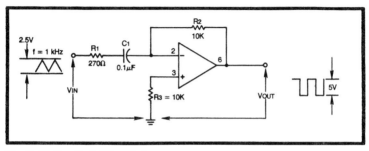

Fig. 2-15. Practical differentiator.

which contributes 90° phase shift to the loop and may cause stability problems even with an amplifier which is compensated for unity gain.

The differentiator circuit of Fig. 2-15 provides an output proportional to the derivative of the input signal. The equation for output voltage is given by the equation:

$$V_{OUT} = -\ R^2 C_1 \frac{dV_1}{dt}$$

A triangular input voltage will produce a square wave output voltage. For a 2.5 V peak to peak triangle wave with a period of 1 ms we have, for the circuit in Fig. 2-15 the following calculations:

$$\frac{dV}{dt} = \frac{2.5V}{0.5\ ms} = 5\ \frac{V}{ms}$$

$$V_{OUT} = -\ (10\ k\Omega)(0.1\ \mu F)\ (5\ V/ms) = 5\ V\ peak\ to\ peak$$

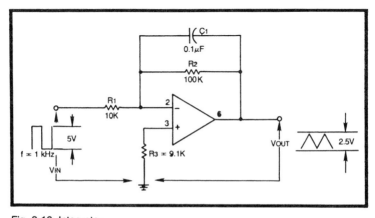

Fig. 2-16. Integrator.

55

The resistor R_1 is needed to limit the high frequency gain of the differentiator. This makes the circuit less susceptible to high frequency noise and assures dynamic stability. The corner frequency where the gain limiting comes into effect is given by the equation:

$$f = \frac{1}{2\pi R_1 C_1}$$

and should be at least 10 times the highest input frequency for accurate operation. A maximum value for the corner frequency is determined by stability criteria. In general, it should be no larger than the geometric mean between $1/2\pi R_2 C_1$ and the gain bandwidth product of the op amp. The differentiator is subject to damage from fast rising input signals, and it is also susceptible to high frequency instability.

INTEGRATOR

The *integrator* circuit is shown in Fig. 2-16. This circuit provides an output that is proportional to the time integral of the input signal. The equation for the output voltage is given as follows:

$$V_{OUT} = -\frac{1}{R_1 C_1} \ V_{IN} \ dt$$

As an example, consider the response of the integrator to a symmetrical square wave input signal with an average value of 0 volts. If the input has a peak amplitude of B V, in the period T, then the peak to peak output can be calculated by integrating over one-half the input period as illustrated by following equation:

$$|V_{OUT}| = \frac{1}{R_1 C_1} \int_0^{1/2} B \ dt = \left(\frac{B}{R_1 C_1}\right) \left(\frac{T}{2}\right) \ V$$

The wave shape will be triangular corresponding to the integral of the square wave. For the component values shown in Fig. 2-16, B = 5 V and T = 1 ms, we have the following results:

$$R_1 C_1 = 10^{-3} \ s$$

$$V_{OUT} = \left(\frac{5}{10^{-3}}\right) \left(\frac{10^{-3}}{2}\right) = 2.5 \ V \ \text{peak to peak}$$

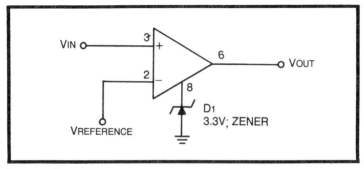

Fig. 2-17. Comparator circuit.

The resistor R_2 is since included to provide DC stabilization for the integrator. Its function is to limit the low-frequency gain of the amplifier and thus minimize drift. The frequency above which the circuit will perform as an integrator is given by the equation:

$$f = \frac{1}{2\pi R_2 C_1}$$

For the best linearity, the frequency of the input signal should be at least 10 times the frequency given in the above equation. The linearity of the circuit illustrated is better than one percent with an input frequency of 1 kHz.

Although it is not immediately obvious, the integrator, if it is to operate reliably, requires both a large common mode and differential

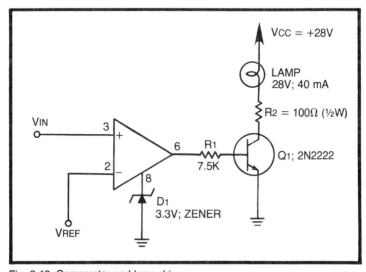

Fig. 2-18. Comparator and lamp drive.

57

mode input voltage range. There are several ways the input voltage limits may be inadvertently exceeded. The most obvious is that transients occurring at the output of the amplifier can be coupled back to the input by the integrating capacitor C_1. Thus, either common mode or differential mode voltage limits can be exceeded.

Another less obvious problem can occur when the amplifier is driven from fast rising or fast falling input signals, such as square waves. The output of the amplifier cannot respond to an input instantaneously. During the short interval before the output reacts, the summing point of the amplifier may not be held at ground potential. If the input signal change is large enough, the voltage at the summing point could exceed safe limits for the amplifier.

VOLTAGE COMPARATOR

A *voltage comparator amplifier* is shown in Fig. 2-17. Notice the circuit is operated open loop. The comparator circuit has a variety of applications, including interface circuits, detectors, and sense amplifiers.

The circuit shown in Fig. 2-17 shows a clamping scheme which makes the output signal directly compatible with *diode transistor logic (DTL)* or *transistor transistor logic* (TTL) ICs. This is accomplished by the breakdown diode with a rating of 3.3V. The input at pin 2 is fixed to a reference voltage. All input signals at pin 3 are compared to the reference voltage, and the output doesn't respond until the reference voltage level is exceeded.

Figure 2-18 shows the connection of an op amp as a comparator and lamp driver. Transistor Q_1 switches the lamp, with resistor R_2 limiting the current surge resulting from turning on a cold lamp. Resistor R_1 determines the base drive to Q_1 while D_1 keeps the amplifier from putting excessive reverse bias on the emitter base junction of the lamp driver when it turns off.

OP AMP CIRCUITS EMPLOYED IN ACTIVE FILTERS

The IC op amp is used as the basic gain device in most active filters. Figure 2-19 illustrates a simple low pass active filter circuit. The op amp provides load isolation and a way to route energy from the supply in the proper amounts at the proper places in a resistor capacitor network to simulate the energy storage of one or more inductors.

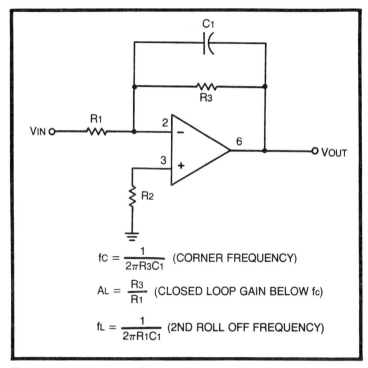

$$f_C = \frac{1}{2\pi R_3 C_1} \quad \text{(CORNER FREQUENCY)}$$

$$A_L = \frac{R_3}{R_1} \quad \text{(CLOSED LOOP GAIN BELOW } f_C)$$

$$f_L = \frac{1}{2\pi R_1 C_1} \quad \text{(2ND ROLL OFF FREQUENCY)}$$

Fig. 2-19. Simple low-pass filter.

The circuit in Fig. 2-19 has a 6 dB/octave roll off after a closed loop 3 dB point defined by f_C. Gain below this corner frequency is defined by the R_3/R_1. The circuit may be considered as an AC integrator at frequencies well above f_C. A gain frequency plot of the circuit response is shown in Fig. 2-20, to illustrate the difference between this circuit and the true integrator.

Op amps suitable for active filter design are often based on the "741" style of device. All of these devices are easy to use, and many cost less than a dollar. Hence, we have included the specifications for the 741 in Fig. 2-21.

The five most popular ways to employ an op amp in active filter design are listed below.

☐ The *voltage follower,* or *unity gain amplifier* which has high input impedance, low output impedance.

☐ As a *noninverting voltage amplifier* providing a gain greater than 1, with high input impedance and low output impedance.

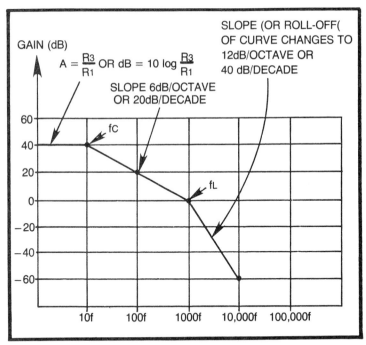

Fig. 2-20. Low-pass filter gain response.

☐ As a *current summing amplifier,* providing any desired gain, moderate input impedance, low output impedance, and signal inversion.

☐ As a *summing block* that combines several input signals— some of which get inverted and some of which do not—a moderate input impedance, and a low output impedance.

☐ As an *integrator amplifier* that gives the integral, or area under the curve of an input signal. Integrators usually invert the signal and have a moderate input impedance and a low output impedance.

Chapter 3
Butterworth and
Chebyshev Transfer Functions

There are many types of low-pass, high-pass, and band-pass filters, but the two most commonly used are the Butterworth and Chebyshev types. Both the Butterworth and Chebyshev filter types have a transfer function which contain all *poles*. Hence, both filter types are called all pole filters. The transfer function of an all pole nth order filter is of the form:

$$G(s) = \frac{Kb_0}{s^n + b_{n-1} s^{n-1} + b_{n-2} s^{n-2} + \bullet\bullet\bullet\bullet\bullet\bullet + b_1 s^1 + b_0}$$

Equation 3-1A

where b_0, b_1,......, b_{n-1}, and K are calculated constants depending upon the order of the transfer function n. The Butterworth and Chebyshev filter circuits differ only by the choice of the coefficients b_i, which yields slightly different response curves. The coefficients for the normalized Butterworth and Chebyshev cases are given in Tables 3-1 through 3-6, for n = 1,2,....,8, and in the Chebyshev case, for ripple widths of 0.1, 0.5, 1, 2, and 3 dB. The remainder of this chapter will be devoted to the study of the two popular filter types in active filter design, namely the Butterworth and Chebyshev.

BUTTERWORTH LOW-PASS FILTER

We are going to consider ways to approximate the ideal response of a low-pass filter by means of a transfer function suggested by a person named Butterworth. We shall also consider that it is sufficient to study the low pass filter case to obtain the general results in the high-pass, band-pass, and band-reject filter circuits.

The amplitude response curve in Fig. 3-1 depicts an ideal, normalized, low-pass filter circuit. An equation can be written which approximates the ideal low-pass filter shown in Fig. 3-1, and is follows:

$$|G(j\omega)|^2 = \frac{K}{1 + f(\omega^2)}$$ **Equation 3-1B**

where $f(\omega^2) >> 1$, $\omega > 1$ **Equation 3-2A**

$[0 \leqslant f(\omega^2) << 1, 0 \leqslant \omega < 1.$ **Equation 3-2B**

Also, for Fig. 3-1, $K=1$ in Equation 3-1. These equations approximate the response in Fig. 3-1, since $0 \leqslant \omega \leqslant 1$, we have $|G(j\omega)|^2 \approx 1$ in the passband, and in the stop band, $\omega > 1$, we have $|G(j\omega)|^2 \approx 0$, when $f(\omega^2)$ is given by Equation 3-2A.

We shall consider various functions of $f(\omega^2)$, which satisfy Equation 3-2A. One such function suitable for use in Equation 3-1 and Equation 3-2A is the Butterworth function:

$$f(\omega^2) = \omega^{2n}$$ **Equation 3-3**

where n = 1, 2, 3,.... If we substitute Equation 3-3 into Equation 3-1, the following result will be obtained.

$$|G(j\omega)|^2 = \frac{K}{1 + \omega^{2n}}$$

Letting $K = 1$, and taking the square root of both sides of the equation results in the following equation:

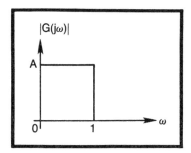

Fig. 3-1. An ideal, normalized low-pass amplitude response.

$$|G(j\omega)| = \frac{1}{\sqrt{1+\omega^{2n}}}$$ **Equation 3-4**

Equation 3-4 is defined as the amplitude resposne of the *nth order Butterworth filter*.

We note that Equation 3-4 has a maximum value of unity (1) when $\omega = 0$. Also, the cutoff point is defined as the normalized value $\omega c = 1$. For ω much greater than one (1), the Butterworth amplitude function of Equation 3-4 is approximated by the following equation.

$$|G(j\omega)| = \frac{1}{\omega^n}$$ **Equation 3-5**

The loss in dB can be found for this equation as follows:

$$A_{dB}(\omega) = 20 \log_{10} \omega^n = 20n \log_{10}\omega$$ **Equation 3-6**

If the loss is plotted versus ω in decades, then for large ω the loss $A_{dB}(\omega)$ has a slope of $20n$ dB/decade. The loss thus increases rapidly for large n, which indicates a good approximation to the ideal case.

Plots of Equation 3-4, $|G(j\omega)|$, and Equation 3-6, $A_{dB}(\omega)$ are shown in Fig. 3-2A and Fig. 3-2B respectively, for various values of n. The curves in Fig. 3-2 illustrate the approximation to how the ideal low pass filter improves as n increases.

BUTTERWORTH TRANSFER FUNCTIONS

Consider next the derivation of the Butterworth transfer function $G(s)$, whose amplitude is defined by Equation 3-4. First, we replace ω^2 by $-s^2$ in Equation 3-4. Also, we note that the product $G(s) G(-s) = |G(j\omega)|$, where $G(-s)$ is the conjugate of $G(s)$. Hence, we can obtain the following transfer function.

$$G(s) G(-s) = \frac{1}{1+(-s^2)^n}$$ **Equation 3-7**

If $n = 2$ in the above equation, we would have a second order Butterworth filter transfer function, whose denominator becomes:

$$D(s) = 1 + (-s^2)^2 = 1 + s^4$$

We can write $D(s)$ as follows:

$$D(s) = 1 + s^4 - 2s^2 + 2s^2$$

63

$$= (s^2 + 1)^2 - (\sqrt{2}\, s)^2$$
$$= (s^2 + \sqrt{2}\, s + 1)(s^2 - \sqrt{2}\, s + 1)$$

Hence, for this example, Equation 3-7 may be written as:

$$G(s)\, G(-s) = \frac{1}{(s^2 + \sqrt{2}\, s + 1)}\ \frac{1}{(s^2 - \sqrt{2}\, s + 1)}$$

This means the first fraction in the previous equation must be $G(s)$.

$$G(s) = \frac{K}{(s^2 + \sqrt{2}\, s + 1)}$$

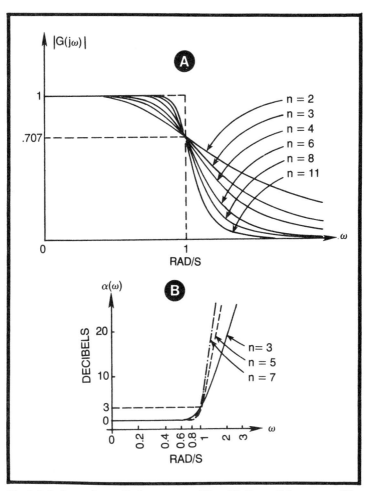

Fig. 3-2. Butterworth amplitude responses (A) and Butterworth loss curves (B).

In general, we can find a $D(s)$ for the transfer function in Equation 3-7 for various values of n, that will yield a $G(s)$ with a denominator $Q(s)$ defined by the following polynomial. In other words, $G(s) = 1/Q(s)$ $Q(s)$ is the polynomial:

$$Q(s) = s^n + b_{n-1} s^{n-1} + \ldots\ldots + b_1 s^1 + b_0$$

The above equation is the so-called Butterworth polynomial, whose constant coefficients b are tabulated in Table 3-1 for n = 1, 2, ..., 8.

As an example of the use of Table 3-1, find the Butterworth polynomial of a third-order Butterworth transfer function. For the third order function, n = 3. We go to Table 3-1 and pick the coefficients b from the table for n = 3. These coefficients are $b_0 = 1$, $b_1 = 2$ and $b_2 = 2$. Therefore, the Butterworth polynomial $Q(s)$ can be written as follows:

$$Q(s) = s^3 + b_2 s^2 + b_1 s^1 + b_0$$
$$= s^3 + 2s^2 + 2s + 1$$

The Butterworth polynomial will be employed to construct active filter circuits.

CHEBYSHEV OR EQUAL RIPPLE LOW-PASS FILTER

The Chebyshev low-pass filter has an amplitude whose general equation is defined by Equation 3-1. Specifically, if the quantity $f(\omega^2)$ $= \epsilon^2 C_n^2(\omega)$ in Equation 3-1, the Chebyshev low-pass filter amplitude equation is defined as follows:

$$|G(j\omega)| = \frac{1}{\sqrt{1 + \epsilon^2 C_n^2(\omega)}} \qquad \textbf{Equation 3-8}$$

where $n = 1, 2, 3, \ldots\ldots$, $\epsilon = $ A constant much smaller than one, that can be called the ripple factor, and $C_n(\omega) = $ The expression that represents the Chebyshev polynomial of the order n.

Table 3-1. Butterworth Filter: $s^h + b_{\eta-1} s^{\eta-1} + \ldots + b_1 s + b_0$.

η	b0	b1	b2	b3	b4	b5	b6	b7
1	1.00000							
2	1.00000	1.41421						
3	1.00000	2.00000	2.00000					
4	1.00000	2.61313	3.41421	2.61313				
5	1.00000	3.23607	5.23607	5.23607	3.23607			
6	1.00000	3.86370	7.46410	9.14162	7.46410	3.86370		
7	1.00000	4.49396	10.09783	14.59179	14.59179	10.09783	4.49396	
8	1.00000	5.12583	13.13707	21.84615	25.68836	21.84615	13.13707	5.12583

η	b_0	b_1	b_2	b_3	b_4	b_5	b_6	b_7
1	6.55222							
2	3.31329	2.37209						
3	1.63809	2.62953	1.93883					
4	0.82851	2.02550	2.62680	1.80377				
5	0.40951	1.43556	2.39696	2.77071	1.74396			
6	0.20713	0.90176	2.04784	2.77908	2.96575	1.71217		
7	0.10238	0.56179	1.48293	2.70514	3.16925	3.18350	1.69322	
8	0.05179	0.32645	1.06667	2.15932	3.41855	3.56485	3.41297	1.68104

During analysis of the amplitude response of the Chebyshev filter in Equation 3-8, we see that for $0 \leqslant \omega \leqslant 1$, $|G(j\omega)|$ attains its maximum value of 1 at the zeros of $C_n(v)$ and attains its minimum value of $1/\sqrt{1 + e^2}$ at the points where the magnitude of $C_{n(\omega)}$ attains its maximum value of 1. Thus there are *ripples* in the passband of ripple width (RW), which are defined by the following equation:

$$RW = 1 - \frac{1}{\sqrt{1 + \epsilon^2}} \qquad \text{Equation 3-9}$$

The Chebyshev filter contains waves or ripples in the passband which are equal in magnitude, hence we hear the name *equiripple filter* given to the Chebyshev filter. The constant ripple width is usually expressed in dB by calculating the loss in dB at the passband minima. This is given by the following equation:

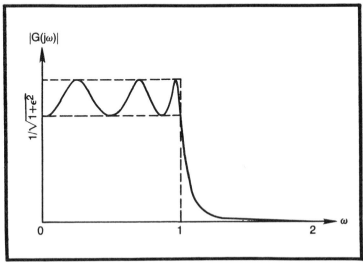

Fig. 3-3. A sixth-order Chebyshev response.

Table 3-3. 0.5 dB Chebyshev Filter ($\epsilon = 0.34931$): $s^{\eta} + b_{\eta-1} s^{\eta-1} + \ldots + b_1 + b_0$.

η	b_0	b_1	b_2	b_3	b_4	b_5	b_6	b_7
1	2.86278							
2	1.51620	1.42562						
3	0.71569	1.53490	1.25291					
4	0.37905	1.02546	1.71687	1.19739				
5	0.17892	0.75252	1.30957	1.93737	1.17249			
6	0.09476	0.43237	1.17186	1.58976	2.17184	1.15918		
7	0.04473	0.28207	0.75565	1.64790	1.86941	2.41265	1.15122	
9	0.02369	0.15254	0.57356	1.14859	2.18402	2.14922	2.65675	1.14608

$$RW_{dB} = -20 \log_{10} \frac{1}{\sqrt{1 + \epsilon^2}}$$

$$RW_{dB} = 10 \log_{10} (1 + \epsilon^2) \qquad \textbf{Equation 3-10}$$

The ripple width in dB given in Equation 3-10 is used to characterize the Chebyshev filter along with the order of the filter n. Looking at Tables 3-2 through 3-6 you will notice that each table refers to the ripple factor ϵ and the corresponding ripple width in dB, which is calculated from Equation 3-10. For example, a 0.1 dB filter is one with $\epsilon = 0.15262$, whose polynomial coefficients are determined by n, the filter order.

The response curve for a Chebyshev filter with the parameters $RW_{dB} = \frac{1}{2}$dB ($\epsilon = 0.3493$), and n = 6 (the filter order) is shown in Fig. 3-3. As is typical of even-order filters, at $\omega = 0$ the ripple value is minimum, in contrast to odd-order filters at $\omega = 0$ the ripple value is maximum, or unity (1). In every case, the amplitude is equal to $1/\sqrt{1 + \epsilon^2}$ as seen in Fig. 3-3.

When ω is arge, then we can say that $\epsilon^2 |C_n(\omega)| >> 1$ we can approximate the amplitude by the following equation:

$$|G(j\omega)| \cong \frac{1}{\epsilon \, C_n(\omega)} \qquad \textbf{Equation 3-11}$$

Table 3-4. 1 dB Chebyshev Filter ($\epsilon = 0.50885$): $s^{\eta} + b_{\eta-1} + \ldots + b_1 s + b_0$.

η	b_0	b_1	b_2	b_3	b_4	b_5	b_6	b_7
1	1.96523							
2	1.10251	1.09773						
3	0.49131	1.23841	0.98834					
4	0.27563	0.74262	1.45392	0.95281				
5	0.12283	0.58053	0.97440	1.68882	0.93682			
6	0.06891	0.30708	0.93935	1.20214	1.93083	0.92825		
7	0.03071	0.21367	0.54862	1.35754	1.42879	2.17608	0.92312	
8	0.01723	0.10734	0.44783	0.84682	1.83690	1.65516	2.42303	0.91981

Table 3-5. 2 dB Chebyshev Filter ($\epsilon = 0.76478$): $s^{\eta} + b_{\eta-1} + \ldots + b_1 s + b_0$.

η	b_0	b_1	b_2	b_3	b_4	b_5	b_6	b_7
1	1.30756							
2	0.82302	0.80382						
3	0.32689	1.02219	0.73782					
4	0.20577	0.51680	1.25648	0.71622				
5	0.08172	0.45935	0.69348	1.49954	0.70646			
6	0.05144	0.21027	0.77146	0.86701	1.74586	0.70123		
7	0.02042	0.16609	0.38251	1.14444	1.03922	1.99353	0.69789	
8	0.01286	0.07294	0.35970	0.59822	1.57958	1.21171	2.24226	0.69606

The loss in dB can be found for the above equation as follows:

$$A_{dB}(\omega) \overset{\sim}{=} 20 \log_{10}\epsilon + 20 \log_{10}C_n(\omega) \qquad \textbf{Equation 3-12}$$

The second term of the above equation can be approximated by $6(n-1) + 20n \log_{10}\omega$, hence we can write Equation 3-12 in the form:

$$A_{dB}(\omega) \overset{\sim}{=} 20 \log_{10}\epsilon + 6(n-1) + 20n \log_{10}\omega \qquad \textbf{Equation 3-13}$$

Comparing the result of Equation 3-13, the Chebyshev loss function, with the Butterworth loss function of Eq. 3-6, we see that the Chebyshev loss function exceeds that of the Butterworth filter by $20 \log_{10}\epsilon + 6(n-1)$. Since ϵ is usually a number between 0 and 1 to limit the ripple width, $\log\epsilon$ is negative. However, this is usually more than compensated for by the term $6(n-1)$, except in the trivial case, when n = 1.

COMPARING THE BUTTERWORTH AND CHEBYSHEV RESPONSES

Increasing the ripple factor ϵ for a fixed-order n improves the stopband characteristics of a Chebyshev filter, while creating a larger ripple. If the ripple factor ϵ is held constant, and the filter order is increased, increasing n increases loss but improves the stopband characteristics by allowing the filter to move from the passband to the stopband faster as seen in Fig. 3-5. These two

Table 3-6. 3 dB Chebyshev Filter ($\epsilon = 0.99763$): $s^{\eta} + b_{\eta-1} + \ldots + b_1 s + b_0$.

	b_0	b_1	b_2	b_3	b_4	b_5	b_6	b_7
1	1.00238							
2	0.70795	0.64490						
3	0.25059	0.92835	0.59724					
4	0.17699	0.40477	1.16912	0.58158				
5	0.06264	0.40794	0.54886	1.41498	0.57443			
6	0.04425	0.16343	0.69910	0.69061	1.66285	0.57070		
7	0.01566	0.14615	0.30002	1.05184	0.83144	1.91155	0.56842	
8	0.01106	0.05648	0.32076	0.47190	1.46670	0.97195	2.16071	0.56695

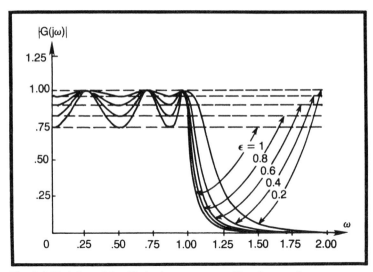

Fig. 3-4. Variation of the Chebyshev response with ϵ, for n = 6.

properties, of increasing the ripple factor ϵ, and increasing the filter order n are illustrated in Fig. 3-4 and Fig. 3-5, respectively.

A comparison of two Chebyshev sixth order (n = 6) responses with ripple factors of 0.1526, and 0.5 is shown with a sixth order Butterworth response in Fig. 3-6. As can be seen from Fig. 3-6, the cutoff and stopband features of the 0.5 ripple factor case are superior to those of the 0.1526 ripple factor case, and both are

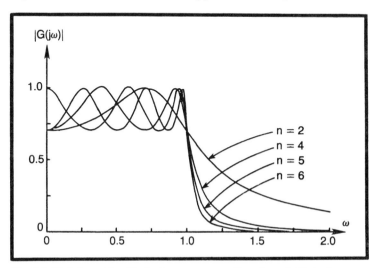

Fig. 3-5. Variation of the Chebyshev response with n, for a 3 dB ripple.

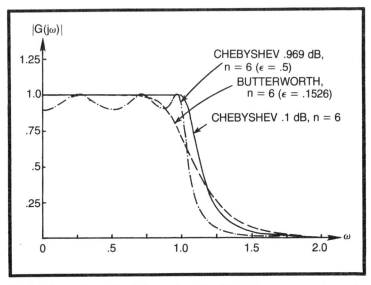

Fig. 3-6. Comparison of the Butterworth and two Chebyshev responses for n = 6.

superior to the Butterworth response. However, in the stopband, the Butterworth filter response has a much flatter response than the Chebyshev filters.

The Chebyshev filter is not only superior to the Butterworth at cutoff and in the stopband, it is the optimum all pole filter in this respect.

CHEBYSHEV FILTER TRANSFER FUNCTIONS

In general, we can find a Chebyshev transfer function $G(s) = 1/Q(s)$, where $Q(s)$ is defined by a polynomial as shown by Equation 3-8 and depends on n, the filter order, and the ripple factor ϵ, or ripple width RW_{dB}. The constant coefficients b of the polynomial for the Chebyshev filter are given in Tables 3-2 through 3-6.

As an example of the use of Tables 3-1 through 3-6 for the Chebyshev filter transfer function, let us find the transfer function of fourth order Chebyshev filter with $RW_{dB} = 0.5$ dB. We go to Table 3-3 for $RW_{dB} = 0.5$ dB labeled at the top of the table, and then look for n = 4 (filter order) in the first column of the table. The numbers in the row for n = 4 are the constant coefficients that fit into the polynomial $Q(s)$. These coefficients are $b_0 = 0.37905$, $b_1 = 1.02546$, $b_2 = 1.71687$, and $b_3 = 1.19739$. Rounding these coefficients to three places, we can write $Q(s)$ as follows:

$$Q(s) = s^4 + b_3 s^3 + b_2 s^2 + b_1 s + b_0$$

$$Q(s) = s^4 + 1.2s^3 + 1.72s^2 + 1.03s + 0.38$$

Now, we can write the transfer function $G(s)$:

$$G(s) = \frac{1}{s^4 + 1.2s^3 + 1.72s^2 + 1.03s + 0.38}$$

The Chebyshev transfer function will be employed to construct active filter circuits.

THE INVERSE CHEBYSHEV FILTER

The Chebyshev filter considered in the early part of this chapter are all-pole filters. If the function $f(\omega^2)$ is a rational function with finite poles, as has been noted earlier the transfer function is a rational function with finite zeros. If the Chebyshev amplitude function

$$|G_C(j\omega)|^2 = \frac{1}{1 + \epsilon^2 C_n^2(\omega)} \qquad \textbf{Equation 3-14}$$

in Equation 3-14 is subtracted from 1, then the resulting function is that of an Inverse Chebyshev filter with ripples in the stopband $0 < \omega < 1$. The function in Equation 3-14 is shown in Fig. 3-7A and 1 minus Equation 3-14 is shown in Fig. 3-7B.

If we now perform a low-pass to high-pass transformation by replacing ω by $1/\omega$, we have the function:

$$|G'(j\omega)|^2 = 1 - |G_C(j/\omega)|^2 \qquad \textbf{Equation 3-15}$$

which is sketched in Fig. 3-8. The function $|G(j\omega)|$ is the inverse Chebyshev amplitude function and is evidently a low-pass function.

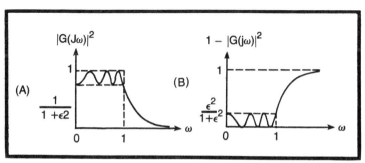

Fig. 3-7. A Chebyshev response $|H_C(j\omega)|^2$ at (A) and $1 - |H_C(j\omega)|^2$ at (B).

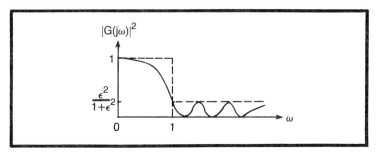

Fig. 3-8. $|H(j\omega)|^2$ for an inverse Chebyshev filter.

We note from Fig. 3-8 that $\omega = 1$ is the beginning of the stop-band ripple channel, and not the cutoff point. This is true in the general case, as is clear from the steps in the development.

From Equations 3-14 and 3-15 we obtain the Inverse Chebyshev function:

$$|Gj\omega)|^2 = \frac{\epsilon^2 C_n^2(1/\omega)}{1 + \epsilon^2 C_n^2(1/\omega)} \qquad \textbf{Equation 3-16}$$

The transfer function of the Inverse Chebyshev filter may be found by considering it the ratio of two polynomials as shown in Equation 3-17:

$$G(s) = \frac{P(s)}{Q(s)} \qquad \textbf{Equation 3-17}$$

where $P(s)$ will have finite zeros in the stop-band response. The polynomial $Q(s)$ may be found readily for a given n and ϵ by first finding its counterpart $Q_C(s)$ for the Chebyshev filter. In other words, we can find the $Q(s)$ of Equation 3-17 as follows:

$$Q(s) = s^n Q_C(1/s) \qquad \textbf{Equation 3-18}$$

This may be seen from the fact that the amplitude functions which yield $Q(s)$ and $Q_C(s)$ are identical except that ω is replaced by $1/\omega$ in one of them.

The numerator polynomial $P(s)$ can be found easily from Equation 3-19 with the aid of Table 3-2.

$$P(s)P(-s) = \omega^{2n} C_n^2(1/\omega)|\omega^2 = -s^2 \qquad \textbf{Equation 3-19}$$

Since $P(s)P(-s)$ will contain only factors like $(s^2 + a)^2$ because C_n is either even or odd with real zeros, both $P(s)$ and $P(-s)$ will contain the factor $s^2 + a$.

As an example, suppose we have a low pass Chebyshev filter transfer function with $Q(s) = s^3 + s^2 + 1.25s + 0.5$, and we wish to transform it into an Inverse Chebyshev filter transfer function as defined by Equation 3-17. The low-pass $Q(s)$ is defined as $Q_C(s)$; in order words:

$$Q_C(s) = s^3 + s^2 + 1.25s + 0.5$$

Then to find the Inverse $Q(s)$ we use Equation 3-18 as follows:

$$Q(s) = s^3 + \frac{1}{s^3} + \frac{1}{s^2} + \frac{1.25}{s} + 0.5$$

$$Q(s) = 0.5(s^3 + 2.5s^2 + 2s + 2)$$

To find $P(s)$ we need $C_3(\omega)$ from Table 3-2. $C_3(\omega) = 4\omega^3 - 3\omega$, and we must substitute $1/\omega$ for each ω in Θ $C_3(\omega)$.

$$P(s)\,P(-s) = \omega^{(2)(3)}\, C_3{}^2(1/\omega)|\omega^2 = -s^2$$

$$= \omega^6 \left[\frac{4}{\omega^3} - \frac{3}{\omega}\right]^2 |\omega^2 = -s^2$$

$$= \left[\frac{4\omega^3}{\omega^3} - \frac{3\omega^3}{\omega}\right]^2 \omega^2 = -s^2$$

$$P(s)P(-s) = \left[4 - 3\omega^2\right]^2|\omega^2 = -s^2$$

$$P(s)P(-s) = (4 + 3s^2)^2$$

$$P(s) = (3s^2 + 4)$$

Table 3-7. Chebyshev polynomials of the first kind.

n	$C_n(\omega)$
0	1
1	ω
2	$2\omega^2 - 1$
3	$4\omega^3 - 3\omega$
4	$8v^4 - 8\omega^2 + 1$
5	$16\omega^5 - 20\omega^3 + 5\omega$
6	$32\omega^6 - 48\omega^4 + 18\omega^2 - 1$
7	$64\omega^7 - 112\omega^5 + 56\omega^3 - 7\omega$
8	$128\omega^8 - 256\omega^6 + 160\omega^4 - 32\omega^2 + 1$

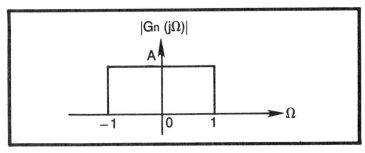

Fig. 3-9. An ideal normalized low-pass response.

Finally, the transfer function is given by

$$G(s) = \frac{K(3s^2 + 4)}{s^3 + 2.5s^2 + 2s + 2}$$

Equation 3-20

In the above equation we have disregarded the factor $\epsilon = 0.5$ in $Q(s)$ and the factor ϵ^2 in Equation 3-16. The ripple factor must be given to obtain the low frequency transfer function. We can lump the constant ϵ^2 with the constnat K in Equation 3-20.

FREQUENCY TRANSFORMATION

Let us assume that we have a normalized, low-pass network, whose transfer function $G_n(s)$ has an amplitude response $|G_n(j\Omega)|$ which satisfactorily approximates the ideal response of Fig. 3-9. Then we shall try to find a frequency transformation

$$S = F(s)$$

Equation 3-21

which applied to $G_n(S)$ results in the transfer function $G(s)$ of a denormalized network having the required amplitude $|G(j\omega)|$. That is,

$$G(s) = G_n[F(s)]$$

Equation 3-22

$$|G(j\omega)| = |G_n(j\Omega)|$$

Equation 3-23

$$\text{where: } j\Omega = F(j\omega).$$

Equation 3-24

As we shall see, the transformation F may be applied directly to the normalized network N_n to obtain the network N, without the intermediate steps of Equations 3-22 and 3-23. We have already considered one example of frequency transformation, that of frequency normalizing.

LOW-PASS TO HIGH-PASS TRANSFORMATION

Suppose the filter N we are seeking is a high pass filter with a cutoff ωc. The ideal response of such a filter is shown in Fig. 3-10, where it is seen that the frequency transformation must map $\Omega = 0$ into $\omega = \infty$, and $\Omega = \pm 1$ into $\omega = \pm \omega c$. Evidently the transformation required is the low pass to high pass transformation which can be described by the equation:

$$S = \frac{\omega c}{s} \qquad \textbf{Equation 3-25}$$

since in this case we have, for $S = j\Omega$ corresponding to $s = j\omega$,

$$\Omega = -\frac{\omega c}{\omega}$$

Thus $S = j0$ maps into $s = \pm j\infty$ and $S = \pm j1$ maps into $s = \pm j\omega c$.

As discussed in a previous section, an all pole normalized low pass function is given by the general equation:

$$G(s) = \frac{Kb_0}{s^n + b_{n-1}s^{n-1} + \ldots\ldots + b_i\,s^1 + b_0} \qquad \textbf{Equation 3-26}$$

where b_1 determines the type of filter (Butterworth or Chebyshev) and K is the gain. Thus the high-pass transfer function obtained from the low-pass prototype function of Equation 3-26 by means of the transformation of Equation 3-25 is given, in the normalized case ($\omega c = 1$), by the following equation:

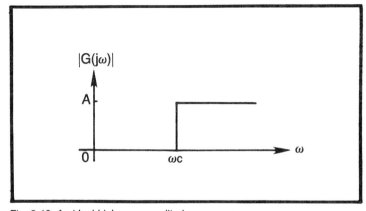

Fig. 3-10. An ideal high-pass amplitude response.

$$G(s) = \frac{Kb_0}{\dfrac{1}{s^n} + \dfrac{b_{n-1}}{s^{n-1}} + \ldots\ldots + \dfrac{b_1}{s_1} + b_0}$$

$$= \frac{Ks^n}{\dfrac{1}{b_0} + \dfrac{b_{n-1}\,s^n}{b_0\,s^{n-1}} + \ldots + \dfrac{b_1 s^n}{b_0 s^1} + \dfrac{b_0 s^n}{b_0}}$$

$$= \frac{Ks^n}{a_0 + a_1 s + \ldots + a_{n-1}s^{n-1} + s^n} \qquad \textbf{Equation 3-27}$$

where

$$a_{n-i} = b_i/b_0; \quad i = 0,1,2,\ldots\text{etc.}$$

Later, it will be shown that transformation from a low-pass active filter to a high-pass active filter requires the replacement of the filter resistors by capacitors, and the replacement of the circuit capacitors by resistors. In other words, Rs will be replaced by Cs, and Cs will be replaced by Rs.

LOW-PASS TO BAND-PASS TRANSFORMATION

To transform a low-pass transfer function into a band-pass filter transfer function with center frequency ω_0 and bandwidth $B = \omega_U - \omega_L$, the transformation $S = F(s)$ must map the ideal low-pass response of Fig. 3-11 into the ideal band-pass response of Fig. 3-12.

In other words, (1) $S = j0$ must map into $s = j\omega_0$; (2). $S = j1$ must map into $s = j\omega_U$; and (3) $S = -j1$ must map into $s = j\omega_L$. Since $s = j\infty$ maps into $s = j\infty$, the function $F(s)$ must be an improper

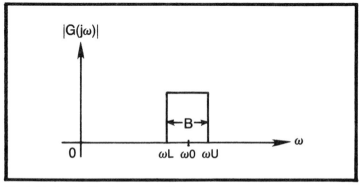

Fig. 3-11. An ideal band-pass amplitude response.

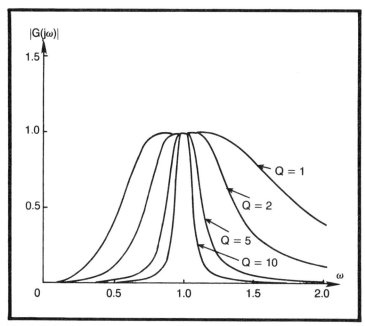

Fig. 3-12. Fourth-order Butterworth band-pass responses.

fraction, (a quadratic over a linear factor is sufficient because of the number of constraints to be satisfied) as shown in Equation 3-29.

$$S = F(s) = \frac{as^2 + bs + c}{\zeta s + e} \qquad \textbf{Equation 3-28}$$

Applying mapping 1 into Equation 3-19 results in

$$\frac{-a\omega_o^2 + jb\omega_o + c}{j\zeta\omega_o + e} = 0.$$

Equating the real and imaginary parts to 0 yields

$$c = a\omega_o^2, \text{ and } b = 0. \qquad \textbf{Equation 3-29}$$

Applying mapping 2 into Equation 3-29 and using the results of Equation 3-20 results in

$$j1(j\zeta\omega_U + e) = -a\omega_U^2 + a\omega_o^2.$$

Solving for e and ζ yields

$$e = 0, \text{ and } \zeta = \frac{a(\omega_U^2 - \omega_o^2)}{\omega_U} \qquad \textbf{Equation 3-30}$$

77

Finally, mapping 3 into Equation 3-28 results in

$$\zeta = \frac{a(\omega_o^2 - \omega_L^2)}{\omega_L} \qquad \text{Equation 3-31}$$

Equating the values of z in Equations 3-30 and 3-31 yields

$$\omega_o^2 = \omega_L \omega_U \qquad \text{Equation 3-32}$$

Thus under this transformation the center frequency ω_o is the geometric mean $\sqrt{\omega_L \omega_U}$. Using Equations 3-20, 3-21, and 3-23, the transformation of Equation 3-19 becomes:

$$S = \frac{a(s^2 + \omega_o^2)}{\dfrac{a(\omega_u^2 - \omega_o^2)s}{\omega_u}}$$

$$= \frac{s^2 + \omega_o^2}{(\omega_u - \omega_L)s}$$

$$= \frac{s^2 + \omega_o^2}{Bs} \qquad \text{Equation 3-33}$$

Thus a transfer function of a second order $(n = 2)$ band-pass filter with center frequency ω_o and bandwidth B is given by Equation 3-1A with s replaced by S given in Equation 3-33. The numerator will be a constant times s^n and the denominator will be a $2n$th-degree polynomial. The gain of a band-pass filter is defined as the value of its transfer function $G(s)$ at the center frequency ω_o. The quality factor Q is defined by the equation

$$Q = \frac{\omega_o}{B} \qquad \text{Equation 3-34}$$

So that in the normalized case, $\omega_o = 1$ rad/s, we have the following transfer function for a band-pass filter.

$$G(s) = \frac{Kb_o}{s^n + b_{n-1}s^{n-1} + \ldots\ldots + b_1 s^1 + b_o} \qquad \text{Equation 3-35}$$

Thus a band-pass filter is a Butterworth or Chebyshev filter type depending on the choice of the coefficients b_i.

As an example, a second order normalized band-pass filter with a specified Q and a gain K is described by the equation

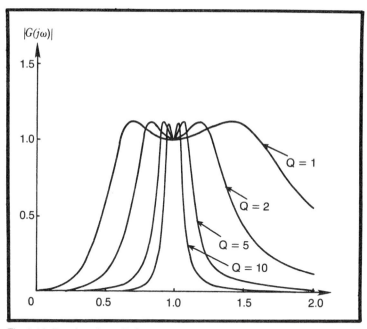

Fig. 3-13. Fourth-order 1 dB Chebyshev band-pass responses for different Qs.

$$G(s) = \frac{K}{s + 1}$$

or

$$G(s) = \frac{\dfrac{Ks}{Q}}{s^2 + \dfrac{1}{Q}s + 1}$$

Equation 3-36

Where $b_0 = 1$ since $K/(s + 1)$ is the transfer function of a normalized first-order low-pass filter with gain K.

As examples of band-pass filter responses, we have plotted, for $Q = 1$, 2, 5, and 10, fourth-order normalized Butterworth and 1-dB Chebyshev amplitude responses in Fig. 3-12 and Fig. 3-13, respectively. The functions were obtained from Equation 3-35 for n = 2 with the constant b_0, b_1, b_2, and b_3 appropriately chosen from Table 3-4. The gain is $K = 1$ in the Butterworth case and is such that the bottom of the passband ripple channel is 1 in the Chebyshev case. Notice that the higher the Q the narrower the bandwidth B.

Chapter 4
Putting Together
An Active Filter Circuit

In this chapter we shall consider a general circuit composed of resistors, capacitors, and one op amp, which can be used to realize second order filter transfer functions. The circuit is shown in Fig. 4-1, where the admittances are either $Y = G = 1/R$, or $Y = sC$, which properly chosen yield low-pass, high-pass, or band-pass filters of order two (n = 2). The circuit is called an infinite gain, multiple feedback network (MFB) because of the multiple feedback paths and the fact that the op amp is operating in an infinite gain mode.

INFINITE GAIN MULTIPLE FEEDBACK FILTERS

In the circuit of Fig. 4-1, we can write a node equation at node a, and the inverting node of the op amp resulting in:

$$(Y_1 + Y_2 + Y_3 + Y_4) V_a - Y_1 V_1 - Y_4 V_2 = 0$$

$$-Y_3 V_a - Y_5 V_2 = 0$$

Eliminating V_a we may write

$$\frac{V_2}{V_1} = \frac{Y_1 Y_3}{Y_5(Y_1 + Y_2 + Y_3 + Y_4) + Y_3 Y_4} \qquad \textbf{Equation 4-1}$$

We note that in all cases the circuit produces an inverting gain.

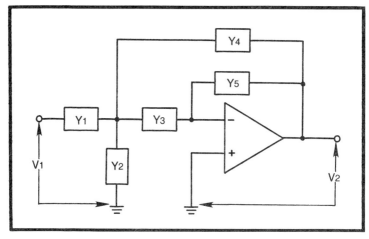

Fig. 4-1. A general second-order infinite gain MFB filter.

If a low-pass second-order filter is desired we need a transfer function with an inverting gain as described by the equation shown below:

$$\frac{V_2}{V_1} = \frac{-kb_0}{s^2 + b_1s + b_0} \qquad \text{Equation 4-2}$$

where k is the gain and b_0 and b_1 determine the type of low-pass filter (Butterworth or Chebyshev). Comparing Equations 4-1 and 4-2, we see that to make the two equations equal then we must have:

$$Y_5 = sC_5 \qquad \text{Equation 4-3}$$

and that Y_1, Y_3, and Y_4 must be constants; that is

$$Y_1 = G_1, \ Y_3 = G_3, \text{ and } Y_4 = G_4. \qquad \text{Equation 4-4}$$

Finally, to achieve the quadratic denominator, it is necessary to have

$$Y_2 = sC_2 \qquad \text{Equation 4-5}$$

The transfer function then becomes:

$$\frac{V_2}{V_1} = \frac{-\dfrac{G_1G_3}{C_2C_5}}{s^2 + \left(\dfrac{G_1 + G_2 + G_4}{C_2}\right)s + \dfrac{G_3G_4}{C_2C_5}}$$

81

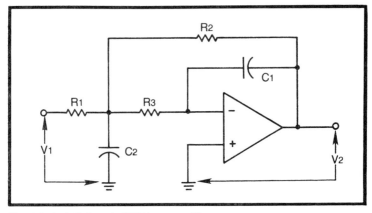

Fig. 4-2. An infinite gain MFB low-pass filter.

Renumbering the elements as shown in Fig. 4-2 yields the transfer function in Equation 4-2, where

$$b_0 = \frac{1}{R_2 R_3 C_1 C_2} \qquad \text{Equation 4-6A}$$

$$b_1 = \frac{1}{C_2} \left(\frac{1}{R_1} + \frac{1}{R_2} + \frac{1}{R_3} \right) \qquad \text{Equation 4-6B}$$

$$K = \frac{R_2}{R_1} \qquad \text{Equation 4-6C}$$

If we wish the active filter circuit of Fig. 4-1 be a high-pass filter, then we must have Equation 4-1 reduced to a transfer function with an inverting gain as described by the following equation:

$$\frac{V_2}{V_1} = \frac{-Ks^2}{s^2 + a_1 s + a_0} \qquad \text{Equation 4-7}$$

Thus both Y_1 and Y_3 must represent capacitors and Y_5 must represent a resistor. These require that Y_4 represent a capacitor and Y_2 a resistor. The circuit, with the elements numbered as shown, is given in Fig. 4-3.

The constants for the circuit in Fig. 4-3 are:

$$a_0 = \frac{1}{R_1 R_2 C_2 C_3} \qquad \text{Equation 4-8A}$$

$$a_1 = \frac{C_1 + C_2 + C_3}{R_2 C_2 C_3} \qquad \text{Equation 4-8B}$$

$$K = \frac{C_1}{C_2} \qquad \text{Equation 4-8C}$$

We may note that the high-pass filter of Fig. 4-3 may be obtained by applying the transformation procedure of section 3.9 to the transfer function of the low-pass filter circuit. Finally to obtain a second order band-pass filter with inverting gain K, center frequency ω_c, and bandwidth B, we must have the transfer function of the form:

$$\frac{V_2}{V_1} = \frac{-KBs}{s^2 + Bs + \omega_0^2} \qquad \text{Equation 4-9}$$

There are several ways of realizing the transfer function of Equation 4-9, one of which is shown in Fig. 4-4. The parameters of the circuit are defined by the following equations:

$$B = \frac{C_1 + C_2}{R_3 C_1 C_2} \qquad \text{Equation 4-10A}$$

$$\omega_0^2 = \frac{1}{R_3 C_1 C_2} + \left(\frac{1}{R_1} + \frac{1}{R_2} \right) \qquad \text{Equation 4-10B}$$

$$K = \frac{R_3 C_2}{R_1 (C_1 + C_2)} \qquad \text{Equation 4-10C}$$

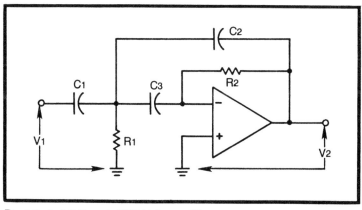

Fig. 4-3. An infinite gain MFB high-pass filter.

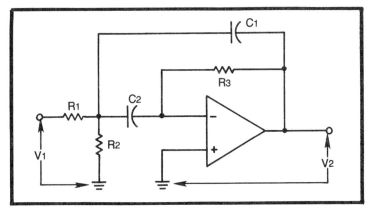

Fig. 4-4. An infinite gain MFB band-pass filter.

Numerical examples of this filter type will be furnished in the latter chapters of the book.

VOLTAGE CONTROLLED VOLTAGE SOURCE (VCVS) FILTERS

Another general filter circuit which may be used to obtain second order low-pass, high-pass, and band-pass active filters is that shown in Fig. 4-5. The circuit is called a *voltage controlled voltage source* (VCVS) *filter* because of the presence of the ideal op amp VCVS with gain $A > 0$. This type filter was first introduced by Sallen and Key in 1955. At this time we shall only consider the low-pass and high-pass filters, and at a latter time give a modification of the circuit of Fig. 4-5, which will realize a band-pass VCVS filter circuit.

From Fig. 4-5, we can write the node equations at nodes a and b, which are given by the following equations.

$$(Y_1 + Y_2 + Y_3)V_a - Y_1V_1 - \frac{Y_2V_2}{A} - Y_3V_2 = 0$$

and

$$(Y_2 + Y_4)\,\frac{V_2}{A} = Y_2V_a$$

where we have noted that $V_b = V_2/A$, and there is no current into the VCVS (ideal op amp). Eliminating V_a and solving for the transfer function yields:

84

$$\frac{V_2}{V_1} = \frac{AY_1Y_2}{(Y_2 + Y_4)(Y_1 + Y_2 + Y_3) - Y_2^2 - AY_2Y_3}$$ **Equation 4-11**

To obtain a low-pass filter, we must have Y_1 and Y_2 constants, and thus for a quadratic denominator, Y_3 and Y_4 must represent capacitors. Numbering the elements as shown in Fig. 4-6, the transfer function becomes:

$$\frac{V_2}{V_1} = \frac{\dfrac{AG_1G_2}{C_1C_2}}{s^2 + \left[\dfrac{C_1(G_1 + G_2) + C_2G_2(1-A)}{C_1C_2}\right]s + \dfrac{G_1G_2}{C_1C_2}}$$ **Equation 4-12**

The gain A of the op amp (VCVS), noninverting amplifier was found in an earlier chapter as

$$A = 1 + \frac{R_4}{R_3}$$ **Equation 4-13**

when applied to the circuit in Fig. 4-6.

Matching the specific transfer function of the VCVS second order active filter found in Equation 4-12 to the general transfer function given in Equation 4-2 of a low-pass Butterworth or Chebyshev filter, we can find the coefficients of Equation 4-2 as stated in Equations 4-14A through C.

$$b_0 = \frac{1}{R_1R_2C_1C_2}$$ **Equation 4-14A**

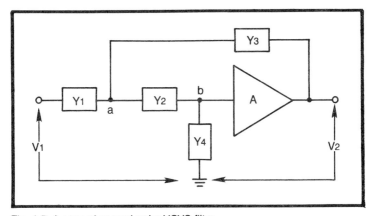

Fig. 4-5. A general second-order VCVS filter.

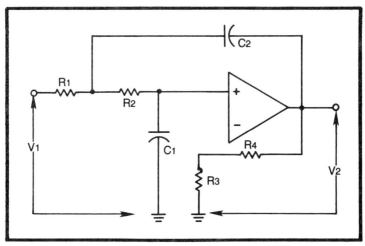

Fig. 4-6. A general second-order VCVS low-pass filter.

$$b_1 = \frac{1}{C_2} + \left(\frac{1}{R_1} + \frac{1}{R_2} \right) + \frac{1}{R_2 C_1} (1 - A) \qquad \textbf{Equation 4-14B}$$

$$A = K = 1 + \frac{R_4}{R_3} \qquad \textbf{Equation 4-14C}$$

Resistor values R_3 and R_4 are arbitrary except that their ratio must be fixed. However, for best operation they should be chosen to minimize the DC offset of the op amp. To see how this is done, consider the circuit of Fig. 4-6 operating in its DC mode; that is, the capacitors are open circuits, and the input and output terminals grounded as illustrated in Fig. 4-7. Ideally there is no voltage $V_a - V_b$, but in order for the practical op amp to operate there must be a slight current flowing into its input terminals. Thus the offset voltage $V_a - V_b$ will be minimized if the resistances $R_1 + R_2$ and the parallel combination of R_3 with R_4 are equal.

From the preceding condition we can write the following equations:

$$R_1 + R_2 = \frac{R_3 R_4}{R_3 + R_4}$$

$$R_3 + R_4 = \frac{R_3 R_4}{R_1 + R_2}$$

$$A = 1 + \frac{R_4}{R_3} = \frac{R_3 + R_4}{R_3}$$

$$A = \frac{R_3 R_4}{R_3(R_1 + R_2)}$$

$$A = \frac{R_4}{R_1 + R_2}$$

$$R_4 = A(R_1 + R_2)$$

$$A = \frac{R_3 + R_4}{R_3}$$

$$AR_3 = R_3 + R_4$$

$$R_4 = R_3(A - 1)$$

$$R_3 = \frac{R_4}{(A - 1)}$$

$$R_3 = \frac{A(R_1 + R_2)}{A - 1} \text{ but } A \neq 1$$

Let $R_{eq} = R_1 + R_2$ **Equation 4-15**

Then $R_3 = \frac{A\,R_{eq}}{A - 1}$ **Equation 4-16**

Figure 4-7 illustrates why we cannot capacitively couple a source into node 1, without allowing a DC return to ground from the noninverting terminal of the op amp. If the DC return path were not

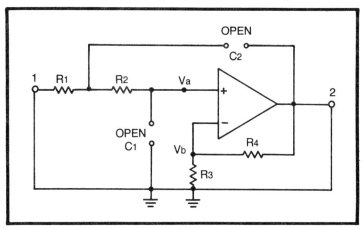

Fig. 4-7. The VCVS filter operating in the DC mode.

employed, no DC current could flow into the op amp and the op amp would not operate. In general, there must always be a DC return path to ground at each input terminal of the op amp.

By a dual development we may obtain a second order VCVS high-pass active filter. From the RC:CR transformation, we know that a high-pass active filter may be obtained from the low-pass active filter shown in Fig. 4-6 by leaving the op amp unchanged and interchanging resistors with capacitors and vice-versa. The stated procedure results in the high-pass active filter circuit illustrated in Fig. 4-8. The transfer function for the circuit in Fig. 4-8 can be shown to be equal to the following equation.

$$\frac{V_2}{V_1} = \frac{As^2}{s^2 + \left[\dfrac{G_2(C_1 + C_2) + C_2 G_1 (1-A)}{C_1 C_2}\right] s + \dfrac{G_1 G_2}{C_1 C_2}} \qquad \text{Equation 4-17}$$

Matching this equation with the general transfer function of a high-pass filter, that is Equation 4-7, results in

$$a_0 = \frac{1}{R_1 R_2 C_1 C_2} \qquad \text{Equation 4-18A}$$

$$a_1 = \frac{1}{R_2}\left(\frac{1}{C_1} + \frac{1}{C_2}\right) + \frac{1}{R_1 C_1}(1 - A) \qquad \text{Equation 4-18B}$$

$$A = K = 1 + \frac{R_4}{R_3} \qquad \text{Equation 4-18C}$$

The DC return to ground is satisfied by R_2, and for minimum offset R_3 and R_4 are given by Equation 4-16, where $R_{eq} = R_2$.

In reality, the high-pass active filter must act like a band-pass active filter since the upper cutoff frequency of the op amp will combine with the passive components to yield an upper and lower cutoff frequency. If the high-pass active filter is to function properly, enough frequency response must be allowed between the lower pass-band limit of the active circuit and the upper limit established by the op amp itself. Very often, the maximum useful frequency limit for an active high-pass filter is much less than for an equivalent low-pass.

Another limitation of high-pass active filters is that they are noisier than low-pass active filters. One obvious reason is that a

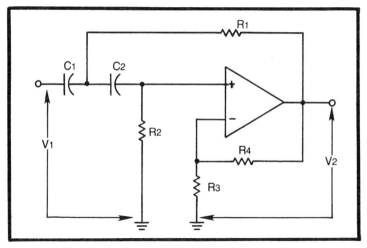

Fig. 4-8. A second-order VCVS high-pass filter.

high-pass filter is a differentiator that responds to sudden changes in inputs and uses this transient information to provide an output. In a high-pass filter, noise above the range of useful signals gets passed on, as do harmonics of rejected waveforms, unlike those in a low-pass filter where they are strongly attenuated. Secondly, the internal high frequency limitations of the op amp tend to decrease stability as frequencies near the upper limits are reached.

BIQUAD ACTIVE FILTER CIRCUIT

We will consider a general second order filter circuit which requires more passive and active elements than either the infinite gain MFB or the VCVS filters of the previous sections, but which has excellent stability and tuning features, and in the case of band-pass filters, is capable of attaining much higher values of Q. The circuit is referred to as a *biquad circuit* because versions of it can be used to realize the general biquadratic (ratio of two quadratics) transfer function.

We will begin by considering the second order high-pass filter transfer function with inverting gain, which we can write in the form

$$\frac{V_2}{V_1} = \frac{-Ks^2}{s^2 + as + b} \qquad \text{Equation 4-19}$$

Equation 4-19 may be written in the form

89

$$\frac{V_2}{V_1} = \left(\frac{-K}{1 + \dfrac{a}{s} + \dfrac{b}{s^2}} \right) \left(\frac{W/K}{W/K} \right) \qquad \textbf{Equation 4-20}$$

where: $\qquad V_2 = -W \qquad\qquad\qquad$ **Equation 4-21A**

$$W = KV_1 - \frac{aW}{s} - \frac{bW}{s^2} \qquad\qquad \textbf{Equation 4-21B}$$

Thus, we can realize Equation 4-19 if we can obtain an active filter circuit which realizes Equation 4-21B with V_2 measured at a node having $-W$ volts.

We can realize the above equations by considering the summing amplifier in Fig. 4-9. To obtain the voltage $-W/s$, we may connect an integrator with a time constant $RC = 1$ from node 4 to a new node 5 which the voltage is W/s. Then an inverter with gain -1 from node 5 to node 2 provides the voltage $-W/s$. Finally, to obtain the voltage $-T/s^2$ at node 3 we need an integrator with $RC = 1$ between nodes 3 and 5. The result is shown in Fig. 4-10, where the additional resistors and capacitors have been given the value of 1. In the normalized case this is a reasonable value.

The circuit is easy to analyze since by inspection we have

$$V_3 = \frac{-V_2}{s}$$

$$V_4 = \frac{-V_3}{s} = \frac{V_2}{s^2}$$

$$V_5 = -V_3 = \frac{V_2}{s}$$

Thus writing a node equation at node 6 in Fig. 4-10, we have

$$-KV_1 - V_2 - \frac{aV_2}{s} - \frac{bV_2}{s^2} = 0$$

Solving for the ratio of V_2/V_1 in the above equation, we have proven that Equation 4-19 follows. Thus, if the output is taken at node 4, we have a high-pass filter. Similarly, if the output is taken as V_3 we have a band-pass function defined by the following equation:

$$\frac{V_3}{V_1} = \frac{Ks}{s^2 + as + b} \qquad\qquad \textbf{Equation 4-22}$$

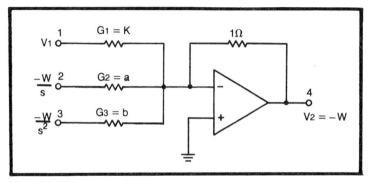

Fig. 4-9. A summing amplifier which realizes a biquad filter.

and if the output is V_4 we have the low-pass function given by the Equation 4-23.

$$\frac{V_4}{V_1} = \frac{-K}{s^2 + as + b} \qquad \textbf{Equation 4-23}$$

The steps outlined in obtaining the filter of Fig. 4-10 are equivalent to another method of obtaining active filters called the state variable method, and may be systematically extended to other filter types as well as to higher order filters. If we are only interested in band-pass and low-pass structures and thus have no need for node 4, we may eliminate one op amp in Fig. 4-10 by combining the operation of summing with that of integrating. This may be seen by considering the summing integrator circuit of Fig. 4-11. From the circuit in Fig. 4-11, we can write the following equation:

$$-KV_1 + \frac{aW}{s} + \frac{bW}{s^2} = sV_0 \qquad \textbf{Equation 4-24}$$

Comparing Equation 4-24 with Equation 4-21B we see that $V_0 = -W/s$. Thus we may connect node 2 of Fig. 4-11 directly to node 4 of Fig. 4-11 (the output node). To obtain $-W/s^2$ at node 3 we need an integrator with RC = 1 between node 4 (the output node) and a new node 5, and then an inverter with gain -1 between new node 5 and node 3. The result is shown in Fig. 4-12.

From the circuit in Fig. 4-12, we can write the following transfer functions.

$$\frac{V_2}{V_1} = \frac{-Ks}{s^2 + as + b} \qquad \textbf{Equation 4-25}$$

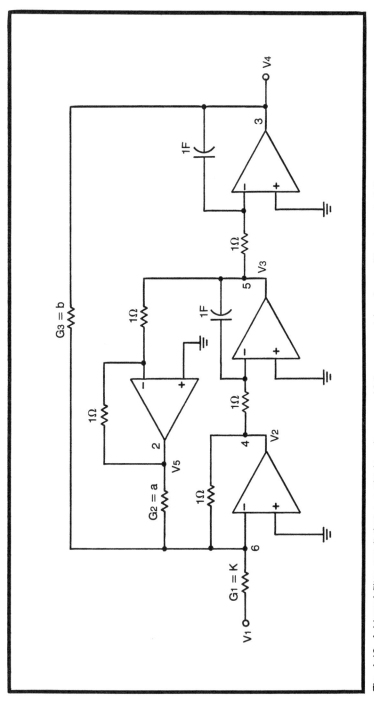

Fig. 4-10. A biquad filter circuit that can obtain a low-pass, high-pass, and band-pass filter characteristic.

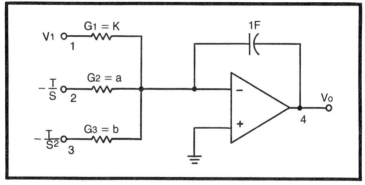

Fig. 4-11. A summing integrator.

Equation 4-25 represents a band-pass filter response.

$$\frac{V_3}{V_1} = \frac{K}{s^2 + as + b}$$ **Equation 4-26**

Equation 4-26 represents a low-pass filter response.

Figures 4-10 and 4-12 are examples of biquad circuits. In both circuits, the parameters K, a, and b may be obtained by adjusting respectively and conductances G_1, G_2, and G_3.

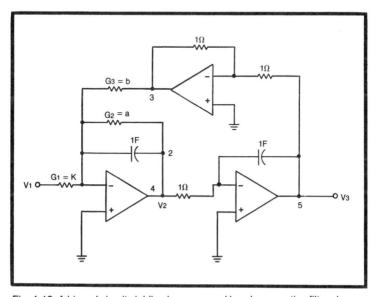

Fig. 4-12. A biquad circuit yielding low-pass and band-pass active filter characteristics.

We shall now consider an all-purpose biquad circuit shown in Fig. 4-13. The circuit has a transfer function of the form shown below:

$$G(s) = \frac{V_0(s)}{V_1(s)} = \frac{-(cs^2 + ds + e)}{s^2 + as + b} \qquad \textbf{Equation 4-27}$$

Where a, b, c, d, and e are real constants, and a, b > 0, with the single exception that (c) $(e) < 0$. The output V_0 may be either V_2 or V_3, depending on the numerator coefficients.

Analysis of the circuit of Fig. 4-13 yields the following equations.

$$\frac{V_2}{V_1} = \frac{-(cs^2 + ds + e)}{s^2 + as + b} \qquad \textbf{Equation 4-28}$$

$$\frac{V_3}{V_1} = \frac{d's + e'}{s^2 + as + b} \qquad \textbf{Equation 4-29}$$

where:

$$a = \frac{G_2G_8 - G_6G_7}{C_1G_8} \qquad \textbf{Equation 4-30}$$

$$b = \frac{G_3G_7G_9}{C_1C_2C_8} \qquad \textbf{Equation 4-31}$$

$$c = \frac{G_4}{G_8} \qquad \textbf{Equation 4-32}$$

$$d = \frac{G_2G_4 - G_1G_7}{C_1G_8} \qquad \textbf{Equation 4-33}$$

$$e = \frac{G_3G_5G_7}{C_1C_2C_8} \qquad \textbf{Equation 4-34}$$

$$d' = \frac{G_4G_9 - G_5G_8}{C_2G_8} \qquad \textbf{Equation 4-35}$$

$$e' = \frac{G_9(G_2G_4 - G_1G_7) - G_5(G_2G_8 - G_6G_7)}{C_1C_2G_8} \qquad \textbf{Equation 4-36}$$

For the normalized case, we choose the following parameters to equal unity (1).

$$C_1 = C_2 = G_7 = G_8 = G_9 = 1. \qquad \textbf{Equation 4-37}$$

Then Equation 4-28 is valid if from Equation 4-30 through Equation 4-34, we have the following

$$G_1 = c(a + G_6) - d \qquad \textbf{Equation 4-38A}$$
$$G_2 = a + G_6 \qquad \textbf{Equation 4-38B}$$
$$G_3 = b \qquad \textbf{Equation 4-38C}$$
$$G_4 = c \qquad \textbf{Equation 4-38D}$$
$$G_5 = e/b \qquad \textbf{Equation 4-38E}$$

The above equations defined by Equation set 4-38A through 4-38E are realizable conductances if the following properties are followed.

The quantity $e \geq 0$, and $c > 0$, since G_6, which is arbitrary, may be chosen so that $G_1 \geq 0$. That is,

$$G_6 \geq \frac{d - ac}{c} \qquad \textbf{Equation 4-39}$$

In the above equation, if $d - ac$ is negative or zero, we choose $G_6 = 0$, which eliminates the resistor R_6 in Fig. 4-13.

The quantity $e < 0$ and $c < 0$, and then we may choose Equation 4-38C except that $G_4 = -c$, $G_5 = -e/b$, and $G_1 = -c(a + G_6) + d$, in which case Equation 4-39 becomes

$$G_6 \geq \frac{ac - d}{c} \qquad \textbf{Equation 4-40}$$

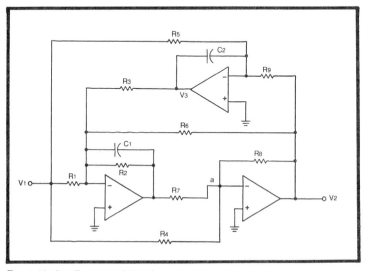

Fig. 4-13. An all-purpose biquad.

This means the original transfer function of Equation 4-28 must be obtained with a sign change. That is, the minus sign of Equation 4-28 must be plus.

The product $ce < 0$; that is, c and e are not equal to zero, and they have opposite signs. A modification of Fig. 4-13 is necessary. In Fig. 4-13, resistor R_8 and capacitor C_2 must be interchanged, and R_6 is removed to connect nodes labeled V_3 and a. Then Equation 4-27 holds for the ratio of V_3/V_1, where $C_1 = C_2 = G_7 = G_8 = G_9 = 1$, then $c = G_5$, $d = G_x - G_4$, $e = G_1 - G_2G_4$, $a = G_2 - G_6$, and $b = G_3 - G_2G_6$.

If we now consider the case when $c = 0$, this requires that

$$G_4 = 0 \qquad \qquad \textbf{Equation 4-41}$$
$$G_1 = -d$$
$$G_2 = a$$
$$G_3 = b$$
$$G_5 = e/b$$

where $d \leq 0$ and $e \geq 0$, and $G_6 = 0$ since it is no longer needed to make G_1 realizable.

If $d \geq 0$ and $e \leq 0$, we may take $G_1 = d$ and $G_5 = -e/b$, resulting is the negative of Equation 4-28.

To obtain $c = 0$ and $de \geq 0$ (both with the same sign), we use Equations 4-29, 4-30, 4-31, 4-35, 4-36, and choosing Equation 4-37, we have the following equations if $G_6 = 0$,

$$a = G_2$$
$$b = G_3$$
$$d' = G_4 - G_5$$
$$e' = G_2G_4 - G_1 - G_2G_5$$

The latter two equations may be written as follows,

$$G_4 = d' + G_5$$
$$G_1 = ad' - e'$$

If d', $e' \geq 0$ and $ad' \geq e'$, these are realizable since G_5 may be selected so that $G_4 \geq 0$. If d', $e' \geq 0$ and $ad' \leq e'$, replace e' and d' by their negatives, obtaining the negative of Equation 4-29. Evidently, if d', $e' \leq 0$, we may replace e' and d' by their negatives and repeat the foregoing procedure.

Finally we note that Fig. 4-13 may be used to obtain a low-pass filter if $c = d = 0$, a band-pass filter if $c = e = 0$, a high-pass filter is $d = e = 0$, a band reject filter if $d = 0$, and $e = bc$, and an all-pass filter if $d = -ac$, and $e = bc$. In the following chapters, we shall consider these special cases.

HIGHER ORDER ACTIVE FILTERS

A higher order active filter is one in which the transfer function is greater than two ($n > 2$). That is the transfer function $G(s)$ is one whose numerator and/or denominator polynomials are of degree greater than two. We shall consider the case of a denominator with degree $n > 2$ and numerator with degree $m \leq n$.

There are two general methods of obtaining higher order transfer functions. One way is to attempt to find a single circuit which realizes the function, such as a state variable realization, or some type of MFB circuit. This method is a generalization of the idea used to obtain the biquad circuits of the previous section.

The second general method is to factor the transfer function $G(s)$ into first and second order functions $G_1(s)$ and $G_2(s)$, then realize each factor with a subnetwork and cascade the subnetworks to obtain the overall network.

The cascaded network has the advantage that the mathematics is relatively simple, requiring only the factoring procedure and the use of familiar subnetworks with which to match the coefficients. Another advantage is that each subnetwork can be tuned separately to the required $G_i(s)$ transfer function.

The primary disadvantage of the cascaded network and one which has led researchers in recent years to seek alternate configurations is the sensitivity properties of active filters. In other words, these researchers examine active filters in terms of the aging, environmental changes, and other causes of circuit changes because of the characteristics of the op amp and the passive elements used in a filter design. These variations may cause an active filter to depart significantly from its desired performance. Employing more components in an active filter design will cause the chances of changing the circuit characteristics over a period of time to increase; hence, it is desirable to employ as few components as possible. However, in the development of higher order active filters, we will illustrate the cascaded network approach in this section.

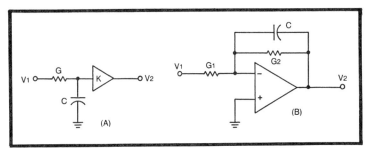

Fig. 4-14. Two first-order low-pass filters.

As a first example, we will consider first order transfer functions for low-pass active filters with noninverting and inverting gains. The transfer functions that we will use are stated below.

$$\frac{V_2}{V_1} = \frac{KG/C}{s + G/C}$$
Equation 4-42

$$\frac{V_2}{V_1} = \frac{-G_1/C}{s + G_2/C}$$
Equation 4-43

The transfer function of Equation 4-42 is shown as a noninverting low-pass active filter circuit in Fig. 4-14A, and the transfer function of Equation 4-43 is shown as an inverting low-pass active filter circuit in Fig. 4-14B.

Next we will consider first order transfer function for high-pass active filters with noninverting and inverting gains. The transfer functions that we will use are stated below.

$$\frac{V_2}{V_1} = \frac{Ks}{s + G/C}$$
Equation 4-44

$$\frac{V_2}{V_1} = \frac{-C_1s/C_2}{s + G/C_2}$$
Equation 4-45

The transfer function of Equation 4-44 is shown as a noninverting high-pass active filter circuit in Fig. 4-15A, and the transfer function of Equation 4-45 is shown as an inverting high-pass active filter circuit in Fig. 4-15B.

A general first order function for a low-pass or high-pass active filter can be written as follows:

$$\frac{V_2}{V_1} = \frac{-(cs + d)}{s + a}$$

Equation 4-46

The circuit in Fig. 4-13 can be employed to implement the transfer function of Equation 4-46 if we compare Equation 4-46 to Equation 4-27. If we make $b = e = 0$ in Equation 4-27, then we have identical equations. Also, we must consider $a, c > 0$, and from Equations 4-38A through 4-38E we have the following conductance values related to the constants in Equation 4-46.

$G_1 = c(a + G_6) - d$	**Equation 4-47A**
$G_2 = a + G_6$	**Equation 4-47B**
$G_4 = c$	**Equation 4-47C**
$G_3 = G_5 = 0$	**Equation 4-47D**

We made $G_3 = 0$ to correspond to $b = e = 0$ in Equation 4-31 and 4-34. We also made $G_5 = 0$ because it plays no role in the other equations. Remember, when a conductance value is zero, the corresponding resistance value is infinity—that is an open circuit. Hence, in Fig. 4-13 $G_3 = G_5 = 0$ disconnects the integrator from the circuit, and we do not have to show it is the final circuit, which is illustrated in Fig. 4-16. The normalized values $C_1 = C_2 = G_7 = G_8 = G_9 = 1$ are used in Equations 4-47A through 4-47D, which results in the circuit of Fig. 4-16.

Thus, given $a, c > 0$, we may select G_6, which is arbitrary, so that $G_1 > 0$. This requires that Equation 4-39 hold. If as before $d - ac \leqslant 0$ we can make $G_6 = 0$, eliminating resistor G_6. Hence, we can find the remaining conductances as follows.

$G_6 = 0$	$G_4 = c$
$G_1 = c(a + G_6) - d = c(a + 0) - d$	$G_3 = G_5 = 0$
$G_1 = ca - d$	$a, c \geqslant 0$
$G_2 = a + 0 = a$	$d - ac \leqslant 0$

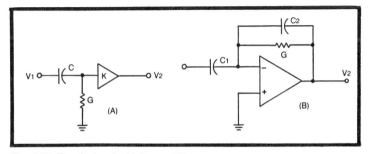

Fig. 4-15. Two first-order high-pass filters.

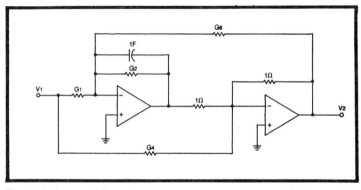

Fig. 4-16. A general first-order section derived from the biquad circuit.

Let $a = 1$ and $c = 1$. Therefore, $d - (1)(1) \leqslant 0$. Now make $d = 0$. Hence, we can find the remaining conductances.

$$G_1 = (1)(1) - (0) = 1$$
$$G_2 = 1$$
$$G_4 = 1$$

Suppose we wish to synthesize a third order Butterworth filter whose transfer function is

$$\frac{V_2}{V_1} = \frac{4}{s^3 + 2s^2 + 2s + 1} \qquad \textbf{Equation 4-48}$$

We factor the third order transfer function to form the product of a second order transfer function (G_2) times the transfer function of a first order network (G_1). In other words, we can write

$$\frac{V_2}{V_1} = G_1 G_2 \qquad \textbf{Equation 4-49}$$

where

$$G_1 = \frac{2}{s + 1}$$

and

$$G_2 = \frac{2}{s^2 + s + 1} \qquad \textbf{Equation 4-50}$$

We may realize G_1 by Fig. 4-14A with $G = C = 1$, and $K = 2$. We may realize G_2 by Fig. 4-6 with $C_1 = C_2 = G_1 = G_2 = 1$, and $K = 2$. Also, $R_{eq} = R_1 + R_2 = 2$, and $R_4 = K(R_{eq}) = 2(2) = 4$, hence $R_3 = R_4 = 4$. The result is shown in Fig. 4-17.

If we wish to construct a fourth-order active filter, we would factor the fourth order transfer function into the product of two

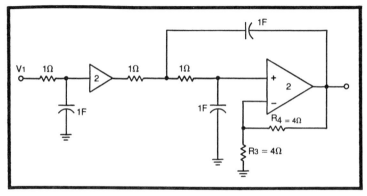

Fig. 4-17. A third-order low-pass Butterworth filter.

second order transfer functions. Then we may obtain the fourth order filter by cascading two networks containing the simulation of a second order filter. This method can be used indefinitely for any order active filter. Remember, if an odd-order active filter is to be simulated a first-order transfer function must be cascaded with as many second-order transfer functions to obtain the odd order active filter circuit.

Table 4-1. Butterworth Filter: $\Pi_i = 1^\eta (s^2 + a_is + b_1)$

η	a_1	b_1	a_2	b_2	a_3	b_3	a_4	b_4
1	1.41421	1.00000						
2	0.76537	1.00000	1.84776	1.00000				
3	0.51764	1.00000	1.41421	1.00000	1.93185	1.00000		
4	0.39018	1.00000	1.11114	1.00000	1.66294	1.00000	1.96157	1.00000

For the designer's convenience the second order denominator factors are given in Tables 4-1 through 4-6 for the more commonly used even order cases of Butterworth and Chebyshev filters.

☐ As an exmaple, construct a 0.1-dB fifth-order low-pass Chebyshev filter. The transfer function of the filter will be the product of two second order transfer functions, and one first order transfer function.

Table 4-2. 0.1 dB Chebyshev Filter: $\Pi_i = 1^\eta (s^2 + a_is + b_1)$

η	a_1	b_1	a_2	b_2	a_3	b_3	a_4	b_4
1	2.37209	3.31329						
2	0.52827	1.32981	1.27536	0.62282				
3	0.22940	1.12953	0.62674	0.69646	0.85614	0.26339		
4	0.12797	1.06964	0.36443	0.79901	0.54540	0.41627	0.64334	0.14563

Table 4-3. 0.5 dB Chebyshev Filter: $\Pi_{i=1}^{\eta}$ ($s^2 + a_i s + b_i$)

η	a1	b1	a2	b2	a3	b3	a4	b4
1	1.42562	1.51620						
2	0.35071	1.06352	0.94668	0.35641				
3	0.15530	1.02302	0.42429	0.59001	0.57959	0.15700		
4	0.08724	1.01193	0.24844	0.74133	0.37182	0.35865	0.43859	0.08805

$$\frac{V_2}{V_1} = H_1 H_2 H_3 \qquad \text{Equation 4-51}$$

The quantity H_1 represents a first order transfer function, and H_2 and H_3 represent second order transfer functions.

$$H_1 = \frac{K_1}{s + b_0}$$

From Table 3-2 we find $b_0 = 6.5522 \cong 6.55$. Hence, the previous equation becomes:

$$H_1 = \frac{K_1}{s + 6.55} \qquad \text{Equation 4-52}$$

Table 4-4. 1 dB Chebyshev Filter: $\Pi_{i=1}^{\eta}$ ($s^2 + a_i s + b_i$)

η	a1	b1	a2	b2	a3	b3	a4	b4
1	1.09773	1.10251						
2	0.27907	0.98650	0.67374	0.27940				
3	0.12436	0.99073	0.33976	0.55772	0.46413	0.12471		
4	0.07002	0.99414	0.19939	0.72354	0.29841	0.34086	0.35200	0.07026

The quantity H_2 represents a second order transfer function which can be written as:

$$H_2 = \frac{K_2}{s^2 + a_1 s + b_1} \qquad \text{Equation 4-53}$$

And the other second order transfer function is written as:

$$H_3 = \frac{K_3}{s^2 + a_2 s + b_2} \qquad \text{Equation 4-54}$$

Table 4-5. 2dB Chebyshev Filter; $\Pi_{i=1}^{\eta}$ ($s^2 + a_i s + b_i$)

η		b1	a2	b2	a3	b3	a4	b4
1		0.80382	0.82325					
2		0.20977	0.92868	0.50644	0.22157			
3		0.09395	0.96595	0.25667	0.53294	0.35061	0.09993	
4		0.05298	0.98038	0.15089	0.70978	0.22582	0.32710	0.26637	0.05650

Table 4-6. 3 dB Chebyshev Filter: $\Pi_i = {}_1{}^{\eta} (s^2 + a_is + b_i)$

η	a_1	b_1	a_2	b_2	a_3	b_3	a_4	b_4
1	0.64490	0.70795						
2	0.17034	0.90309	0.41124	0.19598				
3	0.07646	0.95483	0.20890	0.52182	0.28535	0.08880		
4	0.04316	0.97417	0.12290	0.70358	0.18393	0.32089	0.21696	0.05029

The constants in Equations 4-53 and 4-54 can be found in Table 4-2, for a low-pass Chebyshev filter with $RW_{dB} = 0.1$ dB. From Table 4-2 and n = 2, we find that $a_1 = 0.52827 \cong 0.528$, $b_1 = 1.32981 \cong$ 1.33, $a_2 = 1.27536 \cong 1.28$, and $b_2 = 0.62282 \cong 0.623$. Putting these values in Equations 4-53 and 4-54 yields the following results:

$$H_2 = \frac{K_2}{s^2 + 0.528s + 1.33}$$ **Equation 4-55**

$$H_3 = \frac{K_3}{s^2 + 1.28s + 0.623}$$ **Equation 4-56**

In the following chapters, we will develop techniques that will convert the constants of the transfer functions into actual passive component values.

Chapter 5
Low-Pass Active Filter Design

We will employ mostly Butterworth and Chebyshev active filter circuits in our design approach. Much data is obtainable for these two filter types from Tables 3-1 through 3-6 and Tables 4-1 through 4-6. Since the data in the two tables is for low-pass filters normalized for $\omega c = 1$ rad/s, we shall find it easier to obtain a normalized active filter circuit first. In the normalized circuit the component numbers are convenient to work with when making calculations. We will be using numbers such as 1 F and 1Ω. Eventually, the normalized impedance values will be changed to standard values such as 0.1 F and 10K.

We will select at least one capacitance as $C = 1$ F to begin with, and any other capacitance values should be multiples (for example, 1, 0.1, 2, etc.). Then in the denormalization process, when C is changed from 1 F to a value like 0.01μ F, the others will change to values such as 0.01μF, 0.001 μF, 0.02μF, etc. The denormalization process is carried out, of course, by dividing the normalized capacitances by the frequency normalizing factor u, as was defined in Chapter 1. Then both the capacitances and resistances must be denormalized by the impedance scaling factor (ISF) defined in Chapter 1. Remember that the capacitor normalized values are divided by the ISF and resistor normalized values are multiplied by the ISF.

At this point it is wise to review the equations that will help us in denormalizing a normalized active filter circuit.

$$u = \frac{2\pi f_c}{2\pi f_n} = \frac{\omega_c}{\omega_n}$$

Equation 5-1

u = the frequency normalizing factor
f_c = the desired cutoff frequency of the active filter
f_n = the normalized cutoff frequency usually $1/2\pi$ Hz.
$\omega_c = 2\pi f_c$, the desired cutoff frequency expressed in radians/second
$\omega_n = 2\pi f_n$, the normalized cutoff frequency expressed as 1 radian/second

In most active filter design problems the impedance scaling factor (ISF) is calculated using as a rule of thumb the following equation:

$$\text{ISF} = \frac{f_c}{20\pi}$$

Equation 5-2

Any ISF can be selected as long as the component values of the active filter circuit calculated by your ISF can be easily obtained.

The process of frequency and impedance scaling to obtain denormalized capacitor and resistor values is summarized in the following equations.

$$C_p = \frac{C_n}{(u)\,(\text{ISF})}$$

Equation 5-3

C_p = practical capacitor value
C_n = normalized capacitor value
u = the frequency normalizing factor
ISF = impedance scaling factor

$$R_p = R_n\,(\text{ISF})$$

Equation 5-4

R_p = practical resistor value
R_n = normalized resistor value
ISF = impedance scaling factor

If the denormalized resistances obtained are not suitable, it is well to remember that all of these resistor values may be multiplied by a common factor provided the capacitances are divided by the same common factor. In other words, the designer has changed the ISF. In general, feedback resistances may be much larger relative to the other resistances and still provide good circuit performance.

INFINITE GAIN MULTIPLE FEEDBACK LOW-PASS FILTERS

The basic circuit of the second order infinite gain MFB (multiple feedback) low-pass filter is shown in Fig. 5-1. The transfer function that describes the circuit shown in Fig. 5-1 has the general form shown below.

$$\frac{V_2}{V_1} = \frac{-Kb_0}{s^2 + b_1 s + b_0}$$ **Equation 5-5**

K = the gain of the circuit

b_1, b_0 = constants that can be found in the Tables 3-1 through 3-6 and Tables 4-1 through 4-6 depending if the filter type is a Butterworth or Chebyshev design

V_2 = the filter output voltage

V_1 = the filter input voltage

The constants of the transfer function K, b_0 and b_1 are related to the passive components of the circuit in Fig. 5-1 through the equations that follow.

$$b_0 = \frac{G_2 G_3}{C_1}$$ **Equation 5-6**

$$b_1 = G_1 + G_2 + G_3$$ **Equation 5-7**

$$K = \frac{R_2}{R_1} = \frac{G_1}{G_2}$$ **Equation 5-8**

For each of the above equations the capacitor C_2 was chosen to have a normalized value of 1 F.

The design procedure for the second order low-pass active filter begins with the final statement made in connection with Equations 5-6 through 5-8. The steps outlining the design procedure follow:

1. Select C_2 to have a value of 1 F in the normalizing case.
2. For the type of filter (Butterworth or Chebyshev) and the specific filter requirements find the constants b_0 and b_1 from Tables 3-1 through 3-6 or Tables 4-1 through 4-6. The constant K of the active filter circuit, which represents the circuit gain must be known or chosen depending on the active filter circuit application. Also, the cutoff frequency of the active filter circuit must be known. If the active filter circuit is a Chebyshev filter, the ripple wave factor RW_{dB} must be known.
3. For the given parameters in step 2, we determine the normalized conductances by solving for them using Equa-

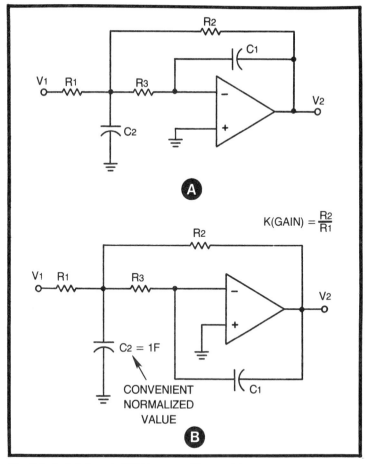

$$K(GAIN) = \frac{R2}{R1}$$

Fig. 5-1. An infinite gain MFB low-pass filter model.

tions 5-6 through 5-8. In other words, we substitute Equation 5-6 and Equation 5-8 into Equation 5-7, and solve for G_2 which results in Equation 5-9.

$$G_2 = \frac{b_1 \pm \sqrt{b_1^2 - 4C_1b_0(1 + K)}}{2(1 + K)} \qquad \textbf{Equation 5-9}$$

The conductance G_2 could have two values that satisfy Equation 5-9 because plus and minus signs appear outside the radical. However, we will use the plus sign on the radical for our solutions to active filter design. The conductance G_2 represents a real resistance; hence, for a given set of values for K, b_0, and b_1, we must select C_1

107

so that calculations under the radical in Equation 5-9 yield a positive number which makes G_2 real.

4. Next, we calculate the other conductances using Equation 5-6 and Equation 5-8 as follows.

$$G_1 = KG_2 \qquad \qquad \textbf{Equation 5-10}$$

$$G_3 = \frac{C_1 b_0}{G_2} \qquad \qquad \textbf{Equation 5-11}$$

5. Finally, we denormalize resistances by multiplying the normalized resistance values by the ISF discussed in the first section of this chapter. Also, we denormalize the capacitance values by dividing the normalized capacitance values by the product of the ISF times u, the frequency normalizing factor.

Example 5-1:

A second order low-pass Butterworth filter must be designed with a gain of 10 at a cutoff frequency of 10 kHz. Find the passive components that will produce the stated requirements.

Solution:

In this section of Chapter 5, we will employ the MFB filter circuit of Fig. 5-1. We will select $C_2 = 1$ F for convenience in the normalized case.

We are going to employ a Butterworth low-pass filter with $n = 2$ (second order). Therefore, we refer to Table 3-1 for $n = 2$, and find the constants $b_0 = 1$ and $b_1 = 1.41421 \cong 1.414$. Remember, the gain $K = 10$.

Next, we find the quantity G_2 using Equation 5-9 and substituting the constants found in step 2.

$$G_2 = \frac{1.414 + \sqrt{(1.414)^2 - 4C_1(1)\,(1 + 10)}}{2(1 + 10)}$$

$$G_2 = \frac{1.414 + \sqrt{2 - 44C_1}}{22}$$

We must select C_1 so that the number under the radical is positive. Let us select $C_1 = 0.01$ F and calculate G_2.

$$G_2 = \frac{1.414 + \sqrt{2 - 44(0.01)}}{22} = \frac{1.414 + \sqrt{2 - 0.44}}{22}$$

$$G_2 = \frac{1.414. + \sqrt{1.56}}{22} = \frac{1.414 + 1.249}{22} = \frac{2.663}{22}$$

$G_2 = 0.1211$ mho

The remaining conductances G_1 and G_3 are calculated using Equations 5-10 and 5-11.

$G_1 = KG_2 = (10)(0.1211)$

$G_1 = 1.211$ mho

$$G_3 = \frac{C_1 b_0}{G_2} = \frac{(0.01)(1)}{(0.1211)}$$

$G_3 = 0.0826$ mho

How much easier it is to calculate capacitance and resistance values that are normalized rather than using powers of ten to calculate these same values!

Finally, we denormalize the resistance and capacitance values. We find the frequency normalizing factor u, and the impedance scaling factor (ISF) from Equations 5-1 and 5-2, respectively.

$$u = \frac{\omega_c}{\omega_n} = \frac{2\pi f_c}{1 \text{ rad/s}} = \frac{2\pi(10,000)}{1}$$

$$= 20,000\pi$$

$$ISF = \frac{f_c}{20\pi} = \frac{10,000}{20\pi}$$

$$= 500/\pi$$

We use the two factors defined above to denormalize first the capacitance values, then the resistor values.

$$C_p = \frac{C_n}{(u)(\text{ISF})}$$

$$C_2 = \frac{1\ F}{(20,000\pi)\ \dfrac{(500)}{\pi}} = \frac{1\ F}{10^{+7}} = 1(10)^{-7}\ F$$

$$= 0.1\ \mu F$$

$$C_1 = \frac{0.01\ F}{10^{+7}} = 0.01\ (10)^{-7}$$

$$= 0.001\ \mu F$$

$$R_1 = \frac{1}{G_1}\ (\text{ISF}) = \frac{1}{1.211}\ (500/\pi) = \frac{159.15}{1.211}$$

$$= 131.42\ \text{ohms}$$

$$R_2 = \frac{\text{ISF}}{G_2} = \frac{159.15}{0.1211} = 1314\ \text{ohms}$$

$$R_3 = \frac{\text{ISF}}{G_3} = \frac{159.15}{0.0826} = 1927\ \text{ohms}$$

The active filter circuit is shown in Fig. 5-2 with the practical values of resistances and capacitances found in this example.

Example 5-2:

A second-order low-pass Chebyshev filter must be designed with a gain of 5 at a cutoff frequency of 15 kHz and a ripple width $RW_{dB} = 0.1$ dB. Find the passive components that will produce the stated requirements.

Solution:

We will employ the MFB filter circuit of Fig. 5-1. We select C_2 = 1 F for convenience in the normalized case.

We are going to employ a Chebyshev low pass filter with n = 2 (second order) and $RW_{dB} = 0.1$ dB, therefore we refer to Table 3-2, and find the constants $b_0 = 3.31329 \cong 3.313$ and $b_1 = 2.37209 \cong$ 2.372. Remember, the gain $K = 5$.

Next, we find the quantity G_2 using Equation 5-9 and substituting the constants found in step 2.

$$G_2 = \frac{2.372 + \sqrt{(2.372)^2 - 4C_1\ (3.313)(1 + 5)}}{2(1 + 5)}$$

$$= \frac{2.372 + \sqrt{5.626384 - 79.512C_1}}{12}$$

We must select C_1 so that the number under the radical is positive. Let us select $C_1 = 0.01$ F and calculate G_2.

$$G_2 = \frac{2.372 + \sqrt{5.626 - 79.512(0.01)}}{12}$$

$$= \frac{2.372 + \sqrt{5.626 - 0.79512}}{12}$$

$$= \frac{2.372 + \sqrt{4.831}}{12} = \frac{4.57}{12}$$

$$= 0.3808 \text{ mho}$$

The remaining conductances G_1 and G_3 are calculated using Equations 5-10 and 5-11.

$$G_1 = KG_2 = (5)(0.3808)$$

$$= 1.904 \text{ mho}$$

$$G_3 = \frac{C_1 b_0}{G_2} = \frac{(0.01)(3.313)}{0.3808} = 0.087 \text{ mho}$$

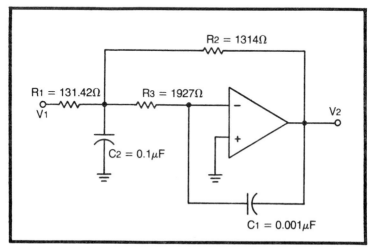

Fig. 5-2. Low-pass Butterworth filter for Example 5-1 where $f_c = 10$ kHz, $n = 2$.

How much easier it is to calculate capacitance and resistance values that are normalized rather than using powers of 10 to calculate these same values.

Finally, we denormalize the resistance and capacitance values. We find the frequency normalizing factor u, and the impedance scaling factor (ISF) from Equations 5-1 and 5-2 respectively.

$$u = \frac{\omega_c}{\omega_n} = \frac{2\pi f_c}{1 \text{ rad/s}} = \frac{2\pi(15,000)}{1}$$

$$= 30,000\pi$$

$$\text{ISF} = \frac{f_c}{20\pi} = \frac{15,000}{20\pi}$$

$$= 750/\pi$$

We use the two factors defined above to denormalize first the capacitance values, then the resistor values.

$$C_p = \frac{C_n}{(u)(\text{ISF})}$$

$$C_2 = \frac{1 \text{ F}}{(30,000\pi)\,\dfrac{(750)}{\pi}} = \frac{1 \text{ F}}{22.5\,(10)^{+6}} = 0.044\,(10)^{-6}$$

$$C_2 = 0.044\ \mu \text{ F}$$

$$C_1 = \frac{0.01 \text{ F}}{22.5\,(10)^{+6}} = 0.00044\,(10)^{-6} = 440\,(10)^{-12}$$

$$C_1 = 440\ p\text{F}$$

$$R_1 = \frac{1}{G_1}\,(\text{ISF}) = \frac{1}{1.904}\,(750/\pi) = \frac{238.73}{1.904}$$

$$R_1 = 126.38 \text{ ohms}$$

$$R_2 = \frac{\text{ISF}}{G_2} = \frac{238.73}{0.3808} = 626.92 \text{ ohms}$$

$$R_3 = \frac{ISF}{G_3} = \frac{238.73}{0.087} = 2744 \text{ ohms}$$

The active filter circuit is shown in Fig. 5-3 with the practical values of resistances and capacitances found in this example.

The infinite gain MFB filter achieves an inverting gain low-pass characteristic with a minimal number of circuit elements. It also has the advantages of low output impedance and good stability.

VOLTAGE CONTROLLED VOLTAGE SOURCE (VCVS) OR SALLEN AND KEY LOW-PASS FILTERS

The basic circuit of the VCVS low-pass filter is shown in Fig. 5-4. The general transfer function that describes the circuit performance of Fig. 5-4 has the general form shown below. The correspondence between the transfer function and the circuit in Fig. 5-4 was developed in Chapter 4, and is repeated at this time.

$$\frac{V_2}{V_1} = \frac{Kb_0}{s^2 + b_1 s + b_0} \qquad \textbf{Equation 5-12}$$

K = the gain of the circuit

b_1, b_0 = constants that can be found in Tables 3-1 through 3-6 and Tables 4-1 through 4-6 depending on whether the filter type is a Butterworth or Chebyshev design

V_1 = the filter input voltage

V_2 = the filter output voltage

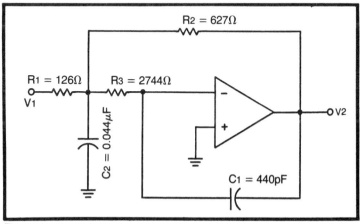

Fig. 5-3 Low-pass Chebyshev filter for Example 5-2 where f_c = 15 kHz, RW_{dB} = 0.1 dB, n = 2.

The constants of the transfer function K, b_0, and b_1 were shown in Chapter 4 to be related to the passive components of the circuit in Fig. 5-4 through the following equations. For the following equations the capacitor C_2 was chosen to have a normalized value of 1 F.

$$K = 1 + \frac{R_4}{R_3}, \text{ for } K \geqslant 1 \qquad \textbf{Equation 5-13}$$

$$b = \frac{G_1 G_2}{C_1} \qquad \textbf{Equation 5-14}$$

$$b_1 = G_1 + G_2 + (1 - K) \frac{G_2}{C_1} \qquad \textbf{Equation 5-15}$$

The steps outlining the design procedure for the VCVS filter follow:

1. Select C_2 to have a value of 1 F in the normalized case.
2. For the type of filter (Butterworth or Chebyshev) and the specific filter requirements find the constants b_0 and b_1 from the Tables 3-1 through 3-6 or Tables 4-1 through 4-6. The constant K of the active filter circuit, which represents the circuit gain must be known or chosen depending on the active filter circuit application. Also, the cutoff frequency of the active filter circuit must be known. If the active filter circuit is a Chebyshev filter, the ripple wave factor RW_{dB} must be known.
3. For the given parameters in step 2, we determine the normalized conductances by solving for them using Equations 5-13 through 5-15. In other words, we substitute Equations 5-13 and 5-14 into Equation 5-15, and solve for G_1 which results in Equation 5-16.

$$G_1 = \frac{b_1 \pm \sqrt{b_1^2 - 4b_0 (C_1 + 1 - K)}}{2} \qquad \textbf{Equation 5-16}$$

The conductance G_1 could have two values that satisfy Equation 5-16 since plus and minus signs appear outside the radical. However, we will use the plus sign on the radical for our solutions to active filter design. The conductance G_1 represents a real resistance; hence, for a given set of values for b_0 and b_1, we must select K greater than $(C_1 + 1)$ so that calculations under the radical in Equation 5-16 yield a positive number which makes G_1 real.

The other conductance G_2 is calculated through Equation 5-14 and the calculated value of G_1 by the following equation:

$$G_2 = \frac{C_1 b_0}{G_1} \qquad \textbf{Equation 5-17}$$

4. Next, we calculate R_3 and R_4 for minimum offset voltage using the equations developed in Chapter 4 and shown below.

$$R_4 = K(R_1 + R_2) \qquad \textbf{Equation 5-18}$$

$$R_3 = \frac{K(R_1 + R_2)}{K - 1}; \quad K = 1 \qquad \textbf{Equation 5-19}$$

In the previous equation, if $K = 1$, then we may take $R_4 = 0$, and $R_3 = \infty$. In Fig. 5-4, this would mean that resistor R_3 would be removed and an open circuit put in its place. In

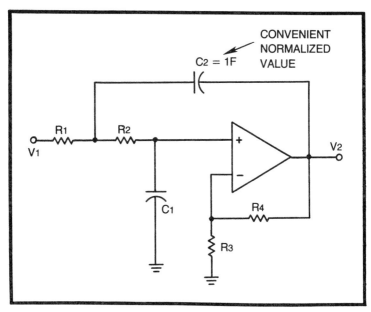

Fig. 5-4. A second-order VCVS (Sallen-Key) low-pass active filter circuit.

addition, the resistor R_4 would be replaced by a short circuit.

5. Finally, we denormalize resistances by multiplying the normalized resistance values by the ISF discussed in the first section of this chapter. Also, we denormalize the capacitance values by dividing the normalized capacitance values by the product of the ISF times u the frequency normalizing factor.

Example 5-3:

A second-order low-pass Butterworth filter must be designed with a gain of unity at a cutoff frequency of $\omega_c = 10^5$ rad/s. Design a VCVS action filter circuit that will meet the stated requirements.

Solution:

We will employ the VCVS circuit shown in Fig. 5-4. Remember the capacitor $C_2 = 1$ F for convenience in the normalized case.

We are going to employ a Butterworth low-pass filter of the second order ($n = 2$). Therefore, we refer to Table 3-1 for $n = 2$, and find the constants $b_0 = 1$ and $b_1 = 1.41421 \stackrel{\sim}{=} 1.414$ Remember the gain $K = 1$.

Next, we find the quantity G_1 using Equation 5-16 and substituting the constants found in step 2.

$$G_1 = \frac{1.414 + \sqrt{(1.414)^2 - 4(1)(C_1 + 1 - 1)}}{2}$$

$$G_1 = \frac{1.414 + \sqrt{2 - 4C_1}}{2}$$

We must select C_1 so that the number under the radical is positive. Let us select $C_1 = 0.5$ F and calculate G_1.

$$G_1 = \frac{1.414 + \sqrt{-4(0.5)}}{2} = \frac{1.414 + \sqrt{2 - 2}}{2}$$

$$G_1 = 0.707 \text{ mho}$$

At this time it is worth while to investigate the limits of selecting C_1 in terms of the constants K, b_0, and b_1 so that the radical in Equation

5-16 is positive. The equation that follows tells us the limits of C_1 so that the radical in Equation 5-16 is positive.

$$0 \leqslant C_1 \leqslant K - 1 + \frac{b_1^2}{4b_0} \qquad \textbf{Equation 5-20}$$

Equation 5-20 allows us to select a C_1 whose value is greater than zero for a gain K that is equal to one or greater than one given a set of constants b_0, and b_1 so that the conductance G_1 is real. In other words, if the restrictions of Equation 5-20 are used, the radical in Equation 5-16 will be positive. Now we can calculate G_2, using Equation 5-17.

$$G_2 = \frac{C_1 b_0}{G_1} = \frac{(0.5)(1)}{0.707} = 0.707 \text{ mho}$$

Next, we calculate R_3 and R_4 for minimum offset voltage using Equations 5-18 and 5-19. However, the gain $K = 1$; hence, in this case, $R_4 = 0$ (a short circuit from the output of the op amp to its inverting terminal), and $R_3 = \infty$ (an open circuit in place of R_4 in Fig. 5-4).

Finally, we denormalize the resistance and capacitance values. We find the frequency normalizing factor u, and the impedance scaling factor (ISF) from Equations 5-1 and 5-2, respectively.

$$u = \frac{\omega_c}{\omega_n} = \frac{10^5 \text{ rad/s}}{1 \text{ rad/s}} = 10^5$$

$$\text{ISF} = \frac{f_c}{20\pi} = \frac{\omega_c/2\pi}{20\pi} = \frac{\omega_c}{40\pi^2} = \frac{10^5}{40\pi^2}$$

$$= 253.3$$

$$C_p = \frac{C_n}{(u)(\text{ISF})}$$

$$C_1 = \frac{0.5 \text{ F}}{10^5 (253.3)} = 0.00197 \, (10^{-5}) = 0.0197 \, (10^{-6})$$

$$C_1 \cong 0.02 \, \mu\text{F}$$

$$C_2 = \frac{1 \text{ F}}{10^5 \, (253.3)} = 0.00394 \, (10^{-5}) = 0.0394 \, (10^{-6})$$

$$\cong 0.04 \, \mu\text{F}$$

$$R_1 = \frac{\text{ISF}}{G_1} = \frac{253.3}{0.707}$$

$$= 358.45 \text{ ohms} \cong 359 \text{ ohms}$$

$$R_2 = \frac{\text{ISF}}{G_2} = \frac{253.3}{0.707}$$

$$= 358.56 \text{ ohms} \cong 359 \text{ ohms}$$

The active filter circuit designed in this example is shown in Fig. 5-5 with the denormalized values of resistances and capacitances found in step 5.

If the designer doesn't like the denormalized values of resistance and capacitance shown in Fig. 5-5, he may decide to change them by choosing a new ISF. For example, if he decides to reduce the capacitor values by a factor 2, then he must increase the resistor values by the same factor. Therefore, the new component values will be $C_1 = 0.01 \, \mu\text{F}$, $C_2 = 0.02 \, \mu\text{F}$, and $R_1 = R_2 = 718$ ohms. Hence, the designer can change the original denormalized values to suit the design to the components he has readily available.

Example 5-4:

A second-order low-pass Chebyshev filter must be designed with a gain of unity at a cutoff frequency of 10 kHz and a ripple width $RW_{dB} = 0.5$ dB. Find the passive components that will produce a VCVS active filter circuit that meets the stated requirements.

Solution:

We will employ the VCVS circuit shown in Fig. 5-4. Remember the capacitor $C_2 = 1$ F for convenience in the normalized case.

We are going to employ a Chebyshev low-pass filter of the second order (n = 2) and $RW_{dB} = 0.5$ dB. Therefore, we refer to Table 3-3 and find the constants $b_0 = 1.51620 \cong 1.516$ and $b_1 = 1.42562 \cong 1.426$. Remember the gain $K = 1$.

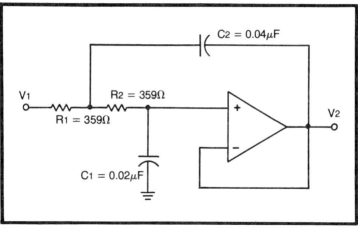

Fig. 5-5. The second-order low-pass Butterworth VCVS active filter circuit for Example 5-3, $\omega_c = 10^5$ rad/s.

Next, we find the quantity G_1 using Equation 5-16 and substituting the constants found in step 2.

$$G_1 = \frac{1.426 + \sqrt{(1.426)^2 - 4(1.516)(C_1 + 1 - 1)}}{2}$$

$$= \frac{1.426 + \sqrt{2.033 - 6.10\, C_1}}{2}$$

We must select C_1 so that the number under the radical is positive. Let us select $C_1 = 0.2$ F and calculate G_1.

$$G_1 = \frac{1.426 + \sqrt{2.033 - 6.10\,(0.2)}}{2}$$

$$= \frac{1.426 + \sqrt{2.033 - 1.2}}{2}$$

$$= \frac{1.426 + \sqrt{0.833}}{2}$$

$$\cong 1.164 \text{ mho}$$

The limits of selecting C_1 so that the radical in Equation 5-16 is positive can be checked by using Equation 5-20 as follows.

119

$$0 \leqslant C_1 \leqslant K - 1 + \frac{b_1^2}{4b_0}$$

$$0 \leqslant C_1 \leqslant 1 - + \frac{(1.426)^2}{4(1.516)}$$

$$0 \leqslant C \leqslant 0.335 \text{ F}$$

Now we can calculate G_2 using Equation 5-17.

$$G_2 = \frac{C_1 b_0}{G_1} = \frac{(0.2)(1.516)}{(1.164)} \cong 0.26 \text{ mho}$$

Next, we calculate R_3 and R_4 for minimum offset voltage using Equation 5-18 and Equation 5-19. However, the gain $K = 1$; hence, in this case $R_4 = 0$ (a short circuit from the output of the op amp to its inverting terminal) and $R_3 = \infty$ (an open circuit in place of R_4 in Fig. 5-4.

Finally, we denormalize the resistance and capacitance values. We find the frequency normalizing factor u, and the impedance scaling factor (ISF) from Equations 5-1 and 5-2, respectively.

$$u = \frac{\omega_c}{\omega_n} = \frac{2\pi(10,000) \text{ rad/s}}{1 \text{ rad/s}} = 20,000\pi$$

$$\text{ISF} = \frac{f_c}{20\pi} = \frac{10,000}{20\pi} = \frac{500}{\pi} = 159.15$$

$$C_p = \frac{C_n}{u(\text{ISF})}$$

$$C_1 = \frac{0.2}{20,000\pi(159.15)} = 0.02 \ \mu\text{F}$$

$$C_2 = \frac{1 \text{ F}}{20,000\pi(159.15)} = 0.1 \ \mu\text{F}$$

$$R_1 = \frac{\text{ISF}}{G_1} = \frac{159.15}{1.164} = 136.73 \text{ ohms}$$

$$R_2 = \frac{159.15}{G_2} = \frac{159.15}{0.26} = 612.11 \text{ ohms}$$

The active filter circuit designed in this example is shown in Fig. 5-6 with the denormalized values of resistances and capacitances found in step 5.

Remember the designer can change the original denormalized values to suit the design to the components he has readily available. The designer must choose a new ISF and multiply the capacitor values by the new ISF, and divide the resistor values by the same ISF.

HIGHER ORDER LOW-PASS FILTER CIRCUITS

We may obtain higher order low-pass Butterworth or Chebyshev filters by cascading two networks or more until the order of filter that the designer desires is attained. In other words, if the designer wants a fourth-order filter, he can cascade two second-order active filter circuits to obtain the fourth-order active filter circuit. If the designer wants an odd order active filter he has to cascade at least one active filter circuit with an order of one, with one or more second-order active filter circuits. For example, if the designer wants a fifth order active filter circuit he would cascade two second order active filter circuits with a single first-order active filter circuit. The methods of the previous sections and those in Chapter 4 will be employed to find the individual filter sections.

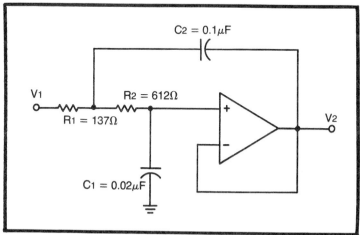

Fig. 5-6. A VCVS Chebyshev low-pass filter circuit with a cutoff frequency of 10 kHz and $RW_{dB} = 0.5$ dB.

Example 5-5:

A fifth-order low-pass Butterworth filter must be designed with a gain of − 10 at a cutoff frequency of 10 kHz. Find the passive components that will produce the stated requirements.

Solution:

1. Consider the overall transfer function $H(s)$ to be the product of three transfer functions. In other words, $H(s) = H_1 H_2 H_3$ where H_1 is a first order transfer function, and H_2 and H_3 are each a second order transfer function. We will employ the VCVS active circuit with a gain of one for each of the two second order VCVS circuits in order to minimize components. The first order active filter section will be the circuit shown in Fig. 4-14B. The general circuit that we will employ is shown in Fig. 5-7.

   The fifth-order transfer function that will describe the action of the circuit in Fig. 5-7 is written as the product of three transfer functions as shown below.

$$H(s) = \left[\frac{-K_0}{s + b_0} \right] \left[\frac{+K_a b_1}{s^2 + a_1 s + b_1} \right] \left[\frac{+K_b b_2}{s^2 + a_2 s + b_2} \right]$$

The constant b_0 is found in Table 3-1 for n = 1; hence, $b_0 = 1$. The other constants are found in Table 4-1 for n = 2; hence, $a_1 = 0.76537 \cong 0.765$, $b_1 = 1$, $a_2 = 1.84776 \cong 1.848$, and $b_2 = 1$. Remember $K_a = 1$, $K_b = 1$, and the product of the three gains equals minus ten, or $K_0 K_a K_b = -10$ which means K_0 must equal minus ten (− 10).

2. Now we will find the passive components that fit the first order transfer function in the equation shown in step 1. We compare the first order transfer function constants of the equation in step 1 to Equation 4-43 which is the transfer function of the first order active filter section of Fig. 5-7. Hence, we can relate the circuit parameters of this active filter section to the constants K_0, and b_0.

$$b_0 = \frac{G_2}{C_1} \qquad \qquad \textbf{Equation 5-21}$$

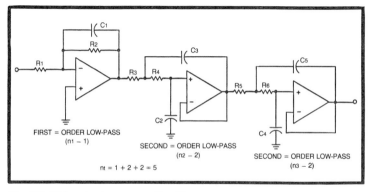

Fig. 5-7. Fifth-order low-pass active filter.

Equation 5-22

$$K_0 = \frac{-G_1}{C_1}$$

For convenience in the normalized case, we will select C_1 = 1 F. Now we can solve for G_1 and G_2 knowing that $b_0 = 1$ and $K_0 = -10$.

$$G_2 = b_0 C_1 = (1)(1)$$
$$= 1 \text{ mho}$$
$$G_1 = -K_0 C_1 = -(-10)(1) = +10$$
$$= 10 \text{ mho}$$

3. Using the method of the previous section in this chapter, we will find the passive components of a low-pass VCVS Butterworth filter as shown in the last two filter sections of Fig. 5-7. The constants of the second order Butterworth transfer function have already been found in step 1 of this example. Thus, we can find the quantity G_3 using Equation 5-16 and substituting the constants found in step 1.

$$G_3 = \frac{a_1 + \sqrt{a_1^2 - 4b_1(C_2 + 1 - K_a)}}{2}$$

$$= \frac{0.765 + \sqrt{(0.765)^2 - 4(1)(C_2 + 1 - 1)}}{2}$$

$$= \frac{0.765 + \sqrt{0.585 - 4C_2}}{2}$$

We must select C_2 so that the number under the radical is positive. Let us select $C_2 = 0.1$ F and calculate G_3.

$$G_3 = \frac{0.765 + \sqrt{0.585 - 4(0.1)}}{2} = \frac{0.765 + \sqrt{0.185}}{2}$$

$$= 0.598 \text{ mho}$$

Remember the capacitor $C_3 = 1$ F for convenience in the normalized case. Now we calculate G_4, using Equation 5-17.

$$G_4 = \frac{C_2 b_1}{G_3} = \frac{(0.1)(1)}{(0.598)}$$

$$= 0.167 \text{ mho}$$

In summary the normalized components for the second section of the active filter shown in Fig. 5-7 are $C_2 = 0.1$ F, $C_3 = 1$ F, $G_3 = 0.598$ mho, and $G_4 = 0.167$ mho.

4. We repeat the steps of step 3 to find the passive components of next second order low-pass VCVS Butterworth filter section shown in Fig. 5-7. The constants a_2 and b_2 of the second order Butterworth transfer function have been found in step 1. For convenience in the normalized case $C_5 = 1$ F. Thus, we can find the quantity G_5 using Equation 5-16 and substituting the constants found in step 1.

$$G_5 = \frac{1.848 + \sqrt{(1.848)^2 - 4(1)(C_4 + 1 - K_b)}}{2}$$

$$G_5 = \frac{1.848 + \sqrt{3.415 - 4C_4}}{2}$$

We must select C_4 so that the number under the radical is positive. Let us select $C_4 = 0.5$ F and calculate G_5.

$$G_5 = \frac{1.848 + \sqrt{3.415 - 4(0.5)}}{2} = \frac{1.848 + 1.415}{2}$$

$$= 1.519 \text{ mho}$$

Now we calculate G_6 using Equation 5-17.

$$G_6 = \frac{C_4 b_2}{G_5} = \frac{(0.5)(1)}{(1.519)} = 0.329 \text{ mho}$$

5. Finally, we denormalize the resistance and capacitance values. In summary the normalized components for the entire active filter circuit shown in Fig. 5-7 are $C_1 = 1\,F$, $C_2 = 0.1\,F$, $C_3 = 1\,F$, $C_4 = 0.5\,F$, $C_5 = 1\,F$, $G_1 = 10\,mho$, $G_2 = 1\,mho$, $G_3 = 0.598\,mho$, $G_4 = 0.167\,mho$, $G_5 = 1.519\,mho$, and $G_6 = 0.329\,mho$. Next, we find the frequency normalizing factor u, and the impedance scaling factor (ISF) from Equation 5-1 and Equation 5-2 respectively.

$$u = \frac{\omega_c}{\omega_n} = \frac{2\pi\,(10,000)}{1\,\text{rad/s}} = 20,000\pi$$

$$\text{ISF} = \frac{f_c}{20\pi} = \frac{10,000}{20\pi} = \frac{500}{\pi} = 159.15$$

$$C_p = \frac{C_n}{u(\text{ISF})}$$

$$C_1 = \frac{1\,F}{20,000\pi\,(159.15)} = 0.1\,\mu F$$

$$C_2 = 0.1C_1 = 0.1(0.1\,\mu F) = 0.01\mu F$$

$$C_3 = C_1 = 0.1\,\mu F$$

$$C_4 = 0.5C_1 = 0.5(0.1\,\mu F) = 0.05\,\mu F$$

$$C_5 = C_1 = 0.1\,\mu F$$

In the above calculations for denormalized capacitance values notice after C_1 was denormalized, the remaining capacitance values are found by comparing their normalized values to the normalized value of C_1. Then the compared fractional value of each capacitance is multiplied by the denormalized value of C_1 to obtain the actual capacitance value.

$$R_1 = \frac{\text{ISF}}{G_1} = \frac{159.15}{10} = 15.915\,\text{ohms}$$

$$R_2 = \frac{ISF}{G_2} = \frac{159.15}{1} = 159.15 \text{ ohms}$$

$$R_3 = \frac{ISF}{G_3} = \frac{159.15}{0.598} = 266.137 \text{ ohms}$$

$$R_4 = \frac{ISF}{G_4} = \frac{159.15}{0.167} = 952.99 \text{ ohms}$$

$$R_5 = \frac{ISF}{G_5} = \frac{159.15}{1.519} = 104.77 \text{ ohms}$$

$$R_6 = \frac{ISF}{G_6} = \frac{159.15}{0.329} = 483.739 \text{ ohms}$$

Notice the denormalized resistor values are far from standard resistor values. If it is critical to obtain these values, the designer must obtain the nearest standard resistor value, measure that resistor on a bridge circuit, and repeat this process until he obtains the value of resistance nearest to the allowable tolerance. This is a tedious process, but if it is necessary it must be accomplished. The final active filter design is shown in Fig. 5-8 for Example 5-5.

If a positive gain is desired, another op amp with a gain of minus one can be cascaded onto the active filter circuit of Fig. 5-8. Al-

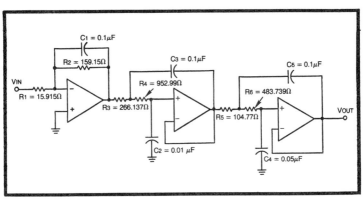

Fig. 5-8. Low-pass active filter circuit for Example 5-5 with f_c = 10 kHz, n = fifth order Butterworth, and a gain of −10.

126

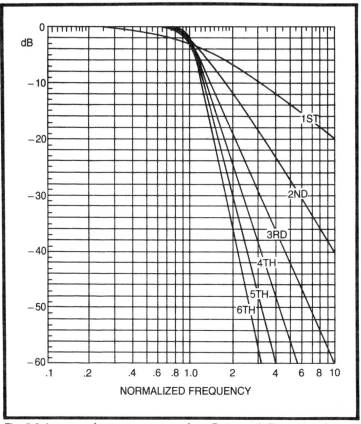

Fig. 5-9. Low-pass frequency response for a Butterworth filter with order n = 1,2,3,4,5, and 6.

though a Butterworth design was employed, a Chebyshev filter design could have been shown using the Chebyshev constant instead of the Butterworth constants.

FREQUENCY RESPONSE

The graph of Fig. 5-9 shows a low-pass frequency response for a Butterworth active filter with filter orders of n = 1, 2, 3, 4, 5, and 6. The dB amplitude response in the stop band decreases linearly with increasing logarithm of frequency. The rate of this decrease (or the slope of the straight line), called the roll-off, is defined by the order of the filter. Above the cutoff frequency, the roll-off of a first order low-pass filter is −6 dB per octave or −20 dB per decade. Remember an *octave* is defined as twice the cutoff frequency, and a

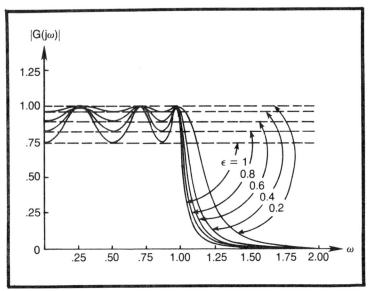

Fig. 5-10. Variation of the Chebyshev response with ϵ, for $n = 6$.

decade is defined as ten times the cutoff frequency when we consider the low-pass frequency response curve. A second order low-pass filter has a roll-off equal to twice that of a first order filter or -12 dB/octave or -20 dB/decade. It follows that a third order filter has a roll-off equal to -18 dB/octave, or -60 dB/decade, and so on for

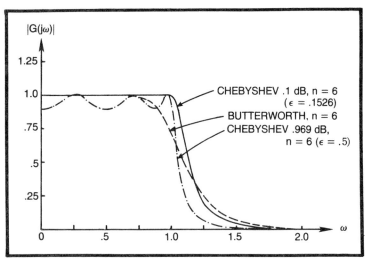

Fig. 5-11. Comparing low-pass Butterworth and Chebyshev filter responses with order $n = 6$.

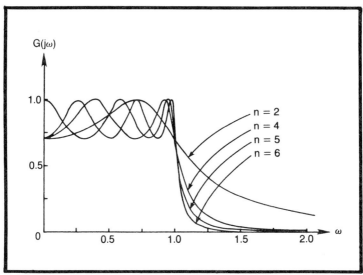

Fig. 5-12. Chebyshev filter response for a fixed ripple width of 3 dB and increasing order n = 2,4,5, and 6.

higher order Butterworth low-pass filters. In general the roll-off for an nth order Butterworth low-pass filter is equal to −6n dB/octave or −20 dB/decade. Regardless of the order of the filter, the curves shown in Fig. 5-9 have a constant, or maximally flat passband, which characterizes the Butterworth filter response.

Also, we may have an amplitude response that looks like the curves shown in Fig. 5-10, which shows ripples in the passband. This type of response is characteristic of a Chebyshev filter. Figure 5-10 illustrates for increasing ripple width (shown as ϵ) for a fixed n improves the stopband characteristics while creating a larger ripple width.

Figure 5-11 compares two Chebyshev sixth order responses with ripple widths of 0.1 dB and 0.969 db to a sixth order Butterworth response. Clearly the cutoff and stopband features of the 0.969 dB Chebyshev filter are superior to those of the 0.1 dB case, and both Chebyshev filters are superior to the Butterworth in cutoff and stopband features. However, the opposite is true in the passband. The Chebyshev filter is the optimum all-pole filter in this respect.

In Fig. 5-12, it is seen that for a fixed ripple width, increasing n for a Chebyshev filter increases the loss and improves the stopband characteristics.

Chapter 6
High-Pass Active Filter Design

In this chapter, we will learn to design mostly high-pass Butterworth and Chebyshev active filters from a first order filter to the highest order filter the designer needs. The basic circuits of this chapter are very similar to the low-pass filter circuits of Chapter 5. In fact, they are the vice versa versions of the same circuits in Chapter 5 with frequency determining capacitors and resistors interchanged.

Two important restrictions on the use of high-pass filters exist. In actual practice, the upper frequency cutoff of the op amp employed in the active filter design will combine with the lower frequency cutoff characteristics of the high-pass filter to give a passband response. If the high-pass active filter is to be useful, we have to design enough useful frequency range between the lower passband limit of the filter and the upper frequency limit set by the op amp. Another limitation of active high-pass filter circuits is that they are inherently noisier than low-pass active filter circuits. There are several obvious reasons for this. A high-pass active filter is a differentiator that responds to sudden changes in inputs and uses this transient information to provide an output. In a high-pass active filter, noise above the range of useful signals gets passed on, as do harmonics of rejected waveforms. This is unlike a low-pass active filter where these components are strongly attenuated. Finally, in some op amp circuits, the internal high-frequency limitations tend to decrease stability as frequencies near the upper limits are reached. The opposite is often true in many low-pass circuits where the op amp increases the damping and adds rolloff to the response.

We will employ mostly Butterworth and Chebyshev active filter circuits in our design approach. Much data is obtainable for these two filter types from the Tables 3-1 through 3-6 and Tables 4-1 through 4-6. Since the data in the two tables are for low-pass filters, we must transform the low-pass data to high-pass data by the methods shown in Chapter 3. At this point, it is wise to review the equations that will help us in transforming the low-pass filter data to high-pass filter data.

An all-pole normalized low-pass transfer function is given by the general equation:

$$G(s) = \frac{Kb_0}{s^n + b_{n-1}s^{n-1} + \ldots + b_1 s^1 + b_0} \quad \textbf{Equation 6-1}$$

where the b_i coefficients are given in the Tables 3-1 through 3-6 and Tables 4-1 though 4-6. An all-pole high-pass transfer function is given by the general equation:

$$G(s) = \frac{Ks^n}{a_0 + a_1 s^1 + \ldots\ldots a_{n-1} s^{n-1} + s^n} \quad \textbf{Equation 6-2A}$$

where:

$$a_{n-i} = \frac{b_i}{b_0} \; ; i = 0, 1, 2, \ldots \text{ etc.} \quad \textbf{Equation 6-2B}$$

and

$$a_0 = \frac{b_n}{b_0} = \frac{1}{b_0} \quad \text{since } b_n = 1. \quad \textbf{Equation 6-2C}$$

We shall find it easier to obtain a normalized active filter circuit first. In the normalized circuit the component numbers are convenient to work with when making calculations. We will be using numbers such as 1 F and 1 Ω. Eventually, the normalized impedance values will be changed to standard values such as 0.1 F and 10 K.

We will select at least one capacitance as C = 1 F to begin with, and any other capacitance values should be multiples; for example 1, 0.1, 2, and so on. Then in the denormalization process, when C is changed from 1 F to a value like 0.01 μF, the others will change to values such as $0.01\mu F$, $0.001\ \mu F$, $0.02\mu F$, and so on. The denormalization process is carried out, of course, by dividing the normalized capacitances by the frequency normalizing factor u, as was illustrated in the preceding chapter. Then both the capacitances and resistances must be denormalized by the impedance scaling factor (ISF), as was illustrated in the preceding chapter. Remember the capacitor normalized values are divided by the ISF, and resistor normalized values are multiplied by the ISF. At this point it is wise to review the equations that will help us in denormalizing a normalized active filter by going back to Chapter 5 and looking at Equations 5-1 through 5-4. Once the denormalized resistances and/or capacitances are obtained, and the designer sees that they are not suitable for whatever reason, he may choose to change their values by multiplying the resistor values by a new ISF and dividing the capacitor values by the new ISF to obtain suitable passive components for his design.

INFINITE GAIN MULTIPLE FEEDBACK HIGH-PASS FILTERS

The basic circuit of the second-order infinite gain MFB (multiple feedback) high-pass filter is shown in Fig. 6-1. If the circuit in Fig. 6-1 is compared to the low-pass filter, infinite gain MFB circuit in Fig. 5-1, you can see that the resistors and capacitors in these two circuits have been interchanged. The transfer function that describes the circuit shown in Fig. 6-1 has the general form shown below.

$$\frac{V_2}{V_1} = \frac{-Ks^2}{a_0 + a_1 s + s^2} \qquad \textbf{Equation 6-3}$$

$K =$ the gain of the circuit

$a_1, a_0 =$ constants that can be found by using the tables in Chapters 3 and 4 depending on whether the filter type is of a Butterworth or Chebyshev design, and using Equation 6-4 to determine a_1 and a_0.

$a_0 = 1/b_0$, for a second order high-pass filter, where b_0 can be found in the tables in Chapters 3 and 4.

$a_1 = b_1/b_0$, for a second order high-pass filter, where b_0 and b_1 can be found in the tables in Chapters 3 and 4.

$V_2 =$ the filter output voltage.

$V_1 =$ the filter input voltage

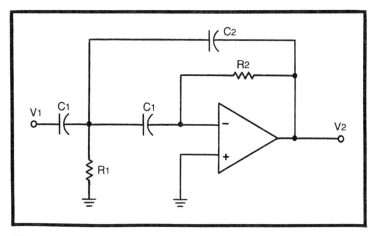

Fig. 6-1. A second-order MFB high-pass active filter.

The constants of the transfer function K, a_0, and a_1 are related to the passive components of the circuit in Fig. 6-1 through the equations that follow, if the capacitor C_1 in Fig. 6-1 is normalized to the value 1 F.

$$a_0 = \frac{G_1 G_2}{C_2} \qquad \text{Equation 6-4}$$

$$a_1 = \frac{G_2(C_2 + 2)}{C_2} \qquad \text{Equation 6-5}$$

$$K = \frac{C_1}{C_2} = \frac{1}{C_2} \text{ , since } C_1 = 1 \text{ F} \quad \text{Equation 6-6}$$

Solving for the normalized circuit elements in Equations 6-6 through 6-8 we have:

$$C_2 = \frac{1}{K} \qquad \text{Equation 6-7}$$

$$G_1 = \frac{a_0 (2K + 1)}{a_1 K} \cdot \qquad \text{Equation 6-8}$$

$$G_2 = \frac{a_1}{(2G + 1)} \qquad \text{Equation 6-9}$$

The steps outlining the design procedure for the MFB second order high-pass active filter follow:

1. Select C_1 to have a normalized value of 1 F.

2. For the type of filter (Butterworth or Chebyshev) and the specific filter requirements, find the constants b_0 and b_1 from Tables 3-1 through 3-6 and Tables 4-1 through 4-6. Convert the constants found in the tables to a_0 and a_1, the constants of a high-pass active filter circuit, by using Equation 6-4. The constant K of the active filter circuit, which represents the circuit gain must be known or chosen depending on the active filter circuit application. Also, the cutoff frequency of the active filter circuit must be known. If the active filter circuit is a Chebyshev filter, the ripple wave factor RW_{dB} must be known.

3. For the given parameters in the second step, we determine the normalized capacitance C_2, and then the normalized conductances G_1 and G_2.

4. Finally, we denormalize resistances by multiplying the normalized resistance values by the ISF discussed in the first section of Chapter 5. Also, we denormalize the capacitance values by dividing the normalized capacitance values by the product of the ISF times u, the frequency normalizing factor.

Example 6-1:

A second-order high-pass Butterworth filter must be designed with a gain of 10 at a cutoff frequency of 10 kHz. Find the passive components that will produce the stated requirements for an infinite gain multiple feedback circuit.

Solution:

We will employ the MFB active filter circuit of Fig. 6-1. We will select $C_1 = 1$ F for convenience in the normalized case.

We are going to employ a Butterworth high-pass filter with n = 2 (second order), therefore we refer to Table 3-1 for n = 2, and find the constants $b_0 = 1$ and $b_1 = 1.41421 \cong 1.414$. Remember, the gain K = 10. We must convert the low-pass filter constants to the high-pass filter constants through the following equation:

$$a_{n-} = \frac{b_i}{b_0,}$$

where $i = 0, 1, 2, \ldots$ etc., until the nth term, which is the filter order. Remember $b_n = 1$.

Let us solve for the term when $i = n$, where n = 2 in our example. Hence, we are solving for $a_{n-i} = a_{n-n} = a_0$ as follows:

$$a_{n-i} = a_{n-n} = a_0 = \frac{b_i}{b_0} = \frac{b_n}{b_0}$$

But $b_n = 1$ and $b_0 = 1$ from the tables in Chapter 3. Hence, we have

$$a_0 = \frac{1}{1} = 1$$

Solving for the constant term when n = 2 and i = 1 we have

$$a_{2-1} = a_1 = \frac{b_1}{b_0} = \frac{1.414}{1} = 1.414$$

Let me caution the designer, that the high-pass filter constants will not always equal the low-pass filter constants. In fact, for the most part the low-pass and high-pass filter constants will NOT be the same. The above solution for equal low-pass and high-pass filter constants is the exception rather than the rule.

Now we can determine the normalized capacitance value for C_2.

$$C_2 = \frac{C_1}{K} = \frac{1 \text{ F}}{10} = 0.1 \text{ F}$$

Next we can find the normalized conductance values G_1 and G_2.

$$G_1 = \frac{a_0 (2K + 1)}{a_1 K} = \frac{1 \left[(2)(10) + 1 \right]}{1.414 (10)} = 14.85 \text{ mhos}$$

$$= \frac{a_1}{(2K + 1)} = \frac{1.414}{(2)(10) + 1} = 0.0673 \text{ mhos}$$

Finally, we denormalize the resistance and capacitance values. We find the frequency normalizing factor u, and the impedance scaling factor (ISF) from Equations 5-1 and 5-2, respectively.

$$u = \frac{\omega_c}{\omega_n} = \frac{2\pi f_c}{1 \text{ rad/s}} = \frac{2\pi(10,000)}{1}$$

$$= 20,000\pi$$

$$\text{ISF} = \frac{f_c}{20\pi} = \frac{10,000}{20\pi}$$

$$= 500/\pi = 159.15$$

We use the two factors defined above to denormalize first the capacitance values, then the resistor values.

$$C_p = \frac{C_n}{(u)(\text{ISF})}$$

$$C_1 = \frac{1\text{ F}}{(20,000\pi)(159.15)} = \frac{1\text{ F}}{10^{+7}} = 1(10^{-7})\text{ F}$$

$$= 0.1\ \mu\text{F}$$

The normalized value of C_2 is one-tenth (1/10) the value of C_1. Hence, it follows that the denormalized value of C_2 is 1/10 the value of C_1. Therefore, we can write the following equation;

$$C_2 = 0.1C_1 = 0.1(0.1\mu\text{F})$$

$$= 0.01\mu\text{F}$$

$$R_1 = \frac{(\text{ISF})}{G_1} = \frac{159.15}{14.85}$$

$$= 10.72\text{ ohms}$$

$$R_2 = \frac{(\text{ISF})}{G_2} = \frac{159.15}{0.0673} = 2364.78\text{ ohms}$$

The second order high-pass Butterworth filter in employing multiple feedback for Example 6-1 is shown with practical values in Fig. 6-2.

Example 6-2:

A second-order high-pass Chebyshev filter must be designed with a gain of five at a cutoff frequency of 15 kHz and a ripple width $RW_{dB} = 0.1$ dB. Find the passive components of a MFB active filter that will produce the stated requirements.

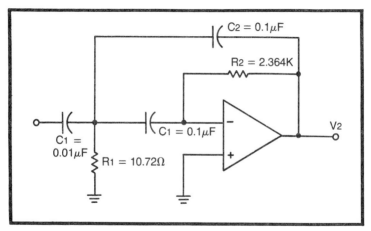

Fig. 6-2. The MFB high-pass Butterworth active filter for Example 6-1, $f_c = 10$ kHz, the gain = 10, and n = 2 (second order).

Solution:

We will employ the MFB active filter circuit shown in Fig. 6-1. We will select $C_1 = 1$ F for convenience in the normalized case.

We are going to employ a Chebyshev high-pass filter with n = 2 and $RW_{dB} = 0.1$ dB; therefore, we refer to Table 3-2 and find the constants $b_0 = 3.31329 \cong 3.313$ and $b_1 = 2.37209 \cong 2.372$. Remember the gain K = 5. We must convert the low-pass filter constants to the high-pass filter constants through the following equation:

$$a_{n-1} = \frac{b_i,}{b_0}$$

where i = 0, 1, 2, ...etc., until the nth term, which is the filter order. Remember $b_n = 1$. Let us solve for the term when $i = n$, where n = 2 in our example. Hence, we are solving for $a_{n-i} = a_{n-n} = a_0$ as follows

$$a_{n\text{-}i} = a_{n\text{-}n} = a_0 = \frac{b_i}{b_0} = \frac{b_n}{b_0}$$

But $b_n = 1$ and $b_0 = 3.313$ from Fig. 3-1. Hence, we have

$$a_0 = \frac{1}{3.313} = 0.302$$

Solving for the constant term when n = 2 and i = 1 we have

$$a_{2-1} = a_1 = \frac{b_1}{b_0} = \frac{2.372}{3.313}$$

$$a_1 = 0.716$$

137

Now we can determine the normalized capacitance value for C_2.

$$C_2 = \frac{C_1}{K} = \frac{1 \text{ F}}{5}$$

$$= 0.2 \text{ F}$$

Next we can find the normalized conductance values G_1 and G_2.

$$G_1 = \frac{a_0 (2K + 1)}{a_1 K} = \frac{0.302 \left[(2)(5) + 1\right]}{(0.716)(5)}$$

$$= 0.928 \text{ mhos}$$

$$G_2 = \frac{a_1}{(2K + 1)} = \frac{0.716}{(2)(5) + 1}$$

$$= 0.0651 \text{ mhos}$$

Finally, we denormalize the resistance and capacitance values. We find the frequency normalizing factor u, and the impedance scaling factor (ISF) from Equations 5-1 and 5-2, respectively.

$$u = \frac{2\pi f_c}{1 \text{ rad/s}} = \frac{2\pi(15,000)}{1}$$

$$= 30,000\pi$$

$$\text{ISF} = \frac{f_c}{20\pi} = \frac{15,000}{20\pi} = 238.73$$

We use the two factors defined above to denormalize first the capacitance values then the resistor values.

$$C_p = \frac{C_n}{(u) \text{ (ISF)}}$$

$$C_1 = \frac{1 \text{ F}}{(30,000\pi)(238.73)} = \frac{1 \text{ F}}{2.25 \; (10^{+7})} = 0.444 \; (10^{-7})$$

$$C_1 = 0.0444 \; \mu\text{F}$$

The normalized value of C_2 is one-fifth (1/5) the value of C_1. Hence, it follows that the denormalized value of C_2 is (1/5) the value of C_1. Therefore, we can write the following equation;

$$C_2 = 0.2C_1 = 0.2(0.0444 \ \mu F)$$

$$= 0.00888 \ \mu F$$

$$R_1 = \frac{ISF}{G_1} = \frac{238.73}{0.928}$$

$$= 257.25 \ \text{ohms}$$

$$R_2 = \frac{ISF}{G_2} = \frac{238.73}{0.0651}$$

$$= 3667.13 \ \text{ohms}$$

The second order high-pass Chebyshev filter employing multiple feedback for Example 6-2 is shown with practical values in Fig. 6-3.

The infinite gain MFB filter achieves an inverting gain high-pass characteristic with a minimal number of circuit elements. It also has the advantages of low output impedance and good stability. Let me again caution the designer when employing a high-pass active filter, care must be taken so that the high frequency cutoff of the op

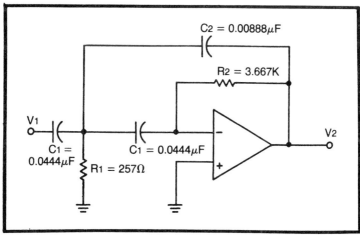

Fig. 6-3. The MFB high-pass Chebyshev active filter for Example 6-2 with $f_c = 15$ kHz, the gain = 5, $RW_{dB} = 0.1$ dB, and n = 2 (second order).

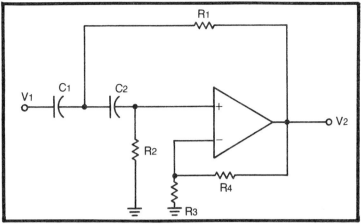

Fig. 6-4. A second-order VCVS high-pass filter circuit.

amp does not influence the characteristics of the high-pass active filter that you wish to employ.

VOLTAGE CONTROLLED VOLTAGE SOURCE (VCVS) OR SALLEN AND KEY HIGH-PASS FILTERS

The basic circuit of the VCVS high-pass active filter is shown in Fig. 6-4. We modify the circuit in Fig. 6-4 by choosing $C_1 = C_2 = C$, and we recall that the gain K is given by the equation:

$$K = \frac{R_4}{R_3} + 1 \qquad \text{Equation 6-10}$$

and for minimum DC offset

$$R_3 = \frac{K(R_1 + R_2)}{(K - 1)}, \; K \neq 1 \qquad \text{Equation 6-11}$$

If K = 1, we would make $R_4 = 0$ (a short circuit) and $R_3 = \infty$ (an open circuit). The modified circuit is shown in Fig. 6-5.

The general transfer function that describes the circuit performance of Fig. 6-5 has the following general form. The correspondence between the transfer function and the circuit in Fig. 6-5 was developed in Chapter 4, and is repeated at this time.

$$\frac{V_2}{V_1} = \frac{Ks^2}{a_0 + a_1 s + s^2} \qquad \text{Equation 6-12}$$

K = the gain of the circuit

140

$a_1, a_0 =$ constants that can be found through Tables 3-1 through 3-6 and 4-1 through 4-6 depending on whether the filter type is of a Butterworth or Chebyshev design, and using Equation 6-2C to determine a_1 and a_0.

$a_0 = 1/b_0$, for a second order high-pass filter, where b_0 can be found in Tables 3-1 through 3-6 and 4-1 through 4-6.

$a_1 = b_1/b_0$, for a second-order high-pass filter, where b_0 and b_1 can be found in Tables 3-1 through 3-6 and 4-1 through 4-6.

$V_2 =$ the filter output voltage

$V_1 =$ the filter input voltage

The constants of the transfer function K, a_0, and a_1 are related to the passive components of the circuit in Fig. 6-5 through the equations that follow.

$$K = \frac{R_4}{R_3} + 1 \qquad \text{Equation 6-13}$$

$$a_0 = \frac{G_1 G_2}{C_1 C_2} \qquad \text{Equation 6-14}$$

$$a_1 = G_2 \left[\frac{1}{C_1} + \frac{1}{C_2} \right] + \frac{G_1}{C_1} (1 - K) \qquad \text{Equation 6-15}$$

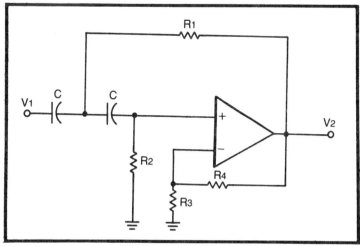

Fig. 6-5. A second-order VCVS high-pass filter circuit with $C_1 = C_2 = C$.

Using the modified circuit in Fig. 6-5 with $C_1 = C_2 = C = 1$ F for a convenient normalized value and substituting 1 F in the above equations where it applies the above equations become:

$$a_0 = G_1 G_2 \qquad \textbf{Equation 6-16}$$

$$a_1 = 2G_2 + G_1 (1 - K) \qquad \textbf{Equation 6-17}$$

Using Equations 6-16 and 6-17 to solve for the conductances in terms of the high-pass filter constants we have:

$$G_1 = \frac{a_0}{G_2} \qquad \textbf{Equation 6-18}$$

$$G_2 = \frac{a_1 + \sqrt{a_1^2 + 8a_0 (K - 1)}}{4} \qquad \textbf{Equation 6-19}$$

Thus for the constant a_0, a_1, and gain K, we may find the normalized conductances, when $C_1 = C_2 = C = 1$ F in the VCVS second order high-pass filter circuit.

The steps outlining the design procedure for the VCVS second order high pass active filter follow:

1. Use the modified VCVS second-order high-pass active filter circuit shown in Fig. 6-5 with a normalized capacitance value of 1 F.

2. For the type of filter (Butterworth or Chebyshev) and the specific filter requirements, find the constants b_0 and b_1 from the tables in Chapters 3 and 4. Convert the constants found in the tables to a_0 and a_1, the constants of a high-pass active filter circuit by using Equation 6-2C. The constant K of the active filter circuit, which represents the circuit gain must be known or chosen depending on the active filter circuit application. Also, the cutoff frequency of the active filter circuit must be known. If the active filter circuit is a Chebyshev filter, the ripple wave factor RW_{dB} must be known.

3. For the parameters in step 2, we determine the conductances G_1 and G_2.

4. Finally, we denormalize resistances by multiplying the normalized resistance values by the ISF discussed in the first section of Chapter 5. Also, we denormalize the capacitance values by dividing the normalized capacitance

142

values by the product of the ISF times u, the frequency normalizing factor.

Example 6-3:

A second-order high-pass Butterworth filter must be designed with a gain of 10 at a cutoff frequency of 10 kHz. Find the passive components that will produce the stated requirements for a VCVS active filter circuit.

Solution:

We will employ the VCVS high-pass filter circuit shown in Fig. 6-5. We will select $C = 1$ F for convenience in the normalized case.

We are going to employ a Butterworth high-pass filter with $n = 2$ (second order); therefore, we refer to Table 3-1 for $n = 2$, and find the constants $b_0 =$ and $b_1 = 1.414121 \cong 1.414$. Remember the gain $K = 10$. We must convert the low-pass filter constants to the high-pass filter constants through Equation 6-2B.

$$a_0 = \frac{b_n}{b_0} = \frac{1}{1} = 1$$

$$a_1 = \frac{b_1}{b_0} = \frac{1.414}{1} = 1.414$$

Let me caution the designer that the high-pass filter constants will not always equal the low-pass filter constants. In fact, for the most part the low-pass and high-pass filter constants will be different.

Remember all the capacitor values in the VCVS high-pass active filter circuit are normalized to 1 F. Hence, we must perform calculations to find the normalized conductances values. First we find G_2 through Equation 19 as follows.

$$G_2 = \frac{1.414 + \sqrt{1.414^2 + 8(1)(10 - 1)}}{4}$$

$$= \frac{1.414 + \sqrt{2 + 72}}{4} = \frac{1.414 + \sqrt{74}}{4}$$

$$= 2.5 \text{ mhos}$$

Next, we find G_1 through Equation 6-18.

$$G_1 = \frac{a_0}{G_2} = \frac{1}{2.5}$$

$$= 0.4 \text{ mhos}$$

To determine the resistors R_3 and R_4 for a gain of 10 and for minimum DC offset, we use Equations 6-1 and 6-11. However, we must first convert the conductances G_1 and G_2 to their normalized resistance values.

$$R_1 = \frac{1}{G_1} = \frac{1}{0.4}$$

$$= 2.5 \text{ ohms}$$

$$R_2 = \frac{1}{G_2} = \frac{1}{2.5}$$

$$= 0.4 \text{ ohms}$$

$$R_3 = \frac{K(R_1 + R_2)}{(K - 1)} = \frac{10(2.5 + 0.4)}{(10 - 1)}$$

$$= 3.22 \text{ ohms}$$

$$R_4 = KR_3 - R_3 = 10(3.22) - 3.22$$

$$= 28.98 \text{ ohms}$$

Finally, we denormalize the resistance and capacitance values. We find the frequency normalizing factor u, and the impedance scaling factor (ISF) from Equations 5-1 and 5-2, respectively.

$$u = \frac{\omega_c}{\omega_n} = \frac{2\pi(10,000 \text{ Hz})}{1 \text{ rad/s}}$$

$$= 20,000\pi$$

$$ISF = \frac{f_c}{20\pi} = \frac{10,000}{20\pi}$$

$$= 159.15$$

$$C_p = \frac{C_n}{(u)(\text{ISF})}$$

$$C = \frac{1\,\text{F}}{(20{,}000\pi)\,(159.15)} = 0.1\ \mu\text{F}$$

$$R_1 = \frac{\text{ISF}}{G_1} = \frac{159.15}{0.4}$$

$$= 397.88\ \text{ohms}$$

$$R_2 = \frac{\text{ISF}}{G_2} = \frac{159.15}{2.5}$$

$$= 63.66\ \text{ohms}$$

$$R_3 = \text{ISF}(3.22) = 159.15(3.22) = 512.46\ \text{ohms}$$

$$R_4 = \text{ISF}(28.98) = 159.15(28.98) = 4612.17\ \text{ohms}$$

The VCVS active filter circuit designed in this example is shown in Fig. 6-6 with the denormalized values of resistances and capacitances found in the fourth step.

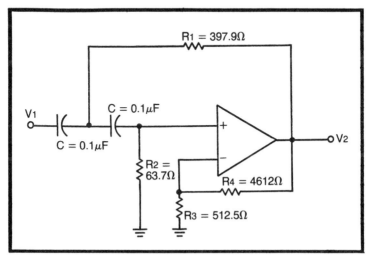

Fig. 6-6. The VCVS high-pass Butterworth active filter for Example 6-3 with f_c = 10 kHz, the gain = 10, and n = 2 (second order).

If the designer doesn't like the denormalized values of resistance and capacitance shown in Fig. 6-6, he may decide to change them by choosing a new ISF. In other words, the designer can change the original denormalized values to suit the design to the components he has readily available. If he decides to decrease the capacitor values by a factor of 10, he must increase the resistor values by the same factor.

Example 6-4:

A second-order high-pass Chebyshev filter must be designed with a gain of 10 at a cutoff frequency of 10 kHz and a ripple width $RW_{dB} = 0.5$ dB. Find the passive components that will produce a VCVS active filter circuit that meets the stated requirements.

Solution:

We will employ the VCVS high-pass filter circuit shown in Fig. 6-5. We will select $C = 1$ F for convenience in the normalized case.

We are going to employ a Chebyshev high-pass filter of the second order (n = 2) and $RW_{dB} = 0.5$ dB; therefore, we refer to Table 3-3 and find the constants $b_0 = 1.5162 \cong 1.516$ and $b_1 = 1.42562 \cong 1.426$. Remember the gain $K = 10$. We must convert the low-pass filter constants to the high-pass filter constants through Equation 6-2B.

$$a_0 = \frac{b_n}{b_0} = \frac{1}{1.516}$$

$$= 0.66$$

$$a_1 = \frac{b_1}{b_0} = \frac{1.426}{1.516}$$

$$= 0.941$$

Remember all the capacitor values in the VCVS high-pass active filter of Fig. 6-5 are normalized to 1 F. Hence, we must perform calculations to find the normalized conductances values. First we find G_2 through Equation 6-19 as follows.

$$G_2 = \frac{0.941 + \sqrt{(0.941)^2 + 8(0.66)(10 - 1)}}{4}$$

$$= \frac{0.941 + \sqrt{0.885 + 47.52}}{4}$$

$$= \frac{0.941 + 6.96}{4} = \frac{7.901}{4}$$

$$= 1.975 \text{ mhos}$$

Next we find G_1 through Equation 6-18.

$$G_1 = \frac{a_0}{G_2} = \frac{0.66}{1.975}$$

$$= 0.334 \text{ mhos}$$

To determine the resistors R_3 and R_4 for a gain of 10 and for minimum DC offset we use Equations 6-10 and 6-11. However, we must first convert the conductances G_1 and G_2 to their normalized resistance values.

$$R_1 = \frac{1}{G_1} = \frac{1}{0.334}$$

$$= 2.99 \text{ ohms}$$

$$R_2 = \frac{1}{G_2} = \frac{1}{1.975}$$

$$= 0.506 \text{ ohms}$$

$$R_3 = \frac{K(R_1 + R_2)}{(K - 1)} = \frac{10(2.99 + 0.506)}{10 - 1}$$

$$= 3.88 \text{ ohms}$$

$$R_4 = KR_3 - R_3 = 10(3.88) - 3.88$$

$$= 34.92 \text{ ohms}$$

Finally, we denormalize the resistance and capacitance values. We find the frequency normalizing factor u and the impedance scaling factor (ISF) from Equations 5-1 and 5-2, respectively.

$$u = \frac{\omega_c}{\omega_n} = \frac{2\pi(10{,}000\ \text{Hz})}{1\ \text{rad/s}}$$

$$= 20{,}000\pi$$

$$\text{ISF} = \frac{f_c}{20\pi} = \frac{10{,}000}{20\pi}$$

$$= 159.15$$

$$C_p = \frac{C_n}{(u)(\text{ISF})}$$

$$C = \frac{1\ \text{F}}{(20{,}000\pi)(159.15)}$$

$$= 0.1\ \mu\text{F}$$

$$R_1 = \frac{\text{ISF}}{G_1} = \frac{159.15}{0.334}$$

$$= 476.5\ \text{ohms}$$

$$R_2 = 0.506\ \text{ohms (ISF)} = 0.506(159.15)$$

$$= 80.53\ \text{ohms}$$

$$R_3 = 3.88\ \text{ohms (ISF)} = 3.88(159.15)$$

$$= 617.5\ \text{ohms}$$

$$R_4 = 34.92\ \text{ohms(ISF)}\ 34.92(159.15)$$

$$= 5557.52\ \text{ohms}$$

The VCVS active filter circuit designed in this example is shown in Fig. 6-7 with the denormalized values of resistances and capacitances found in the fourth step.

If the designer doesn't like the denormalized values of resistance and capacitance shown in Fig. 6-7, he may decide to change them by choosing a new ISF. In other words, the designer can change the original denormalized values to suit the design to the components he has readily available. If he decides to decrease the capacitor values by a factor of 10, he must increase the resistor values by the same factor.

HIGHER ORDER HIGH-PASS FILTER CIRCUITS

We may obtain higher order high-pass Butterworth or Chebyshev filters by cascading two networks or more until the order of filter that the designer desires is attained. In other words, if the designer wants a fourth-order filter, he can cascade two second order active filter circuits to obtain the fourth order active filter circuit. If the designer wants an odd-order active filter he has to cascade at least one active filter circuit with an order of one with one or more second-order active filter circuits. For example, if the designer wants a fifth-order active filter circuit he would cascade two second-order active filter circuits with a single first-order active filter circuit. The methods of the previous sections in this chapter and the topics in Chapter 4 will be employed to find the individual filter sections of a higher order high-pass active filter network.

Example 6-4:

A fifth-order low-pass Butterworth active filter must be de-signed with a gain of -10 at a cutoff frequency of 10 kHz. Find the passive components that will produce the stated requirements.

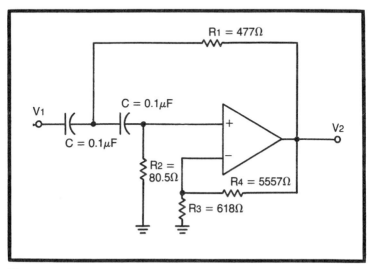

Fig. 6-7. The VCVS high-pass Chebyshev active filter for Example 6-4 with $f_c = $ 10 kHz, the gain = 10, RW$_{dB}$ = 0.5 dB, and n = 2 (second order).

149

Solution:

Consider the overall transfer function $H(s)$ to be the product of three transfer functions. In other words, $H(s) = H_1 H_2 H_3$ where H_1 is a first-order transfer function, and H_2 and H_3 are each a second order transfer function. We will employ the VCVS active circuit with a gain of one for each of the two second-order VCVS circuits in order to minimize components. The first-order active filter section will be the circuit shown in Fig. 4-15B. The general circuit that we will employ is shown in Fig. 6-8.

The fifth-order transfer function that will describe the action of the circuit in Fig. 6-8 is written as the product of three transfer functions as shown below.

$$H(s) = \left(\frac{-K_0 s}{c_0 + s}\right)\left(\frac{+K_a s}{d_1 + c_1 s + s^2}\right)\left(\frac{+K_b s}{d_2 + c_2 s + s^2}\right)$$

To find the high-pass active filter constants c_0, c_1, c_2, d_1 and d_2 in the above equation, we must first find the low-pass active filter constants in Table 3-1 and Table 4-1. Then we convert the low-pass filter constants to the high-pass filter constants by using Equation 6-2B.

In Table 3-1 for n = 1 (first order filter) we see that $b_0 = 1$, and we know that $b_n = 1$; hence, we can find c_0 as follows.

$$c_0 = \frac{b_n}{b_0} = \frac{1}{1} = 1$$

In Table 4-1 for n = 2 (second-order filter) we see that $a_1 = 0.76537 \cong 0.765$, $b_1 = 1$, $a_2 = 1.84776 \cong 1.848$, and $b_2 = 1$, and we know that $b_n = 1$. Hence, we find the remaining high-pass constants as follows.

$$d_1 = \frac{b_n}{b_1} = \frac{1}{1}$$
$$= 1$$

$$c_1 = \frac{a_1}{b_1} = \frac{0.765}{1}$$
$$= 0.765$$

$$d_2 = \frac{b_n}{b_2} = \frac{1}{1}$$

$$= 1$$

$$c_2 = \frac{a_2}{b_2} = \frac{1.848}{1}$$

$$c_2 = 1.848$$

Let me caution the designer that the high-pass filter constants will not always equal the low-pass filter constants. This usually happens in the Butterworth active filter type.

Remember $K_a = 1$, $K_b = 1$, and the product of the three gains equals minus ten or $K_a K_b K_0 = -10$ which means K_0 must equal minus ten (-10).

Now we will find the passive components that fit the first order transfer function in the equation shown in the first step. We compare the first order transfer function constants of the equation in the first step to Equation 4-45, which is the transfer function of the first order active filter section of Fig. 6-8. Hence, we can relate the circuit parameters of this active filter section to the constants K_0 and a_0.

$$a_0 = \frac{G_1}{C_2} \qquad \text{Equation 6-20}$$

$$K_0 = \frac{-C_1}{C_2} \qquad \text{Equation 6-21}$$

For convenience in the normalized case, we will select $C_2 = 1$ F. Now we can solve for G_1 and C_1, knowing that $a_0 = 1$ and $K_0 = -10$.

$$G_1 = a_0 C_2 = (1)(1)$$

$$= 1 \text{ mho}$$

$$C_1 = -K_0 C_2 = -(-10)(1)$$

$$= 10 \text{ F}$$

Using the method developed in the previous sections of this chapter, we will find the passive components of a high-pass VCVS Butterworth active filter, as shown in the last two filter sections of

Fig. 6-8. The constants of the second-order high-pass Butterworth transfer function have already been found in the first step of this example. Thus, we can find the normalized conductance values since all the capacitor values in the VCVS high-pass active filter circuit are normalized to 1 F. First we find G_3 through Equation 6-19 as follows.

$$G_3 = \frac{c_1 + \sqrt{c_1^2 + 8d_1(K_a - 1)}}{4}$$

$$= \frac{0.765 + \sqrt{(0.765)^2 + 8(1)(1 - 1)}}{4}$$

$$= \frac{0.765 + \sqrt{(0.765)^2 + 0}}{4} = \frac{0.765 + 0.765}{4}$$

$$= 0.3825 \text{ mhos}$$

Next, we find G_2 through Equation 6-18.

$$G_2 = \frac{c_1}{G_3} = \frac{0.765}{0.3825}$$

$$= 2 \text{ mhos}$$

For the VCVS active filter circuit, when the gain $K_a = 1$, the feedback path from the output of the op amp to the inverting terminal $(-)$ is a direct connection. In other words, a short from the output of the amplifier to the inverting terminal.

Now we calculate G_5 through Equation 6-19 as follows.

$$G_5 = \frac{c_2^2 + \sqrt{c_2^2 + 8d_2(K_b - 1)}}{4}$$

$$= \frac{1.848 + \sqrt{(1.848)^2 + 8(1)(1 - 1)}}{4}$$

$$= \frac{1.848 + \sqrt{(1.848)^2 + 0}}{4} = \frac{1.848 + 1.848}{4}$$

$$= 0.924 \text{ mhos}$$

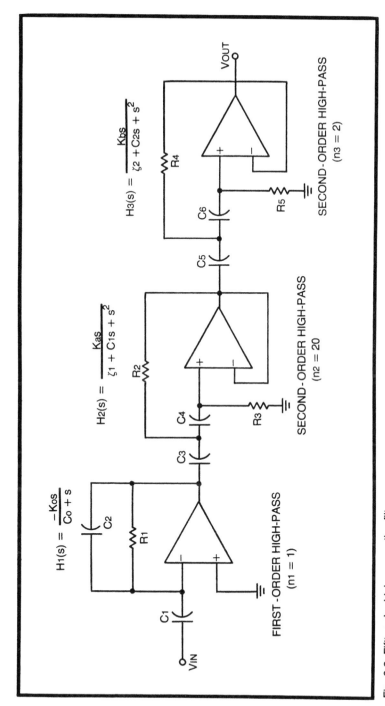

$$H_1(s) = \frac{-K_0 s}{C_0 + s}$$

$$H_2(s) = \frac{K_a s}{\zeta_1 + C_1 s + s^2}$$

$$H_3(s) = \frac{K_b s}{\zeta_2 + C_2 s + s^2}$$

FIRST-ORDER HIGH-PASS
($n_1 = 1$)

SECOND-ORDER HIGH-PASS
($n_2 = 20$)

SECOND-ORDER HIGH-PASS
($n_3 = 2$)

Fig. 6-8. Fifth-order high-pass active filter.

Next, we find G_5 through Equation 6-18.

$$G_4 = \frac{c_2}{G_5} = \frac{1.848}{0.924}$$

$$= 2 \text{ mhos}$$

For the VCVS active filter circuit, when the gain $K_b = 1$, the feedback path from the output of the op amp to the inverting terminal $(-)$ is a direct connection, as shown in Fig. 6-8.

Finally, we denormalize the resistance and capacitance values. In summary, the normalized components for the entire active filter circuit shown in Fig. 6-8 are $C_1 = 10F$, $C_2 = C_3 = C_4 = C_5 = C_6 = 1$ F, $G_1 = 1$ mho, $G_2 = G_4 = 2$ mhos, $G_3 = 0.3825$ mhos, and $G_5 = 0.924$ mhos. Next, we find the frequency normalizing factor u, and the impedance scaling factor (ISF) from Equations 5-1 and 5-2, respectively.

$$u = \frac{\omega_c}{\omega_n} = \frac{2\pi(10{,}000 \text{ Hz})}{1 \text{ rad/s}}$$

$$= 20{,}000\pi$$

$$\text{ISF} = \frac{f_c}{20\pi} = \frac{10{,}000}{20\pi}$$

$$= 159.15$$

$$C_p = \frac{C_n}{(u)(\text{ISF})}$$

$$C_1 = \frac{10 \text{ F}}{(20{,}000\pi)(159.15)}$$

$$= 1.0\mu\text{F}$$

$$C_2 = (0.1)C_1 = 0.1(1.0\mu\text{F})$$

$$= 0.1 \ \mu\text{F}$$

$$= C_3 = C_4 = C_5 = C_6 = 0.1 \ \mu\text{F}$$

In the above calculations for denormalized capacitance values, notice after C_1 was denormalized, the remaining capacitance values are found by comparing their normalized values to the normalized value of C_1. Then the compared fractional value of each capacitance is multiplied by the denormalized value of C_1 to obtain the actual capacitance value.

$$R_1 = \frac{ISF}{G_1} = \frac{159.15}{1}$$

$$= 159.15 \text{ ohms}$$

$$R_2 = \frac{ISF}{G_2} = \frac{159.15}{2}$$

$$= 79.575 \text{ ohms}$$

$$R_3 = \frac{ISF}{G_3} = \frac{159.15}{0.3825}$$

$$= 416.08 \text{ ohms}$$

$$R_4 = R_2 = 79.575 \text{ ohms}$$

$$R_5 = \frac{ISF}{G_5} = \frac{159.15}{0.924}$$

$$= 172.24 \text{ ohms}$$

Looking at the denormalized values of resistors and capacitors, the designer has decided to increase the resistor values by a factor of 10 which means the capacitor values must be decreased by this same factor. The values of capacitance and resistance employed in the final design are listed below.

$C_1 = 0.1\mu F$, $C_2 = C_3 = C_4 = C_5 = C_6 = 0.01 \ \mu F$
$R_1 = 1591$ ohms, $R_2 = R_4 = 795.8$ ohms, $R_3 = 4161$ ohms
$R_5 = 1722$ ohms

Notice the denormalized resistor values are far from standard resistor values. If it is critical to obtain these values, the designer must obtain the nearest standard resistor value, measure it on a bridge circuit, and repeat this process until he obtains the value of resistance nearest to the allowable tolerance. This is a tedious process, but if it is necessary it must be accomplished. The final active filter design for this example is shown in Fig. 6-9.

Another method employed to adjust frequency without obtaining exact passive components is to obtain capacitor trimmers or trim pots and insert them in the active filter circuit to adjust for the exact cutoff frequency.

If a positive gain is desired, another op amp with a gain of minus one can be cascaded onto the active filter circuit of Fig. 6-9. Although a Butterworth design was employed, a Chebyshev filter design could have been shown using the Chebyshev constant instead of the Butterworth constants.

FREQUENCY RESPONSE

The frequency response of a high-pass filter is the opposite frequency response of a low-pass filter. In other words, the high-pass filter rejects signals below the cutoff frequency and allows signals above the cutoff frequency to pass through with little or no attenuation.

The graph of Fig. 6-10 shows a high-pass frequency response for a Butterworth active filter with filter orders of n = 1, 2, 3, 4, 5, and 6. The dB amplitude response in the stop band decreases linearly with decreasing logarithm of frequency. The rate of this decrease (or the slope of the straight line), called the roll-off, is defined by the order of the filter. Below the cutoff frequency, the

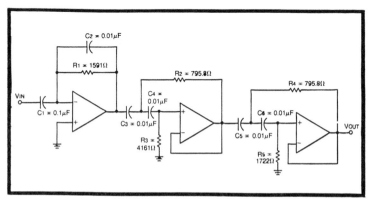

Fig. 6-9. A fifth-order high-pass active Butterworth filter of Example 6-4 with $f_c = 10$ kHz and gain K = −10.

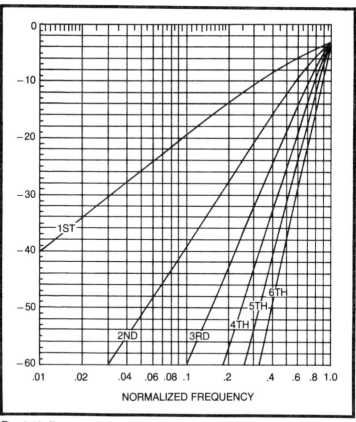

Fig. 6-10. Frequency response of a high-pass Butterworth filter for order n = 1,2,3,4,5, and 6.

roll-off of a first order high-pass filter is −6 dB per octave or −20 dB per decade. Remember an octave is defined as one-half (½) of the cutoff frequency and a decade is defined as one-tenth (1/10) of the cutoff frequency when we consider the high-pass frequency response curve. A second-order high-pass filter has a roll-off equal to twice that of a first order filter, or −12 dB/octave or −20 dB/decade. It follows that a third-order filter has a roll-off equal to −18dB/octave, or −60 dB/decade, and so on for higher order Butterworth high-pass filters. In general, the roll-off for an nth order Butterworth high-pass filter is equal to −6n dB/octave, or −20 dB/decade. Regardless of the order of the filter, the curves shown in Fig. 6-10 have a constant, or maximally flat passband, which characterizes the Butterworth filter response.

The Chebyshev and Butterworth frequency response comparison was made in Chapter 5 for low-pass active filters. The reader is advised to study the "Frequency Response " section of Chapter 5 for the Chebyshev and Butterworth high-pass active filter comparison, since the same information applies to the both the low-pass and high-pass active filters.

Chapter 7
Band-Pass Active Filter Design

A band-pass filter passes a band of frequencies of bandwidth B centered approximately about a center frequency ω_0, and attenuates all other frequencies. Both B and ω_0 may be measured in radians/second. Also, B could be given in Hertz with a center frequency $f_0 = \omega_0/2\pi$ Hertz. An ideal band-pass response is shown in Fig. 7-1 by the broken line, and an approximation to the ideal is represented by the solid line.

The transfer function of a second-order approximation to the characteristic shown in Fig. 7-1 is given in Equation 7-1 as follows.

$$H(s) = \frac{Ks}{s^2 + Bs + \omega_0{}^2} \qquad \textbf{Equation 7-1}$$

Another quantity of interest in a band-pass filter is the quality factor Q, defined by the following equation.

$$Q = \frac{\omega_0}{B} \qquad \textbf{Equation 7-2}$$

Hence, a high Q indicates a highly selective filter since the band of frequencies which pass is narrow compared to the center frequency. The gain of the filter is defined as the amplitude of $H(s)$ at the center frequency f_0, and from Equation 7-1 this amplitude is seen to be K/B.

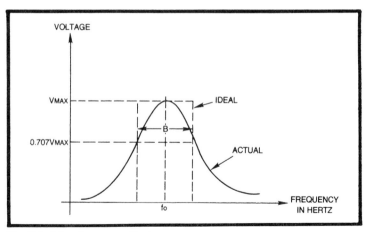

Fig. 7-1. A band-pass amplitude response.

The biggest problem that occurs in the design of band-pass active filters is the highest value of Q compared with the choice of active filter circuit the designer intends to use. In fact, it has been proven that a high performance, high Q band-pass active filter with poles cannot be designed with a single operational amplifier.

If the designer wants to employ one op amp, he limits the value of Q to below 25 with a VCVS circuit. With a MFB (multiple feedback) circuit, the maximum Q is limited to below 10. For Q values greater than 25, the designer must use three or more op amps to get stable and useful responses from a band-pass filter.

INFINITE GAIN MULTIPLE FEEDBACK BAND-PASS FILTERS

The basic circuit of the second order infinite gain MFB (multiple feedback) band-pass filter is shown in Fig. 7-2. The transfer function that describes the circuit shown in Fig. 7-2 has the general form shown below.

$$\frac{V_2}{V_1} = \frac{\dfrac{-Ks}{Q}}{s^2 + \dfrac{1}{Q}s + 1} \qquad \textbf{Equation 7-3}$$

where K = the gain of the circuit

$$Q = \text{quality factor} = \frac{\omega_0}{B},$$

160

where ω_0 is normalized to 1 rad/s in Equation 7-3, and B is the circuit bandwidth.

V_2 = the filter output voltage

V_1 = the filter input voltage

Sometimes $B = 1/Q$ is substituted in Equation 7-3, which results in the following transfer function for the circuit in Fig. 7-2.

$$\frac{V_2}{V_1} = \frac{-KBs}{s^2 + Bs + 1} \qquad \text{Equation 7-4}$$

Remember Equation 7-3 and 7-4 are exactly equal.

The constants of the transfer functions K, Q, and B are related to the passive components of the circuit in Fig. 7-2 through the equations that follow.

$$B = \frac{1}{Q} = \frac{(C_1 + C_2)\, G_3}{C_1 C_2} \qquad \text{Equation 7-5}$$

$$\omega_0^2 = 1 = \frac{G_3(G_1 + G_2)}{(C_1)(C_2)} \qquad \text{Equation 7-6}$$

$$K = \frac{G_1 C_2}{G_3(C_1 + C_2)} \qquad \text{Equation 7-7}$$

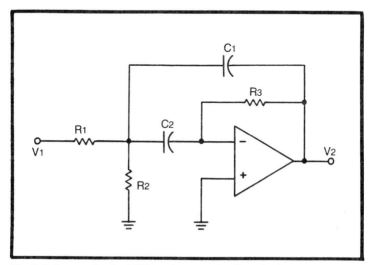

Fig. 7-2. A second-order MFB band-pass active filter circuit.

We can modify the band-pass MFB active filter circuit in Fig. 7-2 and simplify the above equations if we make all of the capacitor values equal, that is $C_1 = C_2 = C$. The modified circuit is shown in Fig. 7-3, and the new equations are listed below the modified circuit.

$$B = \frac{1}{Q} = \frac{2G_3}{C} \qquad \text{Equation 7-8}$$

$$\omega_0^2 = 1 = \frac{G_3 (G_1 + G_2)}{C_2} \qquad \text{Equation 7-9}$$

$$K = \frac{G_1}{2G_3} \qquad \text{Equation 7-10}$$

The circuit in Fig. 7-3 is restricted to values of Q less than 10, since the design of the circuit will yield passive component values that are wide spread. However, the circuit shown in Fig. 7-3 has the nice feature that the designer may specify f_0, Q, and the gain K without much trouble.

We can solve for the conductances G_1, G_2, and G_3 in terms of the parameters C, K, and Q as follows.

$$G_3 = \frac{C}{2Q} \qquad \text{Equation 7-11}$$

$$G_2 = 2QC - \frac{KC}{Q} \qquad \text{Equation 7-12}$$

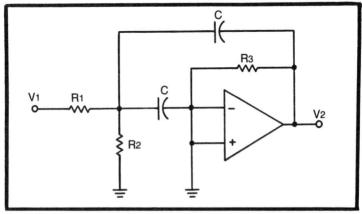

Fig. 7-3. A second-order MFB modified band-pass active filter with all capacitors having equal values ($C_1 = C_2 = C$).

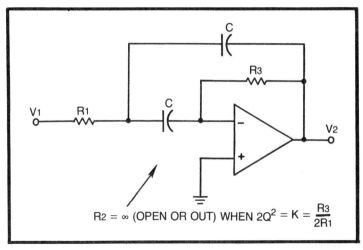

Fig. 7-4. A second-order MFB modified band-pass active filter with capacitors equal and R_2 an open circuit when $2Q^2 = K = R_3/2R_1$.

$$G_1 = 2KG_3 = \frac{KC}{Q} \qquad \textbf{Equation 7-13}$$

In Equation 7-12, the conductance G_2 must be positive; hence, the following equation:

$$2QC > \frac{KC}{Q}$$

$$2Q^2 > K$$

The circuit of Fig. 7-3 can be simplified if $2Q^2 = K$. Then the conductance $G_2 = 0$, which means the resistor $R_2 = \infty$ (an open circuit). Therefore, this means the resistor R_2 in Fig. 7-3 can be removed if $2Q^2 = K$, as shown in Fig. 7-4.

The following example will illustrate the design procedure for a second order band-pass filter employing multiple feedback.

Example 7-1:

A second order MFB band-pass filter must be designed with a center frequency of 500 Hz, and a Q of 7. The gain is not critical in this design.

Solution:
We will select the capacitor value to be 1 F for convenience in the normalized case.

163

Because the gain K is not critical, we will employ the circuit in Fig. 7-4, which means $2Q^2 = K$, and resistor R_2 is an open circuit. If the gain K and the quality factor Q are critical quantities, the designer must use the circuit in Fig. 7-3.

$$2(7)^2 = K$$

$$K = 98$$

Next, we find the conductances G_1 and G_3.

$$G_3 = \frac{C}{2Q} = \frac{1\,F}{2(7)}$$

$$= 0.0714 \text{ mhos}$$

$$G_1 = 2G_3K = 2(0.0714)(98)$$

$$= 13.99 \text{ mhos}$$

Finally, we denormalize the resistance and capacitance values. We find the frequency normalizing factor u, and the impedance scaling factor (ISF) from Equations 5-1 and 5-2, respectively.

$$u = \frac{\omega_0}{\omega_n} = \frac{2\pi f_0}{\omega_n} = \frac{2\pi(500)}{1 \text{ rad/s}}$$

$$= 1000\pi$$

$$\text{ISF} = \frac{f_0}{20\pi} = \frac{500}{20\pi}$$

$$= 7.96$$

We use the two factors found above to denormalize first the capacitance values, then the resistor values.

$$C_p = \frac{C_n}{(u)(\text{ISF})}$$

$$C = \frac{1\,F}{1000\pi(7.96)}$$

$$= 40 \ \mu F$$

Remember all the capacitor values in Fig. 7-4 are the same.

$$R_1 = \frac{ISF}{G_1} = \frac{7.96}{13.99}$$

$$= 0.569 \text{ ohms}$$

$$R_3 = \frac{ISF}{G_3} = \frac{7.96}{0.0714}$$

$$= 111.5 \text{ ohms}$$

Looking at the denormalized value of resistor R_1, the designer has decided that this value is not practical. So the designer is going to multiple the resistor value by 1000 and at the same time divide the capacitor values by 1000. The resulting passive component values are listed below.

$$C = \frac{40 \ \mu F}{1000}$$

$$= 0.04 \ \mu F$$

$$R_1 = 569 \text{ ohms}$$

$$R_3 = 111,500 \text{ ohms} = 111.5K$$

The final active filter design for this example is shown in Fig. 7-5.

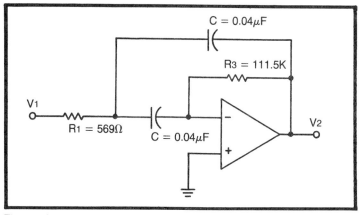

Fig. 7-5. A second-order MFB band-pass active filter for Example 7-1 with $f_o = 500$ Hz, Q = 7, and $2Q^2 = K$.

Our second example will illustrate the design of a MFB band-pass active filter when the center frequency f_0, Q, and K (the gain) are all given. In other words, the three parameters f_0, Q, and K are all critical.

Example 7-2:

A second order MFB band-pass active filter must be designed with a center frequency of 500 Hz, $Q = 7$, and a gain $K = 10$. Find the passive components that will produce the stated requirements.

Solution:
We will select the capacitor value to be 1 F for convenience in the normalized case.

We must make sure that $2Q^2 > K$ so that the conductance G_2 is positive.

$$2(7)^2 = 2(29) = 98 > K = 10$$

Next, we find the conductances.

$$G_3 = \frac{C}{2Q} = \frac{1 \text{ F}}{2(7)}$$

$$= 0.0714 \text{ mhos}$$

$$G_1 = 2KG_3 = 2(10)(0.0714)$$

$$= 1.428 \text{ mhos}$$

$$G_2 = 2QC - \frac{KC}{Q} = 2(7)(1) - \frac{(10)(1)}{(7)}$$

$$= 14 - 1.429$$

$$= 12.571 \text{ mhos}$$

Finally, we denormalize the resistance and capacitance values. We find the frequency normalizing factor u, and the impedance scaling factor (ISF) from Equations 5-1 and 5-2 respectively.

$$u = \frac{\omega_n}{\omega_0} = \frac{2\pi f_0}{\omega_n} = \frac{2\pi(500)}{1 \text{ rad/s}}$$

$$= 1000\pi$$

$$\text{ISF} = \frac{f_0}{20\pi} = \frac{500}{20\pi}$$

$$= 7.96$$

We use the two factors found above to denormalize first the capacitance values, then the resistor values.

$$C_p = \frac{C_n}{(u)(\text{ISF})}$$

$$C = \frac{1\text{ F}}{1000\pi(7.96)}$$

$$= 40 \ \mu\text{F}$$

Remember all the capacitor values in Fig. 7-3 are the same.

$$R_1 = \frac{\text{ISF}}{G_1} = \frac{7.96}{1.428}$$

$$= 5.574 \text{ ohms}$$

$$R_2 = \frac{\text{ISF}}{G_2} = \frac{7.96}{12.571}$$

$$= 0.6332 \text{ ohms}$$

$$R_3 = \frac{\text{ISF}}{G_3} = \frac{7.96}{0.0714}$$

$$= 111.48 \text{ ohms}$$

Looking at the denormalized value of resistor R_2 the designer has decided that this value is not practical. Hence, the designer is going to multiple the resistor value by 1000 and at the same time the designer must divide the capacitor values by 1000. The resulting passive component values are listed below.

$$C = \frac{40\text{ F}}{1000}$$

$$= 0.04 \ \mu\text{F}$$

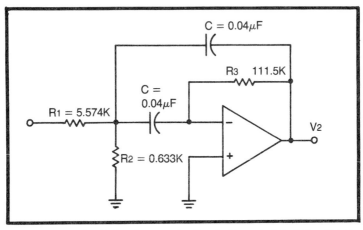

Fig. 7-6. A second-order band-pass active filter for Example 7-1 with $f_0 = 500$ Hz, $Q = 7$ and $K = 10$.

$$R_1 = 5.574K$$
$$R_2 = 633.2 \text{ ohms}$$
$$R_3 = 111.5K$$

The final active filter design for this example is shown in Fig. 7-6.

VOLTAGE CONTROLLED VOLTAGE SOURCE (VCVS) OR SALLEN AND KEY BAND-PASS FILTERS

The basic circuit of the second order VCVS band-pass filter is shown in Fig. 7-7. The transfer function that describes the circuit shown in Fig. 7-7 has the general form shown below.

$$\frac{V_2}{V_1} = \frac{\dfrac{K}{Q}s}{s^2 + \dfrac{1}{Q}s + 1} \qquad \textbf{Equation 7-14}$$

where Q = quality factor $= \dfrac{\omega_0}{B}$,

where ω_0 is normalized to 1 rad/s in Equation 7-14, and B is the circuit bandwidth.

$$V_2 = \text{the filter output voltage}$$
$$V_1 = \text{the filter input voltage}$$

168

Sometimes $B = 1/Q$ is substituted in Equation 7-14, which results in the following transfer function for the circuit in Fig. 7-7.

$$\frac{V_2}{V_1} = \frac{KBs}{s^2 + Bs + 1} \qquad \textbf{Equation 7-15}$$

Remember Equations 7-14 and 7-15 are exactly equal.

The circuit in Fig. 7-7 can be modified by making the two capacitors C_1 and C_2 equal. In other words, we will make $C_1 = C_2 = C$. Also, we will make the resistors R_1, R_2, and R_3 identical. In other words, $R_1 = R_2 = R_3 = R_a$. The resulting modified circuit for a second order VCVS band-pass active filter circuit is shown in Fig. 7-8.

The constants of the transfer function K, Q, and B are related to the passive components of the circuit in Fig. 7-8 through the equations that follow.

$$K = \frac{w}{R_a C} \qquad \textbf{Equation 7-16}$$

$$B = \frac{4 - w}{R_a C} \qquad \textbf{Equation 7-17}$$

$$\omega_0^2 = \frac{2}{R_a^2 C^2}, \qquad \textbf{Equation 7-18}$$

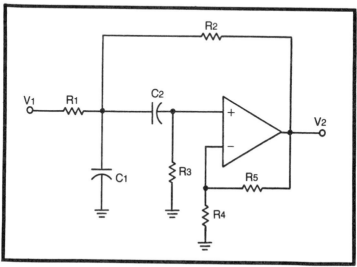

Fig. 7-7. A second-order VCVS (Sallen-Key) band-pass active filter circuit.

$$\text{where } w = 1 + \frac{R_5}{R_4} \qquad \textbf{Equation 7-19}$$

The circuit in Fig. 7-8 operates best for Q values less than 25. The VCVS circuit has serious tuning, gain, and frequency restrictions, as can be seen by Equation 7-17.

$$B = \frac{\omega_0}{Q} = \frac{4 - w}{R_a C} \qquad \textbf{Equation 7-20}$$

$$4 - w = \frac{R_a C \omega_0}{Q}$$

We see from Equation 7-20 that as Q becomes larger and larger the value of $4 - w$ becomes smaller and smaller, which means that the value of w approaches 4. Thus, as Q becomes large the circuit gain decreases; hence, the circuit is quite sensitive to changes in R_4 and R_5. A good feature of the circuit in Fig. 7-8 is that the center frequency f_0 and the chosen value of C determine R_a. Thus, we may obtain a number of bandwidths for a fixed center frequency by changing only R_4 and R_5. The circuit is useful for very low frequency work with small gain requirements. The following example will illustrate the design procedure for the VCVS band-pass filter.

Example 7-3:

A second order VCVS band-pass filter must be designed with a center frequency of 20 kHz, and a Q of 5. Find the passive components that will meet the stated requirements for the circuit shown in Fig. 7-8.

Solution:

We will select a capacitor value of 1 F for convenience in the normalized case.

Since we know that $C = 1$ and $\omega_0 = 1$ for the normalized case we employ Equation 7-18 to find the value of R_a.

$$R_a^2 = \frac{2}{\omega_0^2 C^2}$$

$$R_a^2 = \frac{2}{(1)^2 (1)^2}$$

$$R_a^2 = 2$$

$$R_a = 1.414 \text{ ohms}$$

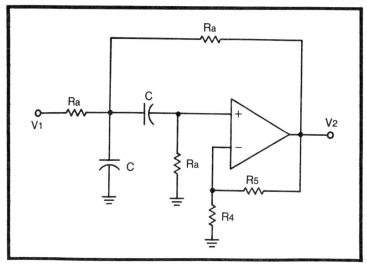

Fig. 7-8. A second-order VCVS band-pass active filter modified to have $C_1 = C_2 = C$, (and $R_1 = R_2 = R_3 = R_a$).

From Equation 7-17, we find the parameter w, since we can find the bandwidth $B = \omega_0/Q = 1/5 = 0.2$ and the parameters R_a and C are known.

$$B = \frac{\omega_0}{Q} = \frac{1}{5} = \frac{4 - w}{R_a\,C}$$

$$0.2 = \frac{4 - w}{(1.414)(1)}$$

$$4 - w = 0.2828$$

$$w = 3.7172$$

Now we can find the resistor values of R_4 and R_5 through Equation 7-19.

$$w = 1 + \frac{R_5}{R_4}$$

We will select $R_4 = 1$ ohm in the normalized case and find the value of R_5 knowing the value of $w = 3.7172$.

$$w = 1 + \frac{R_5}{1}$$

$$3.7172 = 1 + R_5$$
$$R_5 = 3.7172 - 1$$
$$= 2.7172 \text{ ohms}$$

Finally, we denormalize the resistance and capacitance values. We find the frequency normalizing factor u and the impedance scaling factor (ISF) from Equation 5-1 and 5-2, respectively.

$$u = \frac{\omega_0}{\omega_n} = \frac{2\pi f_0}{1 \text{ rad/s}} = \frac{2\pi(20,000)}{1}$$

$$= 40,000\pi$$

$$\text{ISF} = \frac{f_0}{20\pi} = \frac{20,000}{20\pi}$$

$$= 318.31$$

We use the two factors just found to denormalize first the capacitance values, then the resistor values.

$$C_p = \frac{C_n}{(u)\,(\text{ISF})}$$

$$C = \frac{1 \text{ F}}{40,000\,\pi(318.31)}$$

$$= 0.000000025 = 0.025\,(10)^{-6} \text{ F}$$
$$= 0.025\,\mu\text{F}$$

Remember all the capacitor values are the same in Fig. 7-8.
$$R_a = (\text{ISF})\,(1.414 \text{ ohms}) = (318.31)(1.414)$$
$$= 450.1 \text{ ohms}$$
$$R_4 = (\text{ISF})\,(1 \text{ ohm}) = (318.31)(1)$$
$$= 318.31 \text{ ohms}$$
$$R_5 = (\text{ISF})(2.7172 \text{ ohms}) = (318.31)(2.7172)$$
$$= 864.91 \text{ ohms}$$
The final active filter design for this example is shown in Fig. 7-9.

POSITIVE FEEDBACK SECOND ORDER BAND-PASS ACTIVE FILTERS

A high Q band-pass active pole filter can NOT be designed with a single op amp. A circuit using two op amps, which can obtain values

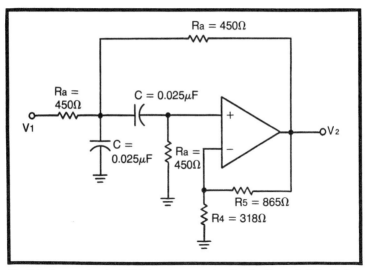

Fig. 7-9. A second-order VCVS band-pass active filter for Example 7-3 with $f_0 =$ 20 kHz and Q = 5.

of Q around 50, is the circuit shown in Fig. 7-10. The circuit in Fig. 7-10 is called a second order band-pass positive feedback active filter, because the second op amp output has its noninverted signal fed back to the input inverting terminal through resistor R_3. In other words, the input signal V_1 is twice inverted 180° by the two op amps, and the output signal V_2 is fed back to the input terminal through R_3.

The transfer function that describes the circuit shown in Fig. 7-10 has the general form already defined in previous sections of this chapter, for example Equations 7-14 and 7-15. The constants of the

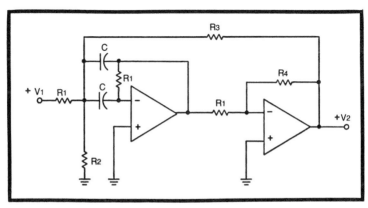

Fig. 7-10. A second-order band-pass positive feedback active filter.

transfer function B, Q, and ω_0 are related to the passive components of the circuit in Fig. 7-10 through the equations that follow.

$$B = \frac{1}{R_1 C}\left(2 - \frac{R_4}{R_3}\right) \qquad \textbf{Equation 7-21}$$

$$\omega_0^2 = \frac{1}{R_1 C^2}\left(\frac{1}{R_1} + \frac{1}{R_2} + \frac{1}{R_3}\right) \qquad \textbf{Equation 7-22}$$

Remember the bandwidth $B = \omega_0/Q$, which can be substituted in Equations 7-21 if necessary.

The following example will illustrate the design procedure for the second order band-pass positive feedback active filter.

Example 7-4:

A second-order band-pass positive feedback active filter must be designed with a center frequency of 20 kHz and a Q of 40. Find the passive components that will meet the stated requirements for the circuit shown in Fig. 7-10.

Solution:

We will select a capacitor value of 1 F for convenience in the normalized case.

Since we know that $C = 1$ and $\omega_0 = 1$ for the normalized case, we employ Equations 7-21 and 7-22 to find the values of resistors R_1, R_2, R_3, and R_4.

$$B = \frac{\omega_0}{Q} = \frac{1}{40} = \frac{1}{R_1(1)}\left[2 - \frac{R_4}{R_3}\right]$$

$$\omega_0^2 = (1)^2 = \frac{1}{R_1(1)^2}\left[\frac{1}{R_1} + \frac{1}{R_2} + \frac{1}{R_3}\right]$$

Rearranging terms in the first of the previous equations, and solving for R_1 we have the following.

$$R_1 = 80 - \frac{40\,R_4}{R_3}$$

Selecting the normalized value of $R_3 = 1$ ohm results in the following equation.

$$R_1 = 80 - 40R_4$$

For the above equation if R_1 is to be positive then 80 must be greater than $40R_4$. Therefore, we can select $R_4 = 1$ ohm in the normalized case and solve for R_1 as follows.

$R_1 = 80 - 40(1)$

$\quad = 40$ ohms

Next we substitute all the known resistor values into the equation that relates ω_0 to the resistor values.

$$\omega_0^2 = (1)^2 = \frac{1}{R_1}\left(\frac{1}{R_1} + \frac{1}{R_2} + \frac{1}{R_3}\right)$$

$$1 = \frac{1}{40}\left(\frac{1}{40} + \frac{1}{R_2} + \frac{1}{1}\right)$$

From the above equation it is obvious that the only resistor that must be found to complete the design is R_2. Hence, we solve for R_2 as follows.

$$40 = 0.025 + \frac{1}{R_2} + 1 = 1.025 + \frac{1}{R_2}$$

$$38.975 = \frac{1}{R_2}$$

$$R_2 = \frac{1}{38.975}$$

$$= 0.02566 \text{ ohms}$$

At this time it is worth while to list the normalized values in order to prepare ourselves for the next step. We have $C = 1$ F, $R_1 = 40$ ohms, $R_2 = 0.02566$ ohms, and $R_3 = R_4 = 1$ ohm.

Finally, we denormalize the resistance and capacitance values. We find the frequency normalizing factor u and the impedance scaling factor (ISF) from Equations 5-1 and 5-2, respectively.

$$u = \frac{\omega_0}{\omega_n} = \frac{2\pi f_0}{1 \text{ rad/s}} = \frac{2\pi(20,000)}{1}$$

$$= 40,000\pi$$

$$\text{ISF} = \frac{f_0}{20\pi} = \frac{20,000}{20\pi}$$

$$= 318.31$$

We use the two factors found above to denormalize first the capacitance values, then the resistor values.

$$C_p = \frac{C_n}{(u)(\text{ISF})}$$

$$C = \frac{1 \text{ F}}{40,000\pi(318.31)}$$

$$= 0.025 \ \mu\text{F}$$

Remember all the capacitor values are the same in Fig. 7-10.

$$R_1 = (\text{ISF})(40 \text{ ohms}) = (318.31)(40)$$
$$= 12,732.4 \text{ ohms}$$
$$R_2 = (\text{ISF})(0.02566) = (318.31)(0.02566)$$
$$= 8.168 \text{ ohms}$$
$$R_3 = R_4 = (\text{ISF})(1) = (318.31)(1)$$
$$= R_4 = 318.31 \text{ ohms}$$

Looking at the denormalized value of resistor R_2, the designer has decided that this value is not practical. Therefore, the designer is going to multiple the resistor values by 100 and at the same time he must divide the capacitor values by 100. The resulting passive component values are listed below.

$$C = 0.00025 \ \mu\text{F} = 0.25 \ n\text{F} = 250 \ p\text{F}$$
$$R_1 = 1.273,240 \text{ ohms} \cong 1.27 \text{ M}$$
$$R_2 = 817 \text{ ohms}$$
$$R_3 = R_4 = 31.8\text{K}$$

The final active filter design for this example is shown in Fig. 7-11.

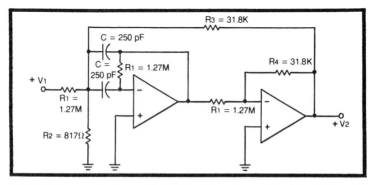

Fig. 7-11. A second-order positive feedback band-pass active filter with $f_o = 20$ kHz and Q = 40.

HIGHER ORDER BAND-PASS ACTIVE FILTERS

The active filter designer may obtain a higher order band-pass filter by cascading low-pass filter sections with high-pass filter sections. If the designer desires a fourth-order band-pass active filter, he could cascade a low-pass second-order filter with cutoff point f_{02}, with a high-pass second-order filter with cutoff point f_{01}, where f_{01} is less than f_{02}. The result is a band-pass active filter with a center frequency approximately equal to the following equation.

$$f_0 = \sqrt{f_{01}\ f_{02}} \qquad \text{Equation 7-23}$$

Also, the bandwidth B can be expressed approximately with the following equation.

$$B = f_{02} - f_{01} \qquad \text{Equation 7-24}$$

The approximations improve as the difference $f_{02} - f_{01}$ increases and hence as the Q decreases. Best results are obtained if f_{01} and f_{02} are at least one octave apart, and therefore for Q not exceeding $\sqrt{2} = 1.414$. Remember an octave is the interval between two frequencies, where one frequency is twice the other frequency. Sharper cutoff features may be obtained by cascading fourth order low-pass and high-pass filters, but this requires more components and op amps. Figure 7-12 illustrates the technique just described to obtain higher order band-pass filters.

In the diagram of Fig. 7-12, if both filter sections are Butterworth filters, the approximation of Equation 7-23 becomes an exact equation. Consider the low- and high-pass active filter sections of Fig. 7-12 to be Butterworth filter and $f_{01} = f_{02}$. Then the center frequency $f_0 = f_{01} = f_{02}$. If $f_{02} = 2f_{01}$, then the center frequency $f_0 = \sqrt{2}\ (f_{01}) = 1.414f_{01}$.

A much sharper band-pass filter may be obtained by cascading two or more identical band-pass second order filters. If Q_1 is the quality factor of a single stage and there are n stages, the Q of the filter is expressed by the following equation.

$$Q = \frac{Q_1}{\sqrt[n]{\sqrt{2}-1}} \qquad \text{Equation 7-25}$$

The values for Q and corresponding bandwidths are shown for n = 1, 2, 3, 4, and 5 in Table 7-1, where B_1 is the bandwidth of a filter with a single stage.

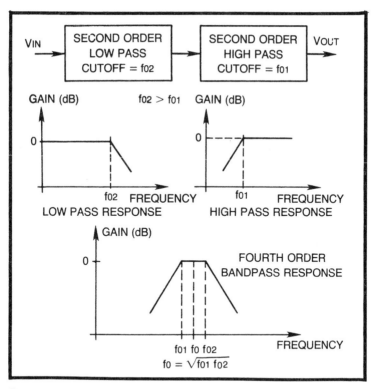

Fig. 7-12. Block diagram of obtaining a higher order band-pass by cascading low-pass and high-pass filter sections.

STATE VARIABLE BAND-PASS ACTIVE FILTER

The state variable filter employed as a band-pass active filter has a block diagram representation shown in Fig. 7-14. The different functions performed by the blocks are summing, two identical integ-

Table 7-1. Bandwidth and selectivity for identical cascaded second-order band-pass filters.

The number of second order identical stages	Bandwidth (B)	Selectivity Q
1	B_1	Q_1
2	$B_2 = 0.644B_1$	$Q_2 = 1.55Q_1$
3	$B_3 = 0.510B_1$	$Q_3 = 1.96Q_1$
4	$B_4 = 0.435B_1$	$Q_4 = 2.30Q_1$
5	$B_5 = 0.386B_1$	$Q_5 = 2.6Q_1$

178

rators, and damping. Because of the manner these functions are employed, we are able to simultaneously have the following filter responses:

☐ A second order low-pass filter.
☐ A second order high-pass filter.
☐ A one-pole band-pass filter. The cutoff frequency of the low-pass and high-pass filter is identical to the center frequency of the band-pass response. In addition, the damping factor a is equal to $1/Q$, and a is the same for all three filter responses.

The block diagram of Fig. 7-13 is now replaced with passive and active components as shown in Fig. 7-14. This circuit shows three op amps two of which are employed as integrators and one op amp is used as a summing amplifier. The circuit is normalized for $\omega_0 = 1$ rad/s and an impedance level of 1 ohm and 1 Farad. The first op amp is the summing block for the input, low-pass and band-pass signals. In series with the summing amplifier are two identical op amp integrators which determine the cutoff and center frequency by the following equations.

$$\omega_0 = \frac{1}{RC} \qquad \text{Equation 7-26}$$

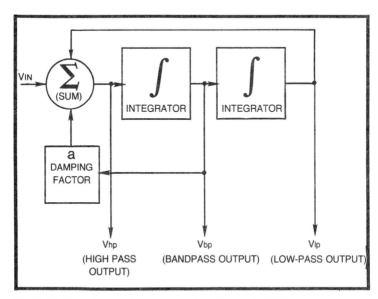

Fig. 7-13. Block diagram for a state variable band-pass filter.

179

$$f_0 = \frac{1}{2\pi RC} \qquad \textbf{Equation 7-27}$$

The damping network is composed of resistors R_1 and R_2. For both the low-pass and high-pass responses to have a second order Butterworth response, the damping factor *(aa)* must be equal to 1.414. Therefore, R_1 must equal to 1.12 ohms when R_2 equals 1.0 ohm. For minimum offset, R_2 should be 0.33 ohms, which is the parallel combination of the two 1-ohm input resistors connected to the inverting input of the summing amplifier, and the 1-ohm feedback resistor. This means the resistor R_1 is equal to 0.37 ohms. However, if the offset voltage can be neglected, the following equations must hold.

$$R_1 = R_2 \left(\frac{3}{a} - 1 \right) \qquad \textbf{Equation 7-28}$$

We can rewrite the above equation since $Q = 1/a$.

$$R_1 = R_2 (3Q - 1) \qquad \textbf{Equation 7-29}$$

In addition, if the offset of the integrators can be neglected, the resistors connected to the noninverting inputs of the two identical integrators may be replaced by short circuits to ground.

It is not possible to obtain the optimum performance with all three outputs, V_{hp}, V_{lp}, and V_{bp} shown in Fig. 7-14. We must therefore compromise. In other words, we should design either for a second order Butterworth low-pass or high-pass response, or for a high Q band-pass response. The following example will illustrate the design procedure for a band-pass state variable active filter employing three op amps.

Example 7-5:

A state variable band-pass active filter must be designed with a center frequency of 1000 Hz and a Q of 40. Find the passive components that will meet the stated requirements for the circuit shown in Fig. 7-14.

Solution:

We will select a capacitor value of C = 1F, and a resistor value of R = 1 ohm for convenience in the normalized case for the circuit shown in Fig. 7-14.

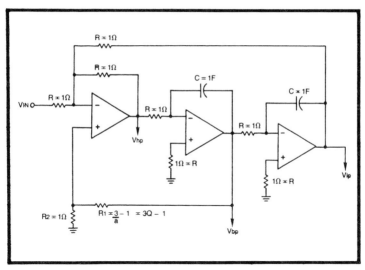

Fig. 7-14. Schematic of a second-order state variable band-pass active filter.

We employ Equation 7-29 to obtain the resistor values for R_1 and R_2, since we know that $Q = 40$.

$$R_1 = R_2(3Q - 1)$$

If Q is greater than 10 we can approximate the above equation as follows.

$$R_1 \cong 3QR_2 = 3(40)R_2$$

Next we select $R_2 =$ ohm in the normalized case and then find R_1.

$$R_1 = 120R_2 = 120(1)$$
$$= 120 \text{ ohms}$$

Next we denormalize the resistance and capacitance values. We find the frequency normalizing factor u and the impedance scaling factor (ISF) from Equations 5-1 and 5-2, respectively.

$$u = \frac{\omega_0}{\omega_n} = \frac{2\pi f_0}{1 \text{ rad/s}} = \frac{2\pi(1000)}{1}$$

$$= 2000\pi$$

$$\text{ISF} = \frac{f_0}{20\pi} = \frac{1000}{20\pi}$$

$$= 15.9155$$

We use the two factors found above to denormalize first the capacitance values, then the resistor values.

$$C_p = \frac{C_n}{(u)(\text{ISF})}$$

$$C = \frac{1\ F}{(2000\pi)(15.9155)}$$

$$= 0.0000099999\ F \cong 0.00001\ F = 10\ (10)^{-6}\ F$$
$$= 10\ \mu F$$
$$R = (\text{ISF})(1\ \text{ohm}) = 15.9155(1)$$
$$= 15.92\ \text{ohms}$$
$$= R_2 = 15.92\ \text{ohms}$$
$$R_1 = 120R_2 = 120(15.92\ \text{ohms})$$
$$= 1910.4\ \text{ohms}$$

Looking at the denormalized value of resistor R and R_2, the designer has decided that this value is not practical. Therefore, the designer is going to multiple the resistor values by 100 and at the same time he must divide the capacitor values by 100. The resulting passive component values are listed below.

$$C = 0.1\ \mu F$$
$$R = R_2 = 1592\ \text{ohms}$$
$$R_1 = 191\ k$$

The final active filter design for this example is shown in Fig. 7-15.

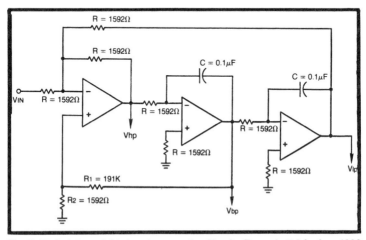

Fig. 7-15. A state variable band-pass active filter for Example 7-5 for $f_o = 1000$ Hz and $Q = 40$.

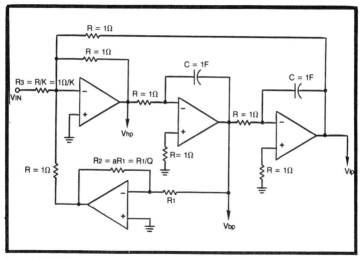

Fig. 7-16. A four op amp state variable band-pass active filter.

The circuit in Fig. 7-14 is a state variable active filter with a pass-band voltage gain of unity. If we wish a pass-band voltage gain of the state variable filter to be greater than unity for the low-pass and high-pass responses, we can just place an additional op amp circuit, which can be either an inverting or noninverting amplifier, after the filter to give the desired gain.

However, if we change the type of summing amplifier and the damping network of the three op amp state variable filter shown in Fig. 7-14, we can then make the gain and damping to be independent of each other. The circuit in Fig. 7-16 is a four-op amp state variable filter for v_0 equal to 1 rad/s and an impedance level of 1 ohm, that will accomplish the objective of increasing the gain above unity and make the gain and damping independent of each other.

The fourth op amp in Fig. 7-16 has its output connected to the summing amplifier. Hence, three inputs are connected to the summing amplifiers inverting input, and the $(3Q - 1)$ damping factor is eliminated. As before, both integrators determine the cutoff/center frequency of the filter. The output of the summing amplifier can be expressed in terms of the three inputs by the following equation.

$$\frac{1}{K}(V_{hp}) = -V_{in} - \frac{1}{K}(V_{lp}) - \frac{(-1)}{K}(V_{bp})$$ **Equation 7-30**

The above equation can be written as follows.

$$KV_{in} = -V_{hp} - V_{lp} + \frac{R_2}{R_1}(V_{bp})$$ Equation 7-31

The resistors R_1 and R_2 are related to Q by the following equation.

$$\frac{R_1}{R_2} = Q$$ Equation 7-32

The voltage gain at center frequency for the band-pass filter is given by the following equation.

$$\frac{V_{bp}}{V_{in}} = KQ$$ Equation 7-33

The following example will illustrate the design procedure for a band-pass state variable active filter employing four op amps.

Example 7-6:

A state variable band-pass active filter must be designed with a center frequency of 1000 Hz and a Q of 40 with a gain at center frequency equal to 100. Find the passive components that will meet the stated requirements for the circuit shown in Fig. 7-16.

Solution:
We will select a capacitor value of C = 1 F, and a resistor value of R = 1 ohm for convenience in the normalized case for the circuit shown in Fig. 7-16.

We employ Equation 7-32 to obtain the resistor values for R_1 and R_2, since we know that Q = 40.

$$R_1 = QR_2$$

We select R_2 = 1 ohm in the normalized case and then find R_1.

$$R_1 = (40)(1 \text{ ohm})$$
$$R_1 = 40 \text{ ohms}$$

Next we must find the input resistance R_3 as defined in the circuit of Fig. 7-16.

$$R_3 = \frac{R}{K}$$ Equation 7-34

The value of R = 1 ohm in the above equation, and the value of K is found through Equation 7-33.

$$\frac{V_{bp}}{V_{in}} = KQ$$

The voltage gain at the center frequency is equal to the voltage ratio in the above equation and the value of the voltage ratio in this example is 100.

$$100 = KQ$$

$$K = \frac{100}{40} = 2.5$$

Therefore, the resistor R_3 can be found as follows from Equation 7-34.

$$R_3 = \frac{1 \text{ ohm}}{2.5}$$

$$R_3 = 0.4 \text{ ohms}$$

Next we denormalize the resistance and capacitance values. We find the frequency normalizing factor u and the impedance scaling factor (ISF) from Equations 5-1 and 5-2, respectively.

$$u = \frac{\omega_0}{\omega_n} = \frac{2\pi f_0}{1 \text{ rad/s}} = \frac{2\pi(1000)}{1}$$

$$= 2000\pi$$

$$\text{ISF} = \frac{f_0}{20\pi} = \frac{1000}{20\pi}$$

$$= 15.9155$$

We use the two factors found above to denormalize first the capacitance values, then the resistor values.

$$C_p = \frac{C_n}{(u)(\text{ISF})}$$

$$C = \frac{1 \text{ F}}{(2000\pi)(15.9155)}$$

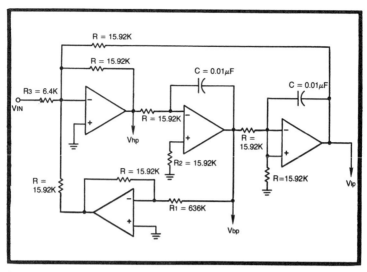

Fig. 7-17. A state variable band-pass active filter for Example 7-6 with Q = 40, fo = 1000 Hz and a gain at fo of 1000.

$$= 10\mu F$$
$$R = (ISF)(1 \text{ ohm}) = (15.9155)(1)$$
$$= 15.92 \text{ ohms}$$
$$= R_2 = 15.92 \text{ ohms}$$
$$R_1 = 40R_2 = (40)(15.92)$$
$$= 636.8 \text{ ohms}$$
$$R_3 = (ISF)(0.4 \text{ ohms}) = (15.9155)(0.4)$$
$$= 6.368 \text{ ohms}$$

Looking at the denormalized value of all the resistors, the designer has decided that these values are not practical. Hence, the designer is going to multiple the resistor values by a factor of 1000 (1K) and at the same time he must divide the capacitor values by the 1000 factor. The resulting passive component values are listed below.

$$C = 0.01 \ \mu F$$
$$R = R_2 = 15.92K$$
$$R_3 = 6.4K$$
$$R_1 = 636K\Omega$$

The final active filter design for this example is shown in Fig. 7-17.

BIQUAD BAND-PASS ACTIVE FILTER

An active filter circuit that resembles the state variable band-pass active filter circuit is shown in Fig. 7-18. The circuit is called a biquad band-pass active filter circuit, and it employs two integrators and an inverter. The input signal to the biquad active filter circuit is applied to one of the integrators instead of the summing amplifier as is the case with the state variable active filter.

In the biquad band-pass active filter circuit, as the frequency changes, the absolute bandwidth remains constant. This characteristic is needed in telephone applications, where a group of identical absolute bandwidth channels is needed at different center frequencies. The center frequency is easily tuned by merely adjusting the value of R_3 in Fig. 7-18. Also, Q may be adjusted by changing the value of R_2, and the gain of the circuit may be changed by adjusting the value of R_1. The biquad circuit is capable of attaining high values of Q, in the neighborhood of 100, and is a much more stable network than those discussed in the previous sections.

The transfer function of the biquad circuit in Fig. 7-19 has the general form shown below.

$$\frac{V_2}{V_1} = \frac{K\omega_0 s/Q}{s^2 + \dfrac{\omega_0}{Q}\, s + \omega_0^2} \qquad \text{Equation 7-35}$$

The constants of the transfer function in Equation 7-35 are related to the passive components of the circuit in Fig. 7-19 through the following equations.

$$R_1 = \cdot\frac{Q}{K\,\omega_0 C} \qquad \text{Equation 7-36}$$

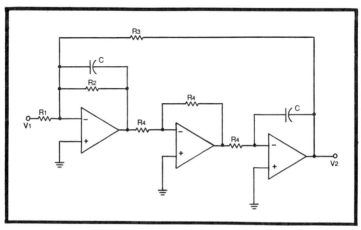

Fig. 7-18. A biquad band-pass active filter circuit.

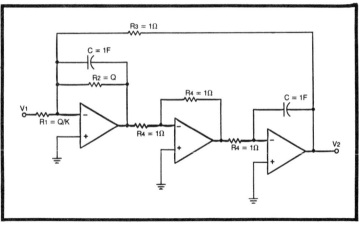

Fig. 7-19. Modified biquad band-pass filter, normalized to $\omega_0 = 1$ rad/s, $R_4 = 1\Omega$, and $C = 1$ F.

$$R_2 = \frac{Q}{\omega_0\, C} \qquad \text{Equation 7-37}$$

$$R_3 = \frac{1}{\omega_0^2\, R_4\, C^2} \qquad \text{Equation 7-38}$$

We can simplify the above equations if we normalize the circuit in Fig. 7-18 by making $\omega_0 = 1$ rad/s, $C = 1$ F, and $R_4 = 1$ Ω. Substituting these values in Equations 7-36 through 7-38 results in the following normalized set of equations.

$$R_1 = \frac{Q}{K} \qquad \text{Equation 7-36A}$$

$$R_2 = Q \qquad \text{Equation 7-37A}$$

$$R_3 = 1 \text{ ohm} \qquad \text{Equation 7-38A}$$

Therefore, we can modify the circuit shown in Fig. 7-18 to the normalized circuit shown in Fig. 7-19.

The following example will illustrate the design procedure for a modified biquad band-pass active filter as shown in Fig. 7-19.

Example 7-7:

A biquad band-pass active filter must be designed with a center frequency of 20,000 Hz, a $Q = 80$, and a gain $K = 10$. Find the passive components that will meet the stated requirements for the circuit shown in Fig. 7-20.

Solution:

We will select a capacitor value of $C = 1$ F, and a resistor value of $R_4 = 1$ ohm for convenience in the normalized case for the circuit shown in Fig. 7-19.

To find the resistor values R_1, R_2, and R_3, we employ Equations 7-36A, 7-37A, and 7-38A as follows.

$$R_1 = \frac{Q}{X} = \frac{80}{10}$$

$$= 8 \text{ ohms}$$

$$R_2 = Q = 80 \text{ ohms}$$
$$R_3 = 1 \text{ ohm}$$

Next we denormalize the resistance and capacitance values. We find the frequency normalizing factor u and the impedance scaling factor (ISF) from Equations 5-1 and 5-2, respectively.

$$u = \frac{\omega_0}{\omega_n} = \frac{2\pi f_0}{1 \text{ rad/s}} = \frac{2\pi(20,000)}{1}$$

$$= 40,000\pi$$

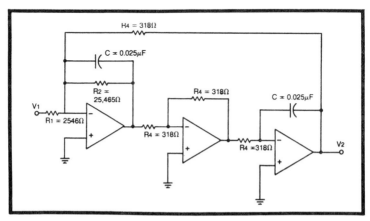

Fig. 7-20. A modified biquad band-pass filter for Example 7-7 with $f_0 = 20,000$ Hz, $Q = 80$, and a gain $K = 10$.

$$\text{ISF} = \frac{f_0}{20\pi} = \frac{20,000}{20\pi}$$

$$= 318.31$$

We use the two factors found above to denormalize first the capacitance values, then the resistor values.

$$C_p = \frac{C_n}{(u)(\text{ISF})}$$

$$C = \frac{1\ \text{F}}{(40,000\pi)(318.31)}$$

$$C = 0.025\ \mu\text{F}$$

$$R_1 = (\text{ISF})(8\ \text{ohms}) = 318.31(8)$$

$$= 2546.48\ \text{ohms}$$

$$R_2 = (\text{ISF})(80\ \text{ohms}) = 318.31(80)$$

$$= 25,464.8\ \text{ohms}$$

$$R_3 = (\text{ISF})(1\ \text{ohm}) = 318.31(1)$$

$$= 318.31\ \text{ohms}$$

$$R_4 = R_3 = 318.31\ \text{ohms}$$

The final active filter design for this example is shown in Fig. 7-20.

Chapter 8
Other Types of Active Filters

In this chapter, we will discuss other active filter designs besides the typical high-pass, low-pass and band-pass Butterworth and Chebyshev filters. Two of the most common active filters that will be illustrated are the *notch filter*, sometimes called the *band-reject*, and the *all-pass filter* sometimes called the *phase shift filter*. As the chapter develops and this book is revised we will present state of the art active filter design by expanding the topics in this chapter.

THE BAND-REJECT OR NOTCH ACTIVE FILTER

The band-reject, or notch filter, is designed into systems for the elimination of a single frequency. This criteria is exactly opposite of the band-pass filter, which is to pass one frequency or a group of frequencies within a given bandwidth. Consequently, there are similarities between the notch filter and the band-pass filter. Both filters have a center frequency and a quality factor Q, which implies a bandwidth B. The response of a notch filter is the mirror image of the band-pass filter about the frequency axis as illustrated in Fig. 8-1.

Figure 8-1 shows the response of a notch filter for a quality factor $Q = 5$. As illustrated in Fig. 8-1, the resonance frequency of the bandpass response will equal the point of zero response of the notch filter. For reasonable Q values (5 to 20), the bandwidth of both responses will be the same. This means that the frequencies at

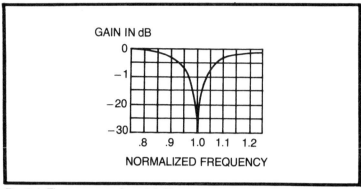

Fig. 8-1. The response of a notch filter.

which the band-pass response is down 3 dB from its maximum resonance value will equal the frequencies at which the notch response is 3 dB down. Therefore, the bandwidth of the band-pass response is equal to the bandwidth of the notch response.

In the following sections, we will illustrate two types of active filters that achieve the notch frequency response. The two circuits we will employ are the VCVS circuit and the infinite gain MFB circuit.

A VCVS NOTCH OR BAND-REJECT ACTIVE FILTER CIRCUIT

A second order VCVS notch or band-reject active filter circuit is shown in Fig. 8-2.

The transfer function that describes the circuit shown in Fig. 8-2 has the general form shown below.

$$\frac{V_2}{V_1} = \frac{K(s^2 + \omega_0^2)}{s^2 + Bs + \omega_0^2} \qquad \textbf{Equation 8-1}$$

K = the gain of the circuit

$B = \omega_0/Q$ the bandwidth of the notch filter, where Q is the quality factor.

$\omega_0 = 2\pi f_0$, where f_0 is the center frequency that is to be rejected.

V_2 = the filter output voltage
V_1 = the filter input voltage

The transfer function in Equation 8-1 can be adapted to the circuit in Fig. 8-2 for the normalized case, $\omega_0 = 1$ rad/s (then $B =$

$1/Q$) and $C = 1$ F, and the gain $K = 1$. Then the transfer function of Equation 8-1 is related to the circuit parameters in Fig. 8-2 by the following equations.

$$\frac{V_2}{V_1} = \frac{s^2 + G_1 G_2}{s^2 + 2G_2 s + G_1 G_2}$$
Equation 8-2

$$G_3 = G_1 + G_2$$
Equation 8-3

$$1 = 2G_2 Q$$
Equation 8-4

$$1 = G_1 G_2$$
Equation 8-5

Solving for the normalized conductances we have the following equations.

$$G_1 = 2Q$$
Equation 8-6

$$G_2 = \frac{1}{2Q}$$
Equation 8-7

$$G_3 = 2Q + \frac{1}{2Q}$$
Equation 8-8

The following example will illustrate the design procedure for a second order VCVS notch (band-reject) active filter circuit that is shown in Fig. 8-2.

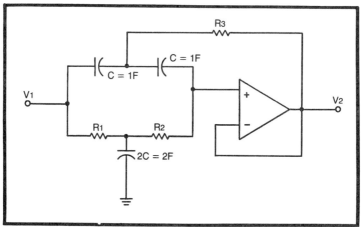

Fig. 8-2. A second-order VCVS notch filter.

Example 8-1:

A second order VCVS notch filter must be designed to reject a center frequency of 1000 Hz with a quality factor of $Q = 10$. Find the components for the circuit in Fig. 8-2.

Solution:

We will use the circuit shown in Fig. 8-2, where $C = 1$ F for convenience in the normalized case, and the gain $K = 1$. Knowing the value of Q_1 we can easily find the conductances.

$$G_1 = 2Q = 2(10)$$

$$= 20 \text{ mhos}$$

$$G_2 = \frac{1}{2Q} = \frac{1}{20}$$

$$= 0.05 \text{ mhos}$$

$$G_3 = G_1 + G_2 = (20 + 0.05) \text{ mhos}$$

$$= 20.05 \text{ mhos}$$

Next we denormalize the resistance and capacitance values. We find the frequency normalizing factor u, and the impedance scaling factor (ISF) from Equations 5-1 and 5-2, respectively.

$$u = \frac{\omega_0}{\omega_n} = \frac{2\pi f_0}{\omega_n} = \frac{2\pi(1000)}{1 \text{ rad/s}}$$

$$= 2000\pi$$

$$\text{ISF} = \frac{f_0}{20\pi} = \frac{1000}{20\pi}$$

$$= 15.92$$

We use the two factors found above to denormalize first the capacitance value, then the resistor values.

$$C_p = \frac{C_n}{(u)(\text{ISF})}$$

$$C = \frac{1 \text{ F}}{(2000\pi)(15.92)}$$

$$= 10 \ \mu F$$

$$R_1 = \frac{\text{ISF}}{G_1} = \frac{15.92}{20}$$

$$= 0.796 \text{ ohms}$$

$$R_2 = \frac{\text{ISF}}{G_2} = \frac{15.92}{0.05}$$

$$= 318.4 \text{ ohms}$$

$$R_3 = \frac{\text{ISF}}{G_3} = \frac{15.92}{20.05}$$

$$= 0.794 \text{ ohms}$$

Looking at the denormalized values of resistors R_1 and R_3 the designer has decided that these values are not practical. Accordingly, the designer is going to multiply the resistor values by 1000 and at the same time he must divide the capacitor value by 1000. The resulting passive component values follow:

$$C = \frac{10 \ \mu F}{1000}$$

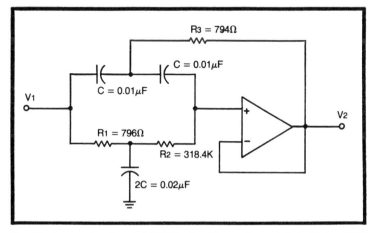

Fig. 8-3. A second-order notch VCVS active filter for Example 8-1 with $f_0 = 1000$ Hz, $Q = 10$, and gain $K = 1$.

195

$$= 0.01 \ \mu\text{F}$$
$$R_1 = 796 \text{ ohms}$$
$$R_2 = 318{,}400 \text{ ohms}$$
$$R_3 = 794 \text{ ohms}$$

The final active filter design for this example is shown in Fig. 8-3.

AN INFINITE GAIN MFB NOTCH OR BAND-REJECT ACTIVE FILTER

The circuit of the previous section is limited to a gain of unity, and for best performance it should not be used for very high quality factors (Q). A notch filter circuit for which the gain may be specified and which is capable of achieving higher values of Q is shown in Fig. 8-4.

Analysis of the circuit in Fig. 8-4 to achieve the transfer function of the notch filter in Equation 8-1, the following equations must hold.

$$K = \frac{G_3}{G_6} \qquad \textbf{Equation 8-9}$$

$$B = \frac{2G_4}{C} \qquad \textbf{Equation 8-10}$$

$$\omega_0^2 = \frac{G_4 (G_1 + G_2)}{C^2} \qquad \textbf{Equation 8-11}$$

provided

$$G_1 G_5 = 2 G_3 G_4 \qquad \textbf{Equation 8-12}$$

For the normalized case when $\omega_0 = 1$ rad/s and $B = 1/Q$, we select $C = 1$ F. Then two of the conductances may be assigned arbitrarily. Next, we find solutions for the conductances in Equations 8-9 through 8-12. The set of equations for conductances which gives relatively good values is given below for two conductances whose values are chosen as $G_3 = 1$ mho, and $G_5 = 0.5$ mho.

$$G_1 = \frac{2}{Q} \qquad \textbf{Equation 8-13}$$

$$G_2 = 2(Q - 1/Q) \qquad \textbf{Equation 8-14}$$

$$G_3 = 1 \text{ mho} \qquad \textbf{Equation 8-15}$$

$$G_4 = \frac{1}{2Q} \qquad \textbf{Equation 8-16}$$

$$G_5 = 0.5 \text{ mhos} \qquad \textbf{Equation 8-17}$$

$$G_6 = \frac{1}{K} \qquad \textbf{Equation 8-18}$$

The following example will illustrate the design procedure for a second order infinite gain MFB notch (band-reject) active filter circuit that is shown in Fig. 8-4.

Example 8-2:

A second order infinite gain MFB notch filter must be designed to reject a center frequency of 1000 Hz with a quality factor of $Q = 10$ and a gain of $K = 5$. Find the components for the circuit in Fig. 8-4.

Solution:

We will use the circuit shown in Fig. 8-4, where $C = 1$ F for convenience in the normalized case.

Knowing the value of Q and the gain K, we can easily find the conductances using Equations 8-13 through 8-18. Remember two conductances have been chosen whose values are $G_3 = 1$ mho and $G_5 = 0.5$ mho.

$$G_1 = \frac{2}{Q} = \frac{2}{10}$$

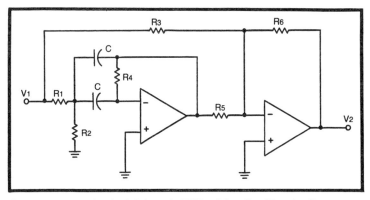

Fig. 8-4. A second-order infinite gain MFB notch active filter circuit.

$$= 0.5 \text{ mhos}$$

$$G_2 = 2\,(Q - 1/Q) = 2(10 - 1/10) = 2(10.1)$$

$$= 20.2 \text{ mhos}$$

$$G_3 = 1 \text{ mho}$$

$$G_4 = \frac{1}{2Q} = \frac{1}{20}$$

$$= 0.05 \text{ mhos}$$

$$G_5 = 0.5 \text{ mhos}$$

$$G_6 = \frac{1}{K} = \frac{1}{5}$$

$$= 0.2 \text{ mhos}$$

Next we denormalize the resistance and capacitance values. We find the frequency normalizing factor u, and the impedance scaling factor (ISF) from Equations 5-1 and 5-2, respectively.

$$u = \frac{\omega_0}{\omega_n} = \frac{2\pi f_0}{\omega_n} = \frac{2\pi(1000)}{1 \text{ rad/s}}$$

$$= 2000\pi$$

$$\text{ISF} = \frac{f_0}{20\pi} = \frac{1000}{20\pi}$$

$$= 15.92$$

We use the two factors found above to denormalize first the capacitance value, then the resistor values.

$$C_p = \frac{C_n}{(u)(\text{ISF})}$$

$$C = \frac{1 \text{ F}}{(2000\pi)(15.92)}$$

$$= 10\mu\text{F}$$

$$R_1 = \frac{ISF}{G_1} = \frac{15.92}{0.5}$$

$$= 31.84 \text{ ohms}$$

$$R_2 = \frac{ISF}{G_2} = \frac{15.92}{20.2}$$

$$= 0.788 \text{ ohms}$$

$$R_3 = \frac{ISF}{G_3} = \frac{15.92}{1}$$

$$= 15.92 \text{ ohms}$$

$$R_4 = \frac{ISF}{G_4} = \frac{15.92}{0.05}$$

$$= 318.4 \text{ ohms}$$

$$R_5 = \frac{ISF}{G_5} = \frac{15.92}{0.5}$$

$$= 31.84 \text{ ohms}$$

$$R_6 = \frac{ISF}{G_6} = \frac{15.92}{0.2}$$

$$= 79.6 \text{ ohms}$$

Looking at the denormalized values of resistors R_2, R_3, R_5, and R_6, the designer has decided that these values are not practical. Therefore, the designer is going to multiply the resistor values by 1000 and at the same time divide the capacitor value by 1000. The resulting passive component values follow:

$$C = \frac{10 \ \mu F}{1000}$$

$$= 0.01 \ \mu F$$
$$R_1 = 31,840 \text{ ohms}$$
$$R_2 = 788 \text{ ohms}$$

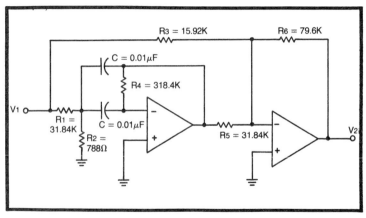

Fig. 8-5. A second-order notch MFB active filter for Example 8-2 with $f_0 = 1000$ Hz, Q = 10, and gain K = 5.

$$R_3 = 15,920 \text{ ohms}$$
$$R_4 = 318,400 \text{ ohms}$$
$$R_5 = 31,840 \text{ ohms}$$
$$R_6 = 79,600 \text{ ohms}$$

The final active filter design for this example is shown in Fig. 8-5.

ALL-PASS OR PHASE SHIFT ACTIVE FILTER

An all-pass active filter is useful where we want a constant amplitude over all frequency of operations, but a controlled varying phase response is required. Important applications are in equalizers and compensation networks.

A second order multiple feedback all-pass filter circuit is shown in Fig. 8-6. The transfer function that describes the circuit in Fig. 8-6 has the general form shown below.

$$\frac{V_2}{V_1} = \frac{K(s^2 - as + b)}{s^2 + as + b} \qquad \textbf{Equation 8-19}$$

And the phase response is given by the following equation.

$$\phi(\omega) = -2 \tan^{-1}\left(\frac{a\omega}{b - \omega^2}\right) \qquad \textbf{Equation 8-20}$$

For the normalized case when $\omega = 1$ the phase shift becomes

$$\phi(1) = -2 \tan^{-1}\left(\frac{a}{b - 1}\right) \qquad \textbf{Equation 8-21}$$

The transfer function in Equation 8-19 can be adapted to the circuit shown in Fig. 8-6 by relating the constants of the transfer function to the circuit parameters by the following equations.

$$R_1 = \frac{a}{2bC}$$ **Equation 8-22**

$$R_2 = \frac{2}{aC}$$ **Equation 8-23**

$$R_3 = \frac{2(a^2 + b)}{abC}$$ **Equation 8-24**

$$R_4 = \frac{2(a^2 + b)}{a^2C}$$ **Equation 8-25**

$$K = \frac{b}{a^2 + b}$$ **Equation 8-26**

In all of the above equations b is greater than zero; that is, b is a positive number. This means that the gain K defined by Equation 8-26 must be less than one.

The following example will illustrate the design procedure for a second order multiple feedback all-pass filter for the circuit shown in Fig. 8-6.

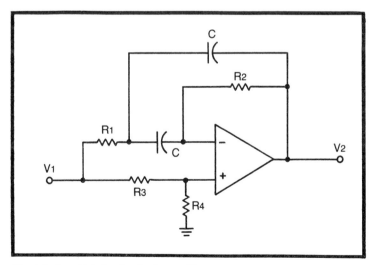

Fig. 8-6. A multiple feedback all-pass filter.

Example 8-3:

A second order multiple feedback all-pass filter must be designed with a gain of 0.1 and a phase shift of $-90°$ at 1000 Hz. Find the components for the circuit in Fig. 8-6.

Solution:

For the circuit in Fig. 8-6, we select $C = 1$ F in the normalized case.

We must find the constants a and b through Equations 8-21 and 8-26. From Equation 8-21 we have:

$$\phi(1) = -90° = -2 \tan^{-1} \frac{a}{b-1}$$

$$45° = \tan^{-1} \frac{a}{b-1}$$

For the previous equation, we know that $\tan(45°) = 1$; hence, we can find the relationship between a and b as follows.

$$1 = \frac{a}{b-1}$$

$$b - 1 = a \qquad\qquad \textbf{Equation 8-27}$$

$$b = a + 1$$

From Equation 8-26 we have the following since the gain $K = 0.1$.

$$K = 0.1 = \frac{b}{a^2 + b}$$

$$\frac{b}{0.1} = a^2 + b$$

$$10b = a^2 + b$$

$$a^2 = 9b$$

Substituting Equations 8-27 into 8-28 we have the following.

$$a^2 = 9(a + 1) = 9a + 9$$
$$0 = a^2 - 9a - 9$$

We can solve for the value of a by using the quadratic equation.

$$a_1, a_2 = \frac{-(-9) \pm \sqrt{(-9)^2 - 4(1)(-9)}}{2(1)}$$

$$a_1, a_2 = \frac{9 \pm \sqrt{81 + 36}}{2} = \frac{9 \pm \sqrt{117}}{2}$$

$$a_1, a_2 = \frac{9 \pm 10.82}{2}$$

$$a_1 = \frac{19.82}{2} = 9.91$$

$$a_2 = \frac{-1.82}{2} = 0.91$$

Using the positive value of a which is 9.91, we can then find the value of b as follows.

$$b = \frac{a^2}{9} = \frac{(9.91)^2}{9}$$

$$b = 10.91$$

Knowing the values of a = 9.91, b = 10.91, and C = 1F, we can easily find the resistance values for the circuit in Fig. 8-6 by using Equations 8-22 through 8-26.

$$R_1 = \frac{a}{2bC} = \frac{9.91}{2(10.91)(1)}$$

$$= 0.454 \text{ ohms}$$

$$R_2 = \frac{2}{aC} = \frac{2}{(9.91)(1)}$$

$$= 0.202 \text{ ohms}$$

$$R_3 = \frac{2(a^2 + b)}{abC} = \frac{2\left[(9.91)^2 + 10.91\right]}{(9.91)(10.91)(1)}$$

$$= 2.02 \text{ ohms}$$

$$R_4 = \frac{2(a^2 + b)}{a^2C} = \frac{2[(9.91)^2 + 10.91]}{(9.91)^2 (1)}$$

$$= 2.22 \text{ ohms}$$

Since we wish to attain the required phase shift at a frequency of 1000 Hz, we will denormalize the resistance and capacitance values at this frequency. We find the frequency normalizing factor u, and the impedance scaling factor (ISF) from Equations 5-1 and 5-2, respectively. These two factors were found in Example 8-2, step 3 and are restated below.

$$u = 2000\pi$$
$$\text{ISF} = 15.92$$

We use the two factors to denormalize first the capacitance value then the resistor values.

$$C_p = \frac{C_n}{(u)(\text{ISF})}$$

$$C = \frac{1 \text{ F}}{(2000 \pi)(15.92)}$$

$$= 10 \text{ } \mu\text{F}$$
$$R_1 = (\text{ISF})(0.454) = (15.92)(0.454)$$
$$= 7.23 \text{ ohms}$$

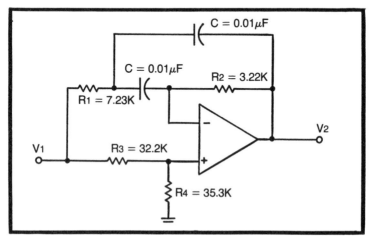

Fig. 8-7. A multiple feedback all-pass filter for Example 8-3 with gain K = 0.1, phase shift is −90° at 1000 Hz.

$$R_2 = (\text{ISF})(0.202) = (15.92)(0.202)$$
$$= 3.22 \text{ ohms}$$
$$R_3 = (\text{ISF})\ (2.02) = (15.92)(2.02)$$
$$= 32.22 \text{ ohms}$$
$$R_4 = (\text{ISF})(2.22) = (15.92)(2.22)$$
$$= 35.34 \text{ ohms}$$

Looking at the denormalized values of resistors R_1 and R_2, the designer has decided that these values are not practical. Consequently, the designer is going to multiply the resistor values by 1000 and at the same time he must divide the capacitor value by 1000. The resulting passive component values are listed below.

$$C = \frac{10 \ \mu F}{1000}$$

$$= 0.01 \ \mu F$$
$$R_1 = 7,230 \text{ ohms}$$
$$R_2 = 3,220 \text{ ohms}$$
$$R_3 = 32,220 \text{ ohms}$$
$$R_4 = 35,340 \text{ ohms}$$

The final active filter design for this example is shown in Fig. 8-7.

Chapter 9
Applications of Active Filters

Most applications of active filter design occur in the areas of audio systems, music, and communication systems. In this chapter, we will discuss in general the different application areas of active filters, and when appropriate go into detail with specific systems. This approach will give us a better understanding of when active filters are employed in electronic systems, and how they are designed into a system, and how they work in a system.

SCRATCH, RUMBLE, AND SPEECH FILTERS

Infinite gain multiple feedback active filters employ high-gain operational amplifiers (e.g. LM387 or LM381) as the active element to make simple low-cost audio filters. Two of the most popular filters found in audio equipment are the *scratch* (low-pass) filter, employed to roll off excess high frequency noise (unwanted signals) appearing as hiss, ticks, and pops from worn records; and the *rumble* (high-pass) filter, employed to roll off low frequency noise associated with worn turntable and tape transport mechanisms. If we combine the low- and high-pass filter sections, we create a broadband band-pass filter, such as that required to limit the audio bandwidth to include only speech frequencies in the range of 300 Hz to 15,000 Hz.

A speech filter consisting of a high-pass filter in cascade with a low-pass filter and its frequency response are shown in Fig. 9-1.

206

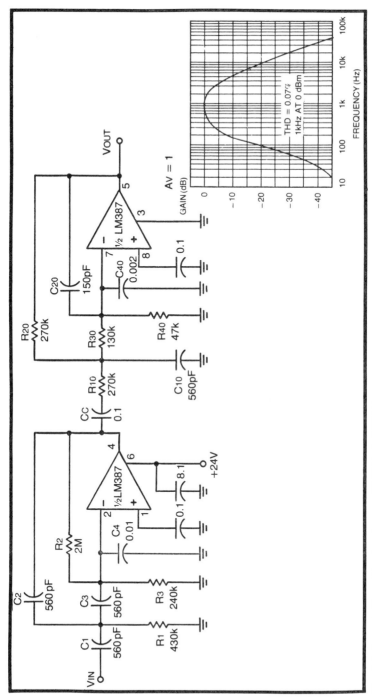

Fig. 9-1. Speech filter with a band-pass of 300 Hz to 3000 Hz.

207

The corner frequencies are 300 Hz and 3000 Hz with roll off of -40 dB/decade beyond the corners. Measured open loop harmonic distortion (THD) was 0.07 percent with a 0 dBm signal of 1000 Hz. Total output noise with input shorted was 150 μV and is due mostly to thermal noise of the resistors yielding S/N of 74 dBm.

OCTAVE EQUALIZER

An octave equalizer offers several bands of tone control, separated an octave apart in frequency with independent adjustment of each. It is designed to compensate for any unwanted amplitude frequency or phase frequency characteristics of an audio system.

Design equations result from a detailed analysis of the circuit shown in Fig. 9-2. Resistor R_3 has been added to supply negative input DC bias current, and to guarantee unity gain at low frequencies. This circuit is particularly suited for equalizer applications since it offers a unique combination of results depending upon the slider position of R_2. With R_2 in the flat position (i.e., centered), the circuit becomes an all-pass active filter with unity gain. Moving resistor R_2 to full boost results in a band-pass characteristic, while positioning R_2 in full cut creates a band-reject (notch) active filter.

The transfer function for the circuit in Fig. 9-2 can be written as follows.

$$\frac{V_0}{V_i} = - \frac{\left[s^2 + \left[\dfrac{2R_1R_2C_1 + R_3(R_1 + R_2)C_2}{R_1R_2R_3C_1C_2} \right] s + \dfrac{2R_1 + R_2}{R_1R_2R_3C_1C_2} \right]}{\left[s^2 + \left[\dfrac{(R_1 + R_2)C_2 + 2R_2C_1 + R_3C_2}{R_2R_3C_1C_2} \right] s + \dfrac{2R_1 + R_2}{R_1R_2R_3C_1C_2} \right]}$$

Equation 9-1

Equation 9-1 has the form shown below.

$$\frac{V_0}{V_i} = - \left[\frac{s^2 + K2\rho\omega_0 s + \omega_0^2}{s^2 + 2\rho\omega_0 s + \omega_0^2} \right] \qquad \text{Equation 9-2}$$

Equating coefficients of Equations 9-1 and 9-2 yield the following equations.

208

$$\omega_0 = \sqrt{\frac{2R_1 + R_2}{R_1 R_2 R_3 C_1 C_2}} \qquad \text{Equation 9-3}$$

$$A_0 = \frac{-(2R_1 R_2 C_1 + R_3(R_1 + R_2)C_2)}{2R_1 R_2 C_1 + R_1(R_2 + R_3)C_2} \qquad \text{Equation 9-4}$$

$$Q = \left(\frac{R_2 R_3 C_1 C_2}{(R_1 + R_2)C_2 + 2R_2 C_1 + R_3 C_2}\right) \sqrt{\frac{2R_1 + R_2}{R_1 R_2 R_3 C_1 C_2}}$$

Equation 9-5

where:

$$A_0 = \text{gain at } f_0 = K, \ \omega_0 = 2\pi f_0 \qquad \text{Equation 9-6}$$

$$Q = \frac{1}{2\rho} \qquad \text{Equation 9-7}$$

In order to reduce the above equations to useful design equations, it is necessary to examine what is required of the final equalizer in terms of performance. For normal home use, ±12 dB of boost and cut is adequate, which means only a moderate amount of pass-band gain is necessary. Since the filters will be centered one

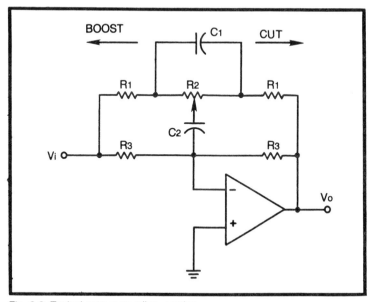

Fig. 9-2. Typical octave equalizer section.

octave apart in frequency, a large Q is not necessary ($Q = 2$ is reasonable). What is desirable is for the pass-band ripple to be less than 3 dB, when all filters are at maximum.

Examination of Equation 9-5 in terms of optimizing the ratio of C_1 and C_2 in order to maximize Q shows a good choice is to make C_1 = $10C_2$. Another design rule that is reasonable is to make $R_3 = 10R_2$, since R_3 is unnecessary for the filter section. Applying these rules to Equation 9-3, 9-4 and 9-5 yields the following results.

$$\omega_0 = 2\pi f_0 = \frac{1}{10R_2C_2}\sqrt{2 + \frac{R_2}{R_1}} \qquad \textbf{Equation 9-8}$$

$$A_0 = 1 + \frac{R_2}{3R_1} \qquad \textbf{Equation 9-9}$$

$$Q = \sqrt{\frac{2R_1 + R_2}{9.61^!R_1}} \qquad \textbf{Equation 9-10}$$

Rewriting Equations 9-9 and 9-10 yields the following equations.

$$R_2 = 3(A_0 - 1)R_1 \qquad \textbf{Equation 9-11}$$

$$R_2 = (9.61Q^2 - 2)R_1 \qquad \textbf{Equation 9-12}$$

Combining Equations 9-11 and 9-12 gives the following equation.

$$A_0 = \frac{9.61Q^2 - 2}{3} + 1 \qquad \textbf{Equation 9-13}$$

From Equation 9-13 it is seen that gain and Q are related and that large gains mean large Qs and vice versa. Equations 9-12 and 9-13 show that R_1 and R_2 are not independent, which means one resistor may be arbitrarily selected and the other calculated if A_0 and/or Q is given. The following example will illustrate the design procedure for a typical octave equalizer section shown in Fig. 9-2.

Example 9-1:

Design a typical octave equalizer section with a gain $A_0 = 4$, and a frequency range of 32 Hz to 16,000 Hz. Tabulate the values of capacitance C_1 and C_2 for each octave of frequency within the desired frequency range.

Solution:

The typical octave equalizer section that we will employ is shown in Fig. 9-2. For each octave (twice the frequency) of frequency one of the circuits in Fig. 9-2 will be employed with different values of capacitors C_1 and C_2. We first select R_2 and as a rule of thumb we find $R_3 = 10R_2$. Let us pick $R_2 = 100K$, and calculate $R_3 = 10K) = 1M$.

Knowing $A_0 = 4$, we find R_1 from Equation 9-9.

$$R_1 = \frac{R_2}{3(A_0 - 1)} = \frac{100\ K}{3(4 - 1)}$$

$$= 11.1\ K$$

Next we calculate the value of Q to determine if Q is less than 2, which is a satisfactory value. We use Equation 9-10 to find Q.

$$Q = \sqrt{\frac{2R_1 + R_2}{9.61R_1}} = \sqrt{\frac{2(10,000) + 100,000}{9.61(10,000)}}$$

$$= 1.12 \text{ which is a workable value.}$$

Next we calculate C_1 and C_2. As a rule of thumb we make $C_1 = 10C_2$, and we calculate C_2 from Equation 9-8 as follows.

$$C_2 = \frac{1}{2pf_0(10R_2)} \quad 2 + \frac{R_2}{R_1}$$

Substituting $R_1 = 100,000$ ohms and $R_2 = 10,000$ ohms into the above equation yields the following equation.

$$C_2 = \frac{1}{2\pi f_0(10)(10,000)} \quad 2 + \frac{100,000}{10,000}$$

$$= \frac{5.513\ (10^{-7})}{f_0}$$

For the first frequency $f_0 = 32$ Hz, we will show a sample calculation for the solution of C_2 and C_1 as follows.

$$C_2 = \frac{5.513\ (10^{-7})}{32} = 0.01723\ \mu F$$

f_0 (Hz)	C_1 (μF)	C_2 (μF)
32	0.18	0.018
64	0.1	0.010
125	0.047	0.0047
350	0.022	0.0022
500	0.012	0.0012
1000	0.0056	0.00056
2000	0.0027	0.00027
4000	0.0015	0.00015
8000	0.00068	0.000068
16000	0.00036	0.000036

Table 9-1. Values of C_1 and C_2 for the typical octave equalizer sections for Example 9-1.

The nearest practical value of capacitance we can obtain to the above value is 0.018 μF. We will use the practical value of C_2 to find C_1.

$$C_1 = 10C_2 = 10(0.018 \ \mu F)$$
$$= 0.18 \ \mu F$$

The remaining values for C_1 and C_2 vs f_0 for each octave of frequency from 32 Hz to 16,000 Hz is tabulated in Table 9-1. Remember the values of capacitance given in Table 9-1 are standard values of capacitance.

The complete octave equalizer design is shown in Fig. 9-4. While it appears complicated, the circuit in Fig. 9-4 consists of only three QUAD IC amplifiers. The circuit is really repetitious since we have 10 duplicate circuits substituting appropriate capacitance values from Table 9-1 to achieve the desired frequency response from 32 Hz to 16,000 Hz.

The IC amplifiers used for the design shown in Fig. 9-3 are National Semiconductor's LM349s. The input buffer amplifier guarantees a low source impedance to drive the equalizer and presents a large input impedance to drive the equalizer and presents a large input impedance for the preamplifier. Resistor R_8 is necessary to stabilize the LM349 while retaining its fast slew rate ($2V/\mu s$). The output amplifier is a unity gain, inverting summer used to add each equalized octave of frequencies back together again. One aspect of the summing circuit that may appear unusual is that the original signal is subtracted from the sum via R_{20}. This is true because each equalizer section inverts the signal relative to the output of the buffer, and R_{20} delivers the original signal without inverting. The reason the subtraction is necessary is in order to maintain a unity gain system. Without the subtraction, the output would equal 10 times the input. That is, an input of 1V, with all pots

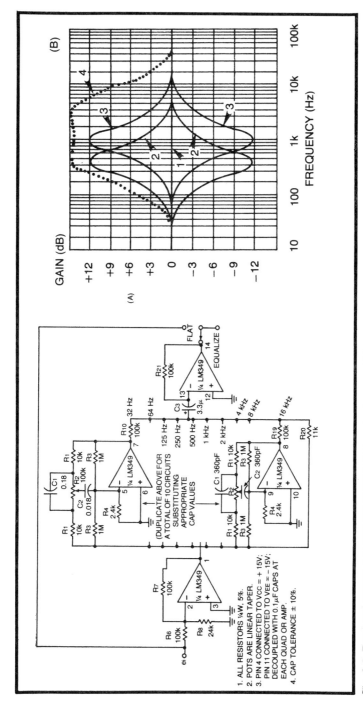

Fig. 9-3. Ten-band octave equalizer (A) and the frequency response (B).

213

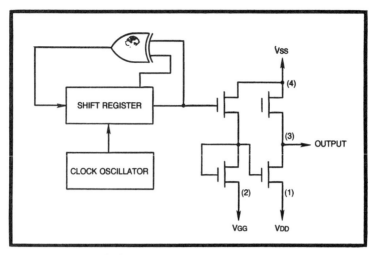

Fig. 9-4. MM5837 MOS/MSI pseudo-random white noise source.

flat, would produce 1V at each equalizer output minus the sum of which is 10V. By scaling R_{20} such that the input signal is multiplied by nine before the subtraction, the output now becomes $10V - 9V = 1V$ output, which means unity gain. The addition of R_4 to each section is for stability. Capacitor C_3 minimizes possibly larger DC offset voltages from appearing at the output. If the driving source has a DC level, then an input capacitor is necessary to block the source DC level. If the lead has a DC level, then an output capacitor is required to couple the load and the equalizer.

PINK NOISE GENERATOR

Once an equalizer is incorporated into a music system, the question arises as to how best to employ the equalizer. The most direct answer is as a super tone control unit, where control is now extended from the familiar 2 or 3 controls to 10 controls (or even 30 if ⅓ octave equalizers are used). While this approach is most useful and the results are dramatic in their ability to liven up a room, there still remains, with many, the desire to have some controlled manner in which to equalize the listening area without resorting to the use of expensive spectrum or real time analyzers.

The first step in generating a self-contained, room-equalizing instrument is to design a pink noise generator to be used as a controlled source of noise across the audio frequency spectrum. With the advent of medium scale integration (MSI) and MOS digital

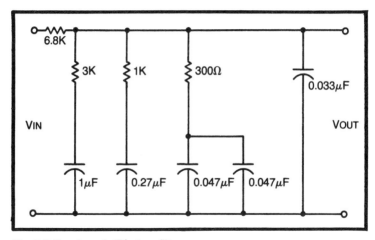

Fig. 9-5. Passive -3 dB/octave filter.

technology, it is quite easy to create a pink noise generator using only one IC and a few passive components.

The National Semiconductor's MM5837 digital noise source is an MOS/MSI pseudo-random sequence generator, designed to produce a broadband white noise signal for audio applications. Unlike traditional semiconductor junction noise sources, the MM5837 provides very uniform noise quality and output amplitude. Originally designed for electronic organ and synthesizer applications it can be directly applied to room equalization. Figure 9-4 shows a block diagram of the internal circuitry of the MM5837.

The output of the MM5837 is broadband white noise. In order to generate pink noise it is necessary to understand the difference between the two noises. White noise is characterized by a +3 dB rise in amplitude per octave of frequency change. Pink noise has flat amplitude response per octave of frequency change. Pink noise allows correlation between successive octave equalizer stages by assuring the same voltage amplitude is used each time as a reference standard. What is required to produce pink noise from a white noise source is simply a -3 dB/octave filter. If capacitive reactance varies at a rate of -6 dB/octave, then how can a slope of less than -6 dB/octave be achieved? The answer is by cascading several stages of lag compensation such that the zeros of one stage partially cancel the poles of the next stages, and so on. Such a network is shown in Fig. 9-5, and exhibits a -3 dB/octave characteristic from 10 Hz to 40,000 Hz.

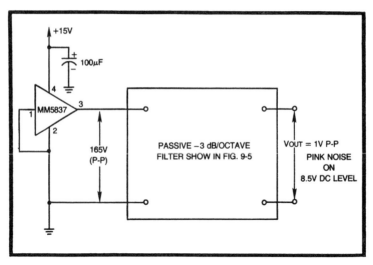

Fig. 9-6. Pink noise generator.

The complete pink noise generator is illustrated in Fig. 9-6. It gives a flat spectral distribution over the audio band of 20 Hz to 20,000 Hz. The output at pin 3 is a 11.5V peak-to-peak random pulse train which is attenuated by the filter, which has an output equal to about 1V peak-to-peak AC pink noise riding on a 8.5V DC level.

ROOM EQUALIZING INSTRUMENT

For a room equalizing instrument, a different type of equalizer section is required than the 10-band octave equalizer section previously designed. The difference lies in the necessary condition that each section must pass only its bandwidth of frequencies. In other words, the all-pass characteristic of the 10-band equalizer section is unacceptable for the room equalizing instrument. The reason for this is that to use the room equalizing instrument, all but one band will be switched out. Under this condition, the pink noise will be passed through the remaining filter, and it must pass only its octave of noise. The filtered noise is passed on to the power amplifier and reproduced into the room by the speaker. A microphone with flat audio band frequency response is used to pick up the noise at some central listening point. The microphone input is amplified and used to drive a VU (volume unit) meter where some arbitrary level is established via the potentiometer of the filter section. This filter

216

section is then switched out and the next one is switched in. Its potentiometer is adjusted such that the VU meter reads the same as before. Each filter section in turn is switched in, adjusted, and switched out, until all 10 octaves have been set. The whole process takes about three minutes. When finished the room response will be equalized flat for each octave of frequencies. From here it becomes personal preference whether the high end is rolled off or the low end is boosted. This allows for greater experimentation since it is very easy to go back to a known (flat) position. It is also easy to correct for new alterations within the listening room (drape changes, new rugs, more furniture, different speaker placement, etc.). Since all adjustments are made relative to each other, the requirement for expensive, calibrated microphones is obviated. Almost any microphone will work if it has flat output over frequency.

For stereo applications, a two-channel instrument is required as diagrammed in Fig. 9-7. The diagrams in Fig. 9-7 shows the typical placement of the equalizer unit within existing systems. For the equalizer section of the room equalizing instrument, any

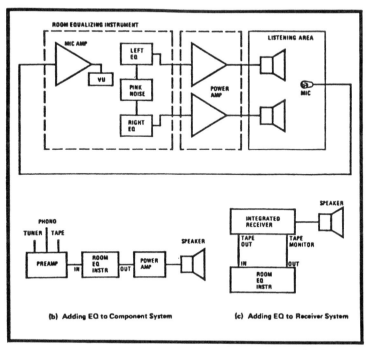

Fig. 9-7. Typical block diagrams of an equalizing instrument application.

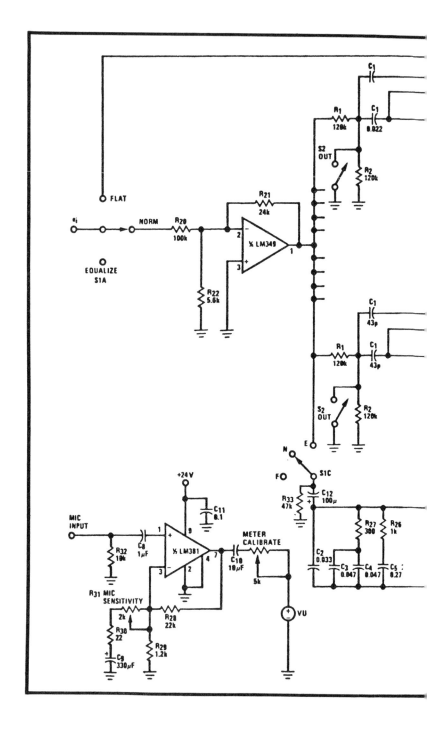

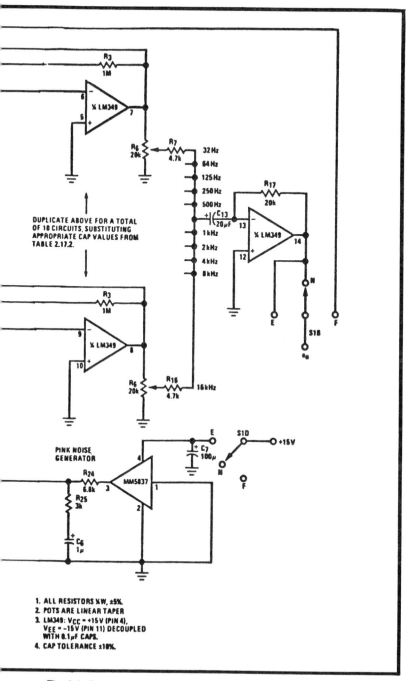

Fig. 9-8. Room equalizing instrument.

219

bandpass filter may be used, but the multiple feedback, infinite gain configuration designed in a previous chapter is chosen for its low sensitivity factor. The complete room equalizing instrument appears in schematic form in Fig. 9-8.

The input buffer and output summer are similar to those in Fig. 9-3 with some important differences. The input buffer acts as an active attenuator with a gain of 0.25, and the output summer has variable gain as a function of slider position. The purpose of these features is to preserve unity gain through a system that is really "cut-only," since the gain of each filter section is fixed, and the output is dropped across the potentiometers. The result is to create a boost and cut effect about the midpoint of the pot which equals unity gain. To see this, consider just one filter section, and let the input to the system equal 1V. The output of the buffer will be 0.25V, and the filter output at the top of potentiometer R_6 will be restored to 1V since the gain is 4. In other words, the gain of the summer is given by R_{17}/R_7 which is approximately equal to four, when the slider of R_6 is at maximum, so the output will be equal to 4V, or + 12 dB relative to the input. With the slider at midposition the 4.7 K summer input resistor R_7 effectively parallels ½ of R_6 for a net resistance from slider to ground of 4700 ohms in parallel with 10,000 ohms, which equals approximately 3200 ohms. The voltage at the top of the pot is attenuated by the voltage divider action of the 10K pot to slider, and the 3.2K slider to ground. This voltage is approximately equal to 0.25V and is multiplied by four through the summer for a final output voltage of 1V, or 0 dB relative to the input. With the slider at minimum, there is no output from this section, but the action of the "skirts" of the adjacent filters tends to create − 12 dB cutoff relative to the input. So the net result is a ±12 dB boost and cut effect from a cut only system.

Typical frequency response of this system is also shown in Fig. 9-8. While the system appears complex, a complete two-channel instrument is made with eight National Semiconductor ICs (six-LM349s, one-LM381, and one-MM5837).

BIAMPLIFICATION

The most common method of amplifying the output of a preamplifier into the large signal required to drive a speaker system is with one large wideband amplifier having a flat frequency response over the entire audio band. An alternate method is to employ two

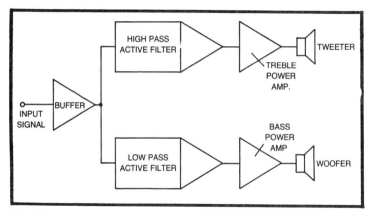

Fig. 9-9. Active crossover, biamp system.

amplifiers, or biamplification, where each amplifier is committed to amplifying only one part of the frequency spectrum. *Biamping* requires splitting up the audio band into two sections and routing these signals to each amplifier. This process is accomplished by using an active crossover network consisting of two active filters as shown in the block diagram of Fig. 9-9.

The most common application of biamping is found in conjunction with speaker systems. Biamping with active crossover networks allows for a more flexible and easier design. It also sounds better, since they have lower distortion than a passive crossover, amp system. In passive crossover systems the high- and low-pass filters require large inductors and capacitors which require more physical space and provide more distortion than the active crossover system.

The lower distortion in the active crossover system is due chiefly to two effects. The first results from the consequence of bass transient clipping. Low frequency signals tend to have much higher transient amplitudes than do high frequencies, so amplifier overloading normally occurs for bass signals. By separating the spectrum, one immediately cleans up half of it and greatly improves the other half, in that the low frequency speaker will not allow high frequency components generated by transient clipping of the bass amplifier to pass, resulting in cleaner sound. Second is a high frequency masking effect, where the low level high frequency distortion components of a clipped low frequency signal are covered up; that is, they are masked by high level undistorted high frequencies. The final advantage of biamping is allowing the use of smaller power amplifiers to achieve the same sound pressure levels.

ACTIVE CROSSOVER NETWORKS

An active crossover network is a system of active filters used to divide the audio frequency band into separate sections for individual signal processing by biamped systems as discussed in the previous section. Active crossovers are audibly desirable because they give better speaker damping and improved transient response, and minimize midrange modulation distortion.

The choice of filter type is based upon the need for good transient and frequency response. The Butterworth characteristics discussed in previous chapters offer the best characteristics for active crossover design.

Intuitively, it is reasonable that if the audio spectrum is split into two sections, their sum should exactly equal the original signal—that is, without change in phase or magnitude. In other words, the vector sum must equal unity. This is known as a constant voltage design. Also it is reasonable to want the same power delivered to each of the drivers (speakers). This is known as constant power design. What is required, therefore, is a filter that exhibits constant voltage and constant power design. Having decided upon a Butterworth filter, what remains to be determined is an optimum order of the filter that satisfies constant voltage and constant power. Experience has shown that the best compromise is to employ a third order (n = 3) Butterworth filter. This filter will exhibit maximally flat magnitude response; that is, no peaking which minimizes the work required by the speakers, and this filter has sharp cutoff characteristics of -18 dB/octave, which minimizes speakers being required to reproduce beyond the crossover point. Also, this filter has flat voltage and power frequency response with a gradual change in phase across the frequency band.

Many active filter designs are possible to yield a third order Butterworth active filter response. However, one of the best circuit designs is the infinite gain multiple feedback circuit that was illustrated in a previous chapter. If the reader desires to design the filter mentioned above, the reader can refer to the chapter on filter design as a design guide.

ELECTRONIC MUSIC

There are two different ways of changing electronic tone sources. If we use a fixed filter system, we are employing formant filtering. The harmonics of each note of differing frequency vary in structure. This is also the case with many conventional musical instruments where their size and shape provide a fixed acoustical filtering response. On the other hand, if we use a voltage controlled filter (VCF), the harmonics of each note can be nearly the same and usually independent of frequency. This creates a distinct electronic or synthesizer sound.

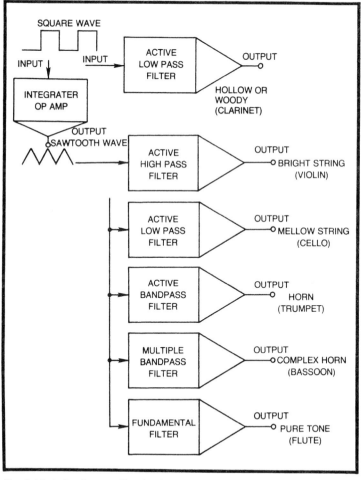

Fig. 9-10. Active formant filter basics.

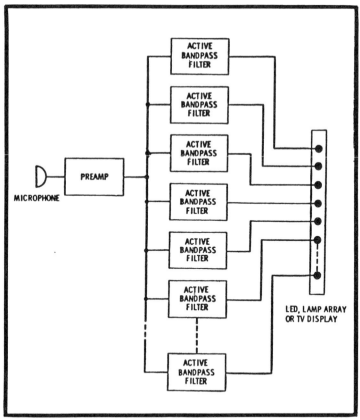

Fig. 9-11. Speech therapy block diagram employing active band-pass filters.

The block diagram of Fig. 9-10 illustrates some of the principles of format filtering that make optimum use of active filters. If we begin with a square wave and filter it lightly with a low-pass filter, we will obtain a group of tone structures that sound hollow or woody, similar to the sound of such instruments as the clarinet. Now we can integrate the square wave and form a sawtooth wave. Minor filter action on a sawtooth wave leads to string voices, made brighter by high-pass filtering or more mellow through low-pass emphasis. The same sawtooth routed through a band-pass filter produces horn sounds. Multiple spectrum instruments (for example, the bassoon, English horn, and oboe) require multiple band-pass filters or a notch filter. Heavy filtering of a sawtooth will recover only the fundamental with slight second harmonic components, characteristics of the flute and some organ voices.

SPEECH THERAPY

Visual feedback of sound is useful as a training aid to help cure speech impediments, such as stuttering and some forms of mental retardation. This is illustrated in the speech therapy system of Fig. 9-11. A microphone pickup is followed by a preamp whose output signal is divided into many narrow audio channels employing band-pass active filter circuits. The energy in each channel is detected and used to control either a single colored lamp or LED, or else to combine the outputs on some sort of bar graph or color TV display. Similar techniques are involved in speech analysis and computer based artificial speech generation circuitry.

MODEMS

A modem is a modulator demodulator that lets you transmit digital data over a phone line or to a cassette recorder. A typical modem setup is shown in Fig. 9-12, and the key frequencies of two popular modem systems are shown in Fig. 9-13.

Active filters greatly simplify modem designs. For modem transmitters, the active filter makes sure that only sine waves of the

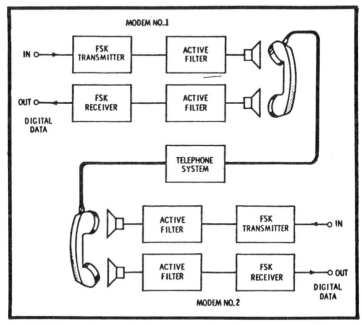

Fig. 9-12. Modem for a digital data transmission over telephone lines.

300 Bits/Second	(Bell 103 Standard)

Two-Way (full duplex), Voice-Grade Line

Originate Mode: "Space" = "0" = 1070 Hz
"Mark" = "1" = 1270 Hz

Answer Mode: "Space" = "0" = 2025 Hz
"Mark" = "1" = 2225 Hz
(Also disables echo suppressors
on phone network)

1200 Bits/Second	(Bell 202 Standard)

One-Way, Voice-Grade Line

"Space" = "0" = 1200 Hz

"Mark" = "1" = 2200 Hz

Fig. 9-13. Standard frequencies for two popular modem systems.

correct frequency are transmitted, eliminating any harmonic problems that could add noise and errors to data systems. At the receiving end, active filters are used to eliminate potential interference from out of band signals. In some circuits, they form the actual tone detection circuitry. A more popular combination combines an active prefilter with a phase-locked loop detector that does the actual tone reception.

Active filters for modems must be designed so that all frequency components of a digital pulse waveform are delayed by an equal amount. Otherwise, portions of the filtered signal will slop over into the available time slot for the next bit of information. This is called the group delay distortion problem. All active filters used in modem receivers must be carefully designed, or else they have to be special versions that carefully control the group delay to acceptable error rate levels.

As we employ active filters in more and more applications, they will become simple, compact, and low-cost. We can expect to see active filters used in automotive electronics, pollution control systems, environmental sciences, and medical electronic applications. Your imagination will be the limiting force in how far active filters can be used in the wonderful world of electronics.

Chapter 10
Active Filter Potpourri

The design of active filter circuits in specific applications such as electronic music circuits or communications becomes a customized procedure based upon the material presented in the first eight chapters of this book. In other words, a designer of active filter circuits knows what response he desires, states the response, and adjusts his circuit to fit the desired response. In this chapter we will illustrate some of the popular active filter designs used in various industries today. My sincerest appreciation is given to Bernie Hutchins of ELECTRONOTES, a newsletter of The Musical Engineering Group, who furnished many of the circuits and applications in this chapter. Any readers interested in the latest developments in electronic music circuitry should contact ELECTRONOTES at 1 Pheasant Lane, Ithaca, NY 14850.

DELIYANNIS BAND-PASS ACTIVE FILTER CIRCUIT

In the design of band-pass filters for filter banks, we are looking for a simple, inexpensive circuit. It should be capable of high-Q, should be stable, and should be relatively easy to design and adjust. Thus, we will concentrate on the design of a single op amp resonator circuit illustrated in Fig. 10-1.

The transfer function as a special case of the final circuit we will be considering is given in Equation 10-1.

$$T(s) = \cfrac{\cfrac{-s}{RC}}{s^2 + \cfrac{2}{BRC}\, s + \cfrac{1}{BR^2C^2}}$$ **Equation 10-1**

As discussed in previous chapters, we defined the terms in the denominator with ω_0, f_0, and Q as follows.

$$\omega_0^2 = \frac{1}{BR^2C^2}$$ **Equation 10-2**

$$f_0 = \frac{1}{2\pi RC\sqrt{B}}$$ **Equation 10-3**

$$Q = \frac{\sqrt{B}}{2}$$ **Equation 10-4**

$$\frac{\omega_0}{Q} = \frac{2}{BRC}$$ **Equation 10-5**

Remember, the quantity Q is called the quality factor of the active filter, and the center frequency of the band-pass active filter is f_0.

The active filter circuit shown in Fig. 10-1, whose transfer function is given in Equation 10-1, appears to be a good filter for Q less than 10, but for higher Qs, it becomes obvious that B will have to be very large. This means that either R is very small, which means the previous stage may be loaded down excessively, or BR will be very large, and the DC bias current flowing through it may cause a large offset current. Hence, we will be looking for a design that will give us a high Q without using large value of B. Before we look for this answer, we want to consider a second problem with the circuit of Fig. 10-1.

We will often be driving our filters with reasonably sized synthesizer voltage levels. For high Q circuits, this means that we will be inserting so much signal into the filter that it will be driven against the power supply rails in most cases. The solution is to provide a smaller signal to the input of the filter. A standard resistor voltage divider will be sufficient to reduce the synthesizer level, but we must be careful to maintain the proper input impedance, or all the filter characteristics will be changed. The circuit illustrated in Fig.

228

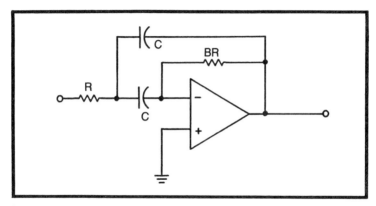

Fig. 10-1. General RC band-pass active filter circuit (courtesy of Electronotes Musical Engineering Group).

10-2 shows the resistor R of Fig. 10-1 replaced with the voltage divider of R_1 and R_2 in Fig. 10-2.

In order for the circuit shown in Fig. 10-2 to function properly, the attenuation ratio $R_2/(R_1 + R_2)$ must give enough drop to the input signal so that the high Q does not drive the output against the supply levels, and the parallel combination of R_1 and R_2 must give a resistance equal to R. The calculations are not difficult and will appear in a design example later in this section. It is also easy to obtain the transfer function of the circuit of Fig. 10-2 by using Equation 10-1 and making use of the considerations discussed previously. We add the attenuation factor as a multiplier, and replace R with the parallel combination of R_1 and R_2. This yields the following transfer function for the classic RC active band-pass filter circuit shown in Fig. 10-2.

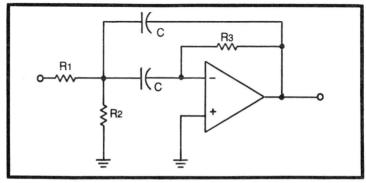

Fig. 10-2. Classic RC band-pass active filter circuit (courtesy of Electronotes Musical Engineering Group).

$$T(s) = \cfrac{\cfrac{-s}{R_1 C}}{s^2 + \cfrac{2s}{R_3 C} + \cfrac{R_1 + R_2}{R_1 R_2 R_3 C_2}}$$ **Equation 10-6**

The circuit of Fig. 10-3 is the same as the one of Fig. 10-1 except positive feedback has been added by means of the voltage divider R_a and R_b on the output. The circuit is used for several electronic music applications and is called the Deliyannis band-pass active filter circuit. The transfer function is carefully derived in ELECTRONOTES publication No. 73, Vol. 9, January, 1977, and is shown below in Equation 10-7.

$$T(S) = \cfrac{\cfrac{-s}{(1 - a)\,RC}}{s^2 + s\,\cfrac{2(1 - a) - aB}{(1 - a)BRC} + \cfrac{1}{BR^2C^2}}$$ **Equation 10-7**

If you compare Equation 10-7 to Equation 10-1, it is easy to see that Equation 10-7 will equal Equation 10-1 when the quantity a equals zero. From Equation 10-7, we can obtain expressions for f_0 and Q by the usual method from the constant term and the s term in the denominator. The equations that follow are Equations 10-8 and 10-9.

$$f_0 = \cfrac{1}{2\pi RC\sqrt{B}}$$ **Equation 10-8**

$$Q = \cfrac{(1 - a)\sqrt{B}}{2(1 - a) - aB}$$ **Equation 10-9**

Equation 10-8 for f_0 is the same equation as Equation 10-3. However, Equation 10-9, which determines the Q, depends on B as before, but also the Q can be controlled by the feedback factor a, which does not appear in the equation for f_0. Thus, once we have determined f_0, the Q can be increased by increasing the value of a independent of f_0. Equations 10-8 and 10-9 are the principal design equations for the Deliyannis band-pass filter shown in Fig. 10-3.

It is reasonably important that Equation 10-8 be well understood. In particular, note that when $2(1 - a) = aB$, the denominator

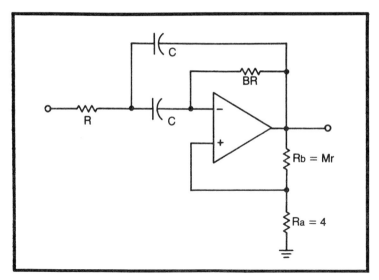

Fig. 10-3. Deliyannis band-pass active filter circuit (courtesy of Electronotes Musical Engineering Group).

goes to zero, and the Q becomes infinite, which means that the filter oscillates. Thus, given a value of B, which sets f_0 and the minimum Q, we can find the value of a which will give the maximum Q. This value of a is defined in Equation 10-10.

$$a_{MAX} = \frac{2}{B + 2}$$ **Equation 10-10**

Equation 10-10 tells us the value of a which will cause oscillation. It also tells us the usable values of a which are those below a_{MAX}. For example, if $B = 1000$, the maximum value for a is only 0.002, while if both resistors in the frequency determining part of the circuit are the same ($B = 1$), then a can reach up to 2/3. Thus, in determining the value of Q, the feedback factor does not give much information, since you must also know where you started; that is, $B =$ what value.

We have not given careful consideration to the Q (sensitivity) of the circuit. If we did this, we might find there is some optimum relationship between a and B which can be employed. Note however that once a minimum Q is set with B, it cannot be decreased by setting a, but only increased.

Before moving on to the development of a design procedure and design examples, we should note that we will usually have in mind the value of f_0 we need and the value of Q we want. Thus, we

231

should solve for the feedback factor in terms of Q. So from Equation 10-9, we have the following equation for a.

$$a = \frac{2Q - \sqrt{B}}{1Q + BQ - \sqrt{B}} \qquad \textbf{Equation 10-11}$$

As a practical matter, we need a resistor ratio rather than the factor a. Thus, we choose resistors r and Mr giving $a = 1/(1 + M)$ and solving for M using Equation 10-11, we have the following equation.

$$M = \frac{BQ}{2Q - \sqrt{B}} \qquad \textbf{Equation 10-12}$$

Finally, we also want to know the pass-band gain (the gain of the filter at its center frequency f_0). To obtain this, we substitute $s = j\omega_0$ into Equation 10-7 and the result is the following equation.

$$G = \frac{B}{2(1 - a) - aB} \qquad \textbf{Equation 10-13}$$

Hence, for a sine wave input of 5V, the output sine wave at frequency f_0 will be $G(5V)$, which can easily exceed the power supply limits. Thus, if we desire unity pass-band gain for the active filter circuit, as is often reasonable, we have to attenuate the input by a factor of $1/G$. This is essentially the same process that gave us Fig. 10-2 from Fig. 10-1. Here we will be looking for an attenuator formed from resistors R_{11} and R_{22} as shown in Fig. 10-4.

The equations that relate the center frequency gain G to the resistors R, R_{11}, and R_{22} follow:

$$\frac{1}{G} = \frac{R_{22}}{R_{11} + R_{22}} \qquad \textbf{Equation 10-14}$$

$$R = \frac{R_{11} \quad R_{22}}{R_{11} + R_{22}} \qquad \textbf{Equation 10-15}$$

The above equations are easily solved for resistors R_{11} and R_{22}, which give the following equations.

$$R_{11} = GR \qquad \textbf{Equation 10-16}$$

$$R_{22} = \frac{GR}{G - 1} \qquad \textbf{Equation 10-17}$$

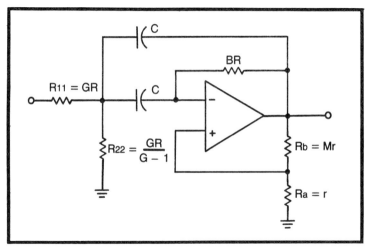

Fig. 10-4. Deliyannis band-pass with attenuator input of R_{11} and R_{22} (courtesy of Electronotes Musical Engineering Group).

The following steps outline the design procedure for the Deliyannis Band-pass Active Filter Circuit shown in Fig. 10-4:

1. Select f_0 and Q.
2. Choose a convenient value for C.
3. Choose B = to a number that is a perfect square for convenience of calculation (e.g., 4, 9, ... 100, 121, etc.).
4. From Equation 10-8, calculate R as shown by the following equation.

$$R = \frac{1}{2\pi f_0 C \sqrt{B}} \qquad \textbf{Equation 10-18}$$

5. From Equation 10-12 calculate M.
6. Select resistors $R_a = r$ and $R_b = Mr$ such that their sum is greater than 20,000 ohms and less than 200,000 ohms.
7. If the pass-band gain G is not going to be a problem, leave out R_{22} and make $R_{11} = R$. However, if you want to assure unity pass-band gain calculate G by the following equation.

$$G = \frac{Q(M + 1)\sqrt{B}}{M} \qquad \textbf{Equation 10-19}$$

Next, calculate R_{11} and R_{22} by using Equations 10-16 and 10-17.

8. Select appropriate standard valued resistors. Try to balance out your errors. If R has to be a little low, make BR a little high. This will in turn make B a little larger than you planned, so make the feedback factor a little lower (assuming you have the choice of making it higher or lower with about equal error). Otherwise, use the calculated value if the error is small.

Example 10-1:

A Deliyannis band-pass filter circuit must be designed with a center frequency $f_0 = 200$ Hz and a $Q = 12$. Find the passive components that will produce the stated requirements.

Solution:

The problem states that the center frequency must be $f_0 = 200$ Hz and the $Q = 12$.

Next, we select a convenient value for capacitance $C = 0.05$ μF.

Let us select $B = 25$ a perfect square, so that $\sqrt{B} = 5$. We calculate R from Equation 10-18.

$$R = \frac{1}{2\pi f_0 C \sqrt{B}} = \frac{1}{2\pi(200)(0.05)(10^{-6})(\sqrt{25})}$$

$$= 3180 \text{ ohms}$$

We also calculate BR = (5)(3180 ohms) = 79,600 ohms.

From Equation 10-12 we calculate M.

$$M = \frac{BQ}{2Q - \sqrt{B}} = \frac{(25)(12)}{2(12) - \sqrt{25}}$$

$$= 15.8$$

Next, we select resistors $R_a = r$ and $R_b = Mr$ such that their sum is greater than 20,000 ohms but less than 200,000 ohms. Let $R_a = r = 2700$ ohms, which means $R_b = Mr = (15.8)(2700 \text{ ohms})$ so $R_b = 42,660$ ohms. Therefore, make $R_b = 47,000$ ohms, a practical value.

If we want amplification at the center frequency f_0, we make R_{11} = R = 3180 ohms, and leave out R_{22}.

However, if we want unity pass-band gain we calculate the value for G by using Equation 10-19.

$$G = \frac{Q(M + 1)\sqrt{B}}{M} = \frac{(12)(15.8 + 1)(5)}{15.8}$$

$$= 63.8$$

Next, we calculate R_{11} and R_{22} by using Equations 10-16 and 10-17.

$$R_{11} = GR = (63.8)(79,600)$$

$$= 203,000 \text{ ohms}$$

$$R_{22} = \frac{GR}{G - 1} = \frac{203,000 \text{ ohms}}{63.8 - 1}$$

$$= 3,230 \text{ ohms}$$

Selecting standard 5 percent resistor values, the completed circuit is illustrated in Fig. 10-5.

The results of an actual measurement on the circuit of Fig. 10-5 are shown in the table at the right of the figure. The agreement is quite good as can be seen, and this is most likely because we were using 1 percent capacitors in the circuit. Probably the results won't

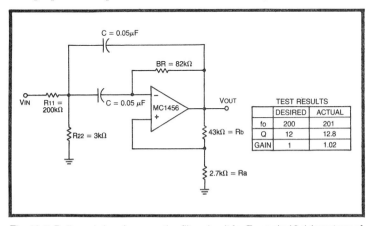

Fig. 10-5. Deliyannis band-pass active filter circuit for Example 10-1 (courtesy of Electronotes Musical Engineering Group).

be quite as good for 5 or 10 percent capacitors. Here, we wanted to test the calculations so we had to use accurate components. Note that since we had to use an 82,000-ohm resistor for the design value of 79,600 ohms, we used the lower choice; that is, 3000 ohms for the resistor R_{22}. This, of course, makes the value of B a little high, and is probably the reason Q was a little high. In general one can probably expect the measured value of f_0 to come out more accurately than the value of Q. Fortunately, it is easy to adjust the Q. In Fig. 10-5, you could use a 2200-ohm resistor with a series trim potentiometer of a few hundred ohms, and increase the series trim potentiometer resistance until the desired Q is reached. After the desired Q is attained, the trim pot resistance can be measured along with the exact resistance of the 2200-ohm resistance, and one resistor can be purchased replacing the exact ohmic value of the trim potentiometer resistance plus the 2200-ohm resistance.

Just what happens when you build these circuits and observe their response? In general, things won't work as expected the first time. The Q may be too low, or the filter may oscillate at f_0. If the center frequency is off, you should try adjusting the resistor BR to put the active filter on center frequency. The next step is to trim up the Q by adjusting the resistors R_a and R_b. You may want to use a trim pot in series with R_a in order to adjust the Q. The final step is adjusting the gain. You will probably be able to make the necessary adjustment to R_{11} without disturbing the rest of the circuit. The reason is that for high Q the gain is high and R_{11} will be much greater than R_{22}, and will have little effect on either f_0 or Q.

The Deliyannis filter is employed in filter banks, since the passive components are held to a minimum with a band-pass active filter that can attain very high Qs. One of these banks is the more or less traditional "resonator" bank which serves to impart formant structure on synthesized sounds. The second band will be a "responding" bank. This will be a 12-channel band set at approximately equal tempered positions in an upper octave. The output of this band will be rectified and will provide a control signal that is an indication of how well the input signal is aligned with the formants. In this way, the input signal can be made to respond to the formant structure.

TESTING THE DELIYANNIS CIRCUIT

A Deliyannis band-pass active filter circuit was described, and the necessary design procedure was given in the previous section.

In this section we want to give an example of the same type of filter, and to discuss the problems that occur with the Deliyannis filter during construction and testing.

The high-Q band-pass filter has a much greater sensitivity to component variations than the low-Q version. Nonetheless, the structure of the Deliyannis band-pass filter has been found empirically to be one of the best for the Qs achieved, comparing very well with the state-variable filter which requires three op amps instead of the one used with the Deliyannis design. When building a filter with a W of 50 or 100 or higher, you usually have the choice of using very precise components, or trimming the fixed resistors employed in the design with series or parallel additions, or employing trim pots. Any one of these methods will work. In the discussion that follows, we will use the second method mentioned—trimming the fixed resistors.

Suppose we need a band-pass filter with a Q of 100 and a center $f_0 = 30$ Hz. We can apply the design procedure of the previous section, and obtain the final circuit shown in Fig. 10-6. The filter in Fig. 10-6 has unity gain at the center frequency, 1 percent tolerance for the capacitor values, and 5 percent tolerance for the resistor values.

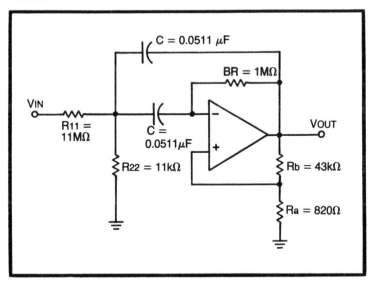

Fig. 10-6. Deliyannis band-pass active filter circuit with $Q = 100$ and a center frequency $f_0 = 30$ Hz with unity gain (courtesy of Electronotes Musical Engineering Group).

The next step is to build the filter and apply power to it. Let me caution the experimenter to solder all connections before testing to avoid spurious oscillations. Even without an input (except the DC supply voltage) there may be an output. If the Q is too high, the filter will be oscillating. For the circuit shown in Fig. 10-6, the feedback factor (a) is calculated in the following manner.

$$a = \frac{R_a}{r} = \frac{R_a}{R_a + R_b} = \frac{820}{43,820}$$

$$= 0.0187$$

It was shown in the previous section that the maximum feedback factor, beyond which oscillation will occur is

Equation 10-10

$$a_{MAX} = \frac{2}{B + 2}$$

$$= \frac{2}{100 + 2} = 0.0196$$

A 5 percent variation in the feedback resistors R_a and R_b can easily cause enough feedback voltage for oscillation. If the circuit is oscil-

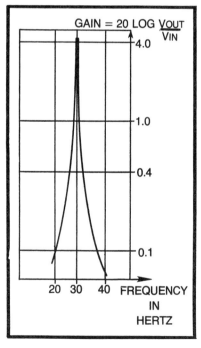

Fig. 10-7. Response for the circuit in Fig. 10-6 (courtesy of Electronotes Musical Engineering Group).

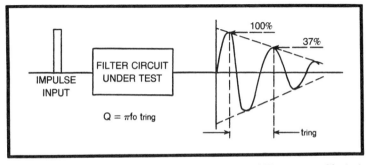

Fig. 10-8. Test circuit for measuring t_{RING} (courtesy of Electronotes Musical Engineering Group).

lating you probably can stop the oscillation by adding a couple of thousand ohms in series with the 43,000-ohm resistor R_b. Now you should have a filter which should have no output.

Next connect a sine wave signal generator at V_{IN} in Fig. 10-6, and an oscilloscope and frequency counter at V_{OUT}. There will be very little signal observed at the output terminals except around 30 Hz. A measured response curve of V_{OUT}/V_{IN} versus frequency is illustrated in Fig. 10-7. If the center frequency is not exactly on the designed value, it is a relatively simple matter to adjust either BR or R_{22} to obtain the desired center frequency. If you have to adjust BR by increasing its value or if you have to adjust R_{22} by decreasing its value, there is a chance oscillation will again start up, and a few more thousand ohms should be added in series with the 43,000-ohm resistor to stop the unwanted oscillation. With proper adjustments, the desired response function can be attained with the proper center frequency and the desired gain value.

The next requirement is to adjust the Q to the desired value. This task is not particularly easy. It requires creativity and patience because such high Qs are difficult to measure by the standard method of "center frequency divided by bandwidth." At this point we will introduce a different technique using "ringing" of the filter circuit to determine its Q.

The test circuit of Fig. 10-8 illustrates the method we will use to determine the circuit Q. A sharp impulse is applied to the input terminals of the active filter circuit. The impulse is obtained from any type of function generator that supplies an impulse function. The impulse makes the filter ring as shown by the output waveform in Fig. 10-8. Next, you must measure the time it takes a decaying sinusoid to go from 100 percent of its maximum value to 37 percent (1/e) of its maximum value. An oscilloscope with an accurate time base is essential for this measurement. Also, a storage scope would be most convenient, since the storage scope can record the ringing effect on its face after the impulse function has been applied, and the observer can casually take the proper data to measure the ringing time (t_{RING}) as shown in Fig. 10-8. A function generator that repeats the impulse function over and over will achieve the same affect as the storage scope.

Once the ring time is determined, the Q is determined by the following equation.

$$Q = \pi f_0\, t_{RING} \qquad\qquad \textbf{Equation 10-20}$$

f_0 = the center frequency of the filter in Hertz

t_{RING} = the ringing time in seconds

Using the method described, the ringing time was found to be 0.9434 seconds and the center frequency from previous discussions was found to be 29.7 Hz. Hence, a Q of 88 is calculated using Equation 10-20. This value of Q is not far from the desired value of 100. A few more ohms placed in series with the resistor $R_a = 820$ ohms should achieve a higher Q. Once this added resistance is placed in series with the 820-ohm resistor, the test procedure for measuring t_{RING} and the calculation of Q is repeated. If the second resistance value doesn't achieve the closeness of Q that you desire, keep repeating and repeating and repeating, this procedure until you are satisfied, which is a true test of patience.

The final step is to adjust the gain to the value of unity at the center frequency. Since we employed a 11,000-ohm resistor instead of the 10,600-ohm resistor design value, the gain is a little low. The R_{11} resistor was changed from 11 M to 10 M with better results. If more accurate results are required, a few hundred ohms could be put in series with the 10 M resistor.

In some applications, it may be useful to have the filter serve as an oscillator as well as a filter. When the filter oscillates, it oscillates at the center frequency of the filter. Adding a few tens of ohms up to about 100 ohms in series with the 820-ohm resistor is sure to make the circuit oscillate. The waveform will be nearly sinusoidal. The amplitude will be the full range between the positive and negative power supply limits. In fact, it is the clipping against the power supply that limits the buildup of oscillation. The value of the series resistor should be adjusted so as to maintain oscillation and minimize the distortion that will be evident as a flat spot on the peak of the waveform.

JUMP RESONANCE IN BAND-PASS ACTIVE FILTER CIRCUITS

When a band-pass filter circuit is designed, there may be limitations due to the actual design properties, such as those limitations to obtain a high-Q and high band-pass frequency at the same time. The kind of deleterious occurrence we except are losses of Q and downward shifts of resonant frequency. These occurrences we can design around by using a faster op amp, or sometimes just by treating the situation with contempt and designing a little high to

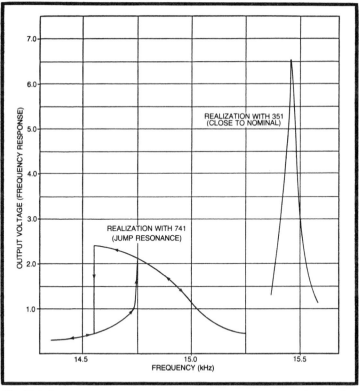

Fig. 10-9. Comparison of 351 and 741 realization of Deliyannis band-pass, $Q =$ 250 and $f_o = 15.5$ kHz (courtesy of Electronotes Musical Engineering Group).

begin with. Often enough we will be able to get satisfactory processing of audio signals in such cases. However, one case that we cannot tolerate is the case where the response makes a sudden resonance jump for no change in input signal, or as a result of a minute change in input signal.

Jump resonance was simulated by building a Deliyannis bandpass active filter circuit as shown in Fig. 10-3, and employing a type LF351 op amp (fast) and then substituting a MC1741 op amp (slow) with the results shown in Fig. 10-9. The arrows on the curves at the left show the direction of frequency change as the curve was plotted. Going up, there is a sudden jump up of substantial magnitude, and coming down, the response remains high even below the jump-up point, and then makes an even greater jump down at some lower frequency. Of course, we also see the expected downward shift in frequency, and loss of response and of circuit Q as we shift to the slower op amp, but the double region—looking somewhat like a hysteresis curve—is unexpected.

Jump resonance is explained in a paper by P. Bowron and M. A. Mohamed titled "Amplifier Nonlinearities in the Multiple-Negative-Feedback Bandpass Filter" in *International J. of Circuit Theory and Applications*, Vol. 6, pg. 121, (1978) published by J. Wiley & Sons Ltd. We will discuss some of the findings of this paper in a moment, but first we will describe the circuit used to obtain the data of Fig. 10-9.

The circuit employed was the Deliyannis Bandpass Active Filter Circuit of Fig. 10-3. The design procedure of the first section of this chapter was used setting Q at 250, and a center frequency of 16.5 kHz with a gain of about 2 so that a 5V sine wave generator would cause the output to slew to a 10V level. The LF351 with a slew rate of 13V/microsecond has no apparent trouble bringing the response up close to nominal. The slightly low frequency and peak voltage is probably due to component tolerance. The most important thing is that the curve with the LF351 is generally what we expect, while the curve with the MC1741 has a vastly different shape, and is subject to discrete *jumps in response*. Since the MC1741 has a slew rate of 0.5V/microsecond, it can only deliver the 6.5V signal level up to a frequency of a little over 12 kHz, so the MC1741 clearly has slew-rate problems if it tries to keep up with the LF351 in this application. Furthermore, if we reduce the input signal, the jump resonance goes away. All this indicates that jump resonance is a result of slew rate limiting, and indeed, this seems to be the cause.

The paper by Bowron and Mohamed obtains results which apply to the multiple feedback band-pass filter (the Deliyannis circuit without positive feedback) so we cannot directly relate the results of this paper to the Deliyannis circuit, although it is clear that qualitatively the results are the same.

VOLTAGE CONTROLLED STATE VARIABLE FILTER

The state variable filter is virtually unchallenged as a "first" filter for a general, patchable, basic synthesizer system. It gives a low-pass, band-pass, high-pass and notch response all from the same unit. The four-pole low-pass filter is a popular second filter for a patchable system, and may be the only filter in certain small prepatched synthesizers. The third most popular VCF (voltage controlled filter) would probably be the four-pole high-pass filter, which we shall consider shortly.

First, we should take a careful look at the way the state variable filter is controlled by the CA3080 OTA (operational transconductance amplifier). One implementation of the voltage-controlled integrator is shown in Fig. 10-10. The reader should note that since we are using the $(-)$ input of the CA3080, and the second op amp forms an inverting integrator, which is a positive integrator overall. The basic equation of the CA3080 is:

$$I_{OUT} = (19.2)I_{ABC}V_1 \qquad \textbf{Equation 10-21}$$

Note that the 100,000-ohm and 220-ohm resistors form a voltage divider (ideally no current enters the inputs of the CA3080, as with any op amp considered ideal) so that we have:

$$V_1 \stackrel{\sim}{=} 0.0022 \, V_{IN} \qquad \textbf{Equation 10-22}$$

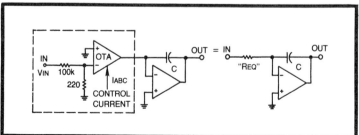

Fig. 10-10. Voltage controlled integrator and equivalent (courtesy of Electronotes Musical Engineering Group).

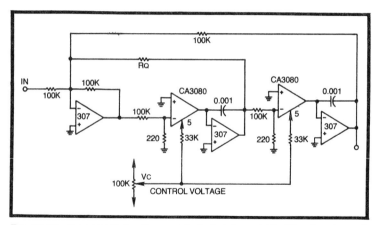

Fig. 10-11. Experimental voltage controlled state variable filter (courtesy of Electronotes Musical Engineering Group).

We can thus calculate an equivalent resistance for the OTA as follows.

$$R_{EQ} = \frac{V_{IN}}{I_{OUT}} = \left(\frac{V_1}{0.0022}\right)\left(\frac{1}{(19.2)I_{ABC}V_1}\right)$$

$$= \frac{23.7}{I_{ABC}} \qquad \text{\textbf{Equation 10-23}}$$

An example of a simple state variable VCF is shown in Fig. 10-11.

The filter shown in Fig. 10-11 provides low-pass, band-pass, and high-pass functions as shown on the experimental plot of Fig. 10-12. A notch response can be easily added by summing the high-pass and low-pass functions. A sharp notch is obtained due to a phase cancellation at the center frequency. Since pin 5 of the CA3080 remains only about one diode drop (0.7V) above the negative supply voltage (-15V), it is possible to calculate I_{ABC} as ($V_c +$ 14.3)/33,000. From this value of I_{ABC}, the value of R_{EQ} can be determined and the center frequency of the state variable is expressed by the following equation.

$$f_c = \frac{1}{2\pi R_{EQ}C} \qquad \text{\textbf{Equation 10-24}}$$

For practical electronic music circuits, the control current I_{ABC} will be supplied by an exponential current source.

The Q of the state variable filter is determined by the amount of feedback from the band-pass output back to the input. The Q can be made voltage controlled by using the OTA. A detailed discussion showing how the Q is determined can be found in Appendix A.

The main purpose of reviewing the state variable filter is to show how two or more such filters can be cascaded to give sharper filter responses. In the past, when persons have asked how to obtain a four-pole high-pass response, this cascade was suggested and several designers have used it successfully. For this report, two sections of the type shown in Fig. 10-11 were used. To sharpen the

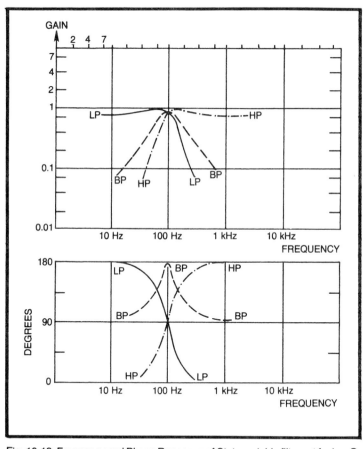

Fig. 10-12. Frequency and Phase Response of State variable filter set for low Q. Redrawn from actual experimental plot to show the different curves, LP, BP, and HP more clearly. The Phases are 180° out due to the inverting nature of the input to the filter. For example, the actual phase of the LP goes from 0° to 180° as frequency increases (courtesy of Electronotes Musical Engineering Group).

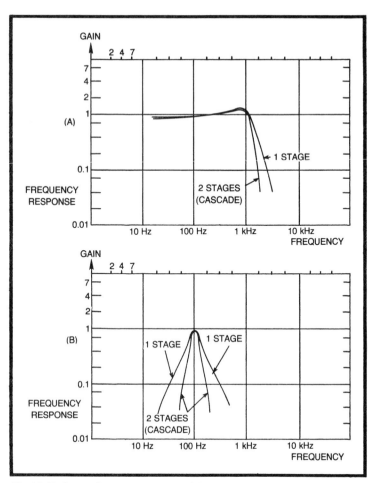

Fig. 10-13. One and two stage state variable low-pass response (A) and one and two stage state variable band-pass response with the input amplitude lower for two stages due to higher Q (B) (courtesy of Electronotes Musical Engineering Group).

response, the appropriate output of the first section is fed to the input of the second, and the corresponding output of the second section is used. The Q controls of the two sections are set to the same positions. The improved responses of the cascaded sections for low-pass and band-pass can be seen from the graphs in Fig. 10-13.

The cascade configuration results in stable high Q filter responses. While it is possible to obtain high Qs with a single state variable section, the cascade gives a better asymptotic roll-off, and since both sections are of a lower Q by themselves, the overall system is more stable. The two sections must track each other very closely. Slight mismatches can be corrected by trimming the 220-ohm resistors on one section if necessary.

Obtaining a 24-dB high-pass filter is simply a matter of cascading the two high-pass sections. Figure 10-14 shows experimental plots for the single and double state variable. A small amount of corner peaking has been added by increasing the Q slightly above its Butterworth value. Additional corner peaking can be used as shown in Fig. 10-15. This sort of corner peaking is sometimes not possible with other four-pole high-pass filters where the corner is peaked using positive feedback.

If we decide to make electronic music VCFs using this cascading technique, there are several approaches we can take. The

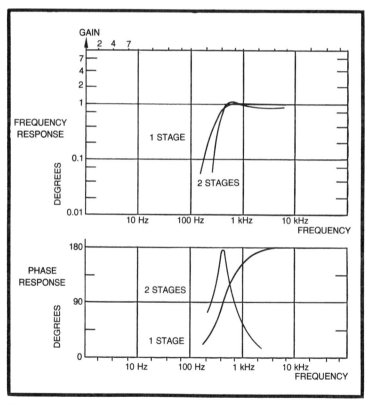

Fig. 10-14. Amplitude and phase response of state variable filter showing one and two cascaded high-pass sections (courtesy of Electronotes Musical Engineering Group).

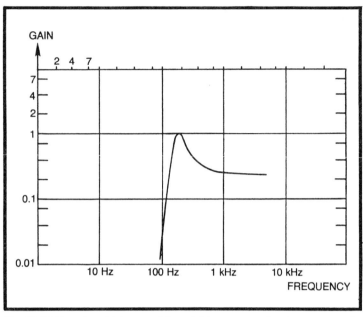

Fig. 10-15. Two stage high-pass state variable response showing corner peaking resulting from increased Q (courtesy of Electronotes Musical Engineering Group).

easiest to set up is the case where two state variable filters exist already, and can be simply patched together. When building a new filter, there are three main considerations:

☐ How is the tracking implemented? Should the two state variable sections be cascaded and hard wired to track, or should the tracking be made variable so that other types of responses are possible?

☐ Some switching arrangement is necessary. This is because to work in different modes, the input of the second section must be connected to different outputs of the first section.

☐ How should the Q be controlled? It could be by a dual pot (or if voltage controlled, the two could be controlled in parallel). Alternatively, the two Q controls could remain independent.

One possible setup is indicated in Fig. 10-16. A single exponential current source drives a four-output multiple current mirror to drive the four CA3080's (two in each filter section). Also shown is a

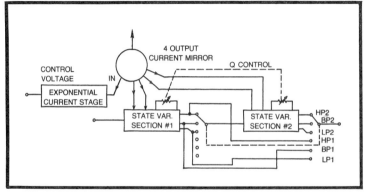

Fig. 10-16. A possible setup of a cascaded state variable filter (courtesy of Electronotes Musical Engineering Group).

switching arrangement that permits either a single or double state variable response according to the switch position. We have also shown here a Q control for the overall filter formed from a dual pot.

TRANSCONDUCTANCE CONTROLLED
LOW-PASS, HIGH-PASS, OR ALL-PASS FILTERS

An interesting active filter has been described by Dennis Colin in US Patent No. 3,805,091 assigned to ARP Instruments, Inc. The patent describes a transconductance controlled network useful as a low-pass, high-pass, or all-pass filter. The general form of the network is given in Appendix B for the interested reader. The low-pass configuration of the network is shown in Fig. 10-17. A

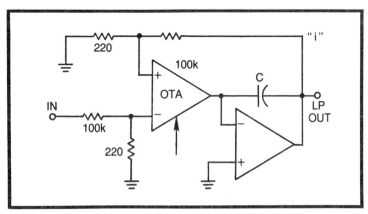

Fig. 10-17. Transconductance controlled first-order LP stage (courtesy of Electronotes Musical Engineering Group).

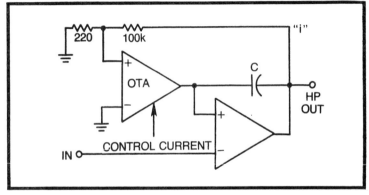

Fig. 10-18. Transconductance controlled first-order HP stage (courtesy of Electronotes Musical Engineering Group).

high-pass configuration is shown in Fig. 10-18. Note that transformation from low-pass to high-pass is basically an exchange of input and ground connections. Note also that no attenuator is used on the input of the "real" (as opposed to OTA) op amp. Bear in mind that the actual input to the OTA is the input to the attenuator marked "i".

The ease with which this single section can be converted from low-pass to high-pass suggests a simple experimenter's filter as shown in Fig. 10-19, where the unit has low-pass and high-pass inputs, and a single output. The inputs can be used simultaneously.

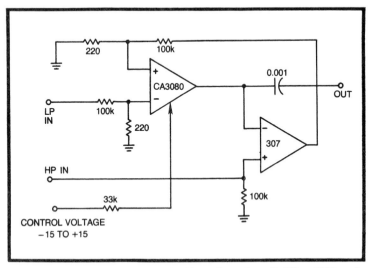

Fig. 10-19. An experimenter's circuit with configuration with LP and HP mode (courtesy of Electronotes Musical Engineering Group).

250

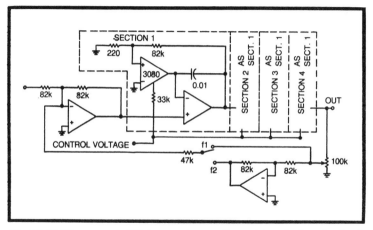

Fig. 10-20. Four cascaded high-pass stages with provisions for loop feedback (courtesy of Electronotes Musical Engineering Group).

This permits the filter to be used in a manner similar to that which could be obtained with two parallel filters and a voltage controlled mixer.

A four-pole high-pass filter analogous to the four-pole low-pass can be formed by cascading sections like those in Fig. 10-18. Such an interconnection is indicated in the experimental circuit of Fig. 10-20, where two feedback paths can be selected by means of a switch. Figure 10-21 shows the experimental measurements on the cas-

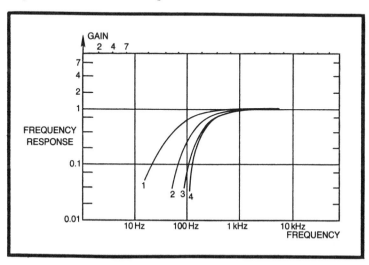

Fig. 10-21. One, two, three, and four cascaded high-pass stages (courtesy of Electronotes Musical Engineering Group).

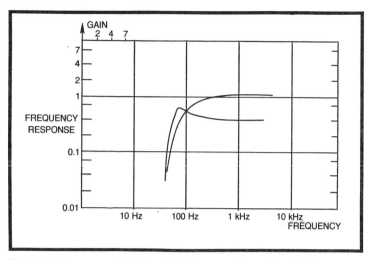

Fig. 10-22. Four cascaded first-order high-pass sections with and without corner peaking (courtesy of Electronotes Musical Engineering Group).

caded sections without any feedback. Note the sharper roll-off for the higher orders.

If corner peaking of the circuit in Fig. 10-20 is attempted, things are not as nice as they are in the low-pass case. With the switch in the f1 feedback position, corner peaking as shown in Fig. 10-22 is obtained for a loop feedback (output of the last stage to the summing node input) of 1.4. In this particular configuration, if one attempts to go beyond the feedback factor of 1.4, an oscillation of about 300 kHz is superimposed on the waveform. This is evidently due to the excessive phase shift across some of the components at 300 kHz. The fact that real op amps are being used means that the filter response is not a true high-pass and the limitations of the components cause the response to come down somewhere on the high end. Thus, the 300-kHz oscillations can be related to the desirable quadrature oscillations obtained, since the origin is basically the same. In other configurations with different components, this oscillation with the high-pass may not appear or be any problem. Indeed, the 300-kHz oscillation observed is only about 100 mV superimposed on about a 5V signal, and its frequency makes it inaudible.

The inclusion of the f2 feedback position is basically to avoid any tedious consideration of the direction of the phase shifts across the filter (we didn't know which one we would use ahead of time).

Peaking with the f2 input does occur but is not too useful since substantial shifts in the cutoff frequency (nearly two decades) do occur as feedback is increased. A feedback factor of 0.7 actually gives less slope on the original cutoff region, and a band-pass-like peak starts to form about a factor of 40 higher in frequency. This sharpens into a band-pass response when the feedback approaches 1.0. If the feedback exceeds 1.0, the circuit becomes a "tone burst generator" giving out bursts at a rate determined by the input frequency to the filter, and at a frequency that increases as feedback increases.

Appendix A
The Q of a State Variable Filter

The Q of a state variable filter depends on the amount of signal fed back from the bandpass output to the input. The most general form of the state variable filter is shown in Fig. A-1, where the network is shown in terms of two integrators and a summer. The integrator has a transfer function of $1/s$. Thus:

$$E_B = (1/s)E_H \text{ and: } E_L = (1/s)E_B = (1/s^2)E_H$$

The equation for the summer is:

$$E_H = E_{IN} + E_L + gE_B$$

Solving for the band-pass transfer function E_B/E_{IN} we get:

$$E_B/E_{IN} = \frac{s}{s^2 - gs - 1}$$

The general form of the denominator of a band-pass transfer function is (see for example J. Graeme et al, *Operational Amplifiers— Design and Applications*, McGraw-Hill (1971), pg. 286):

$s^2 + (1/Q)s + 1$ (normalized for unity frequency)

From this, we can determine that $Q = -1/g$

Experimental measurement of Q is very simple. First one varies the input frequency until the center frequency (maximum amplitude) of the band-pass is found. Next the frequency is lowered

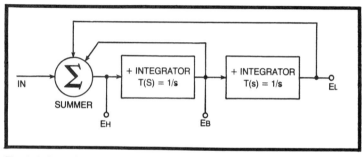

Fig. A-1. Basic form of state variable network (courtesy of Electronotes Musical Engineering Group).

until the amplitude drops to 70% the maximum value (actually 0.707....). This is the lower 3dB point: FL_{3db}. In a similar manner, the upper 3db point is found by going back through the maximum and up to a frequency where the amplitude drops to 70% on the high side. This is FH_{3db}. The Q is then:

$$Q = \frac{F_{center}}{FH_{3db} - FL_{3db}}$$

Any convenient state-variable network can be used to make the experimental test. We will, for sake of illustration use the contrived network of Fig. A-2. Note that this uses two inverting integrators A2 and A3. The two inversions cancel as far as the E_L

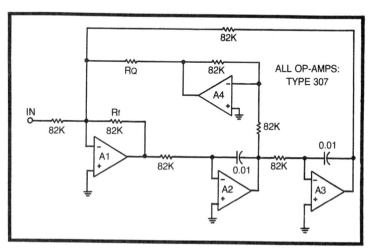

Fig. A-2. State variable network using inverter to simplify the feedback calculation (courtesy of Electronotes Musical Engineering Group).

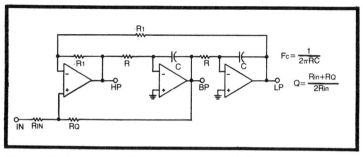

Fig. A-3. Most common configuration of state variable filter (courtesy of Electronotes Musical Engineering Group).

output is concerned. However, the E_B output is inverted, and requires the inverter A4 to look like a positive integrator in the feedback scheme. A3 is a negative summer, and this will supply the $(-)$ sign for the $-g$. In the simpler form of the state variable, the inverter is avoided by using the $(+)$ input to the summer. This will be discussed later. In the circuit of Fig. 10-11 we have only to switch the inputs to the 3080 to invert the integrator, so there is no problem. In the circuit of Fig. A2, we use the inverter so that it is very clear what the feedback factor is due to our familiarity with the summing node. The feedback is just R_f/R_Q.

From this, we can compare experimental and theoretical results. These are shown in Table A-1. Thus, we can see that the agreement is quite good.

It remains to look at some other state variable configurations. Determination of the Q will be a matter of accurately calculating the form of the gain $-g$. The most common form of the state variable and the expression for its Q are shown in Fig. A-3. Another configuration is shown in Fig. A-4. In both these, the feedback from the BP to the $+$ input of the summer is determined by a voltage divider. From that point, the first circuit has an additional gain of 2 while the

Table A-1. Experimental and Theoretical Results.

R_Q	F_{center}	FL_{3db}	FU_{3db}	$Q_{exptl.}$	$Q_{theory} = 82$ k/R_Q
56K	140 Hz	50	2 .0	0.67	0.68
100K	140 Hz	90	210	1.17	1.22
220K	140 Hz	115	170	2.55	2.68
440K	140 Hz	127	153	5.38	5.37
1 M	140 Hz	135	146	12.7	12.2

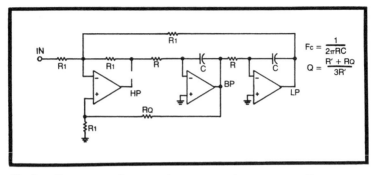

Fig. A-4. Alternative configuraton of state variable filter (courtesy of Electronotes Musical Engineering Group).

second circuit has a gain of 3. These gains are determined by considering all the input (or feedback from later stages) resistors as though they were in parallel and the ends away from the (−) input were grounded.

Appendix B
The General Transconductance Controlled Network

A general form for a transconductance network has been described by D. Colins in US Patent 3,805,091, and by David Friend at the Spring 1975 AES Convention. The general form of the network is shown in Fig. B-1.

Analysis of the network is straightforward and can be understood by an examination of the network with node voltages as marked, and then examining the following development:

$$I = (BV_{IN} - V_{OUT})sC = G_mV' = G_m(DV_{IN} + AV_{OUT})$$

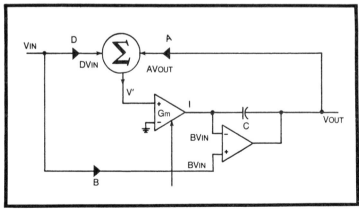

Fig. B-1. General form of the transconductance controlled network (courtesy of Electronotes Musical Engineering Group).

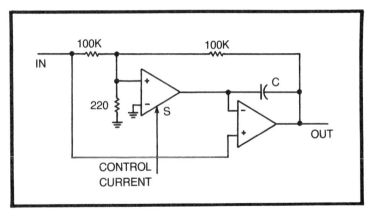

Fig. B-2. Transconductance controlled all-pass (voltage-controlled phase shifter) (courtesy Electronotes Musical Engineering Group).

which is easily solved for the transfer function:

$$V_{OUT}/V_{IN} = \frac{BsC - G_mD}{sC + G_mA}$$

When B = 0 (the + input of the op-amp is grounded), we have a low-pass filter transfer function of which the examples in the text are typical. When B = 1 and D = 0, we have the high-pass configuration discussed in the text. A final example worth considering is the all-pass network formed when B = 1 and A = D. This is an all-pass suitable for use as a voltage-controlled phase shifter. It is convenient in this case to implement the voltage summer required by simply adding currents with the 200Ω resistor, which is possible in this case because 220 is much less than 100K, and the two 100K resistors serve as current sources in this case. One implementation of the all pass is shown in Fig. B-2.

This circuit might well be the basis of a phase shift module. For a phase shift module, it is likely that substantially more phase shift than a total of 180° will be required. Thus, we would have to cascade units of the above type. The question then is one of selecting the capacitor values of the individual sections. We might for example select them so that they roll in sequence, or some other arrangement might prove musically more valauble.

Appendix C
LM108/LM208
Operational Amplifiers

The LM108 and LM208 are precision operational amplifiers having specifications a factor of ten better than FET amplifiers over a −55°C to 125°C temperature range. Selected units are available with offset voltages less than 1.0 mV and drifts less than 5μV/°C, again over the military temperature range. This makes it possible to eliminate offset adjustments, in most cases, and obtain performance approaching chopper stabilized amplifiers.

The devices operate with supply voltages from ±2V to ±20V and have sufficient supply rejection to use unregulated supplies. Although the circuit is interchangeable with and uses the same compensation as the LM101A, an alternate compensation scheme can be used to make it particularly insensitive to power supply noise and to make supply bypass capacitors unnecessary. Outstanding characteristics include:

- [ ] Maximum input bias current of 3.0 nA over temperature
- [ ] Offset current less than 400 pA over temperature
- [ ] Supply current of only 300μA, even in saturation
- [ ] Guaranteed drift characteristics

The low current error of the LM108 series makes possible many designs that are not practical with conventional amplifiers. In fact, it operates from 10 MΩ source resistances, introducing less error than devices like the 709 with 10 kΩ sources. Integrators with

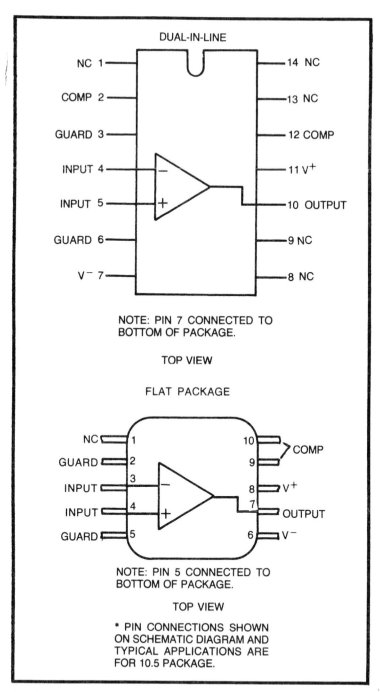

Fig. C-1. Connection diagrams.

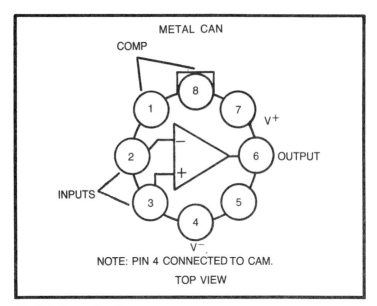

Fig. C-2. Connection diagram.

drifts less than 500μV/sec and analog time delays in excess of one hour can be made using capacitors no larger than 1 μF.

The LM208 is identical to the LM108, except that the LM208 has its performance guaranteed over a $-25°$C to 85°C temperature range, instead of $-55°$C to 125°C.

DEFINITION OF TERMS

INPUT OFFSET VOLTAGE: That voltage which must be applied between the input terminals through two equal resistances to obtain zero output voltage.

INPUT OFFSET CURRENT: The difference in the currents into the two input terminals when the output is at zero.

INPUT VOLTAGE RANGE: The range of voltages on the input terminals for which the offset specifications apply.

INPUT BIAS CURRENT: The average of the two input currents.

COMMON MODE REJECTION RATIO: The ratio of the input voltage range to the peak-to-peak change in input offset voltage over this range.

Table C-1. Electrical Characteristics.

PARAMETER	CONDITIONS	MIN	TYP	MAX	UNITS
INPUT OFFSET VOLTAGE (NOTE 5)	$T_A = 25°C$		0.7	2.0	mV
INPUT OFFSET CURRENT	$T_A = 25°C$		0.05	0.2	nA
INPUT BIAS CURRENT	$T_A = 25°C$		0.8	2.0	nA
INPUT RESISTANCE	$T_1 = 25°C$	30	70		mΩ
SUPPLY CURRENT	$T_A = 25°C$		0.3	0.6	mA
LARGE SIGNAL VOLTAGE GAIN	$T_A = 25°C$, $V_S = ±15V$ $V_{OUT} = ±10V$, $R_L \geqslant 10$ kΩ	50	300		V/mV
INPUT OFFSET VOLTAGE (NOTE 5)				3.0	mV
AVERAGE TEMPERATURE COEFFICIENT OF INPUT OFFSET VOLTAGE (NOTE 5)			3.0	15	μV/°C
INPUT OFFSET CURRENT				0.4	nA
AVERAGE TEMPERATURE COEFFICIENT OF INPUT OFFSET CURRENT			0.5	2.5	pA/°C
INPUT BIAS CURRENT				3.0	nA
SUPPLY CURRENT	$T_A = +125°C$		0.15	0.4	mA
LARGE SIGNAL VOLTAGE GAIN	$V_S = ±15V$, $V_{OUT} = ±10V$ $R_L \geqslant 10$ kΩ	25			V/mV
OUTPUT VOLTAGE SWING	$V_S = ±15V$, $R_L = 10$kΩ	±13	±14		V
INPUT VOLTAGE RANGE	$V_S = ±15V$	±13.5			V
COMMON MODE REJECTION RATIO		85	100		dB
SUPPLY VOLTAGE REJECTION RATIO		80	96		dB

Note 1: The maximum junction temperature of the LM107 is 150*C, while that of the LM208 is 100*C. For operating at elevated temperatures, devices in the TO-5 package must be derated base on a thermal resistance of 150*CPW, junction to ambient, or 45* C/W, junction to case. For the flat package, the derating is based on a thermal resistance of 185° C/W when mounted on a 1/16-inch-thick epoxy glass board with ten, 0.03-inch-wide, 2-ounce copper conductors. The thermal resistance of the dual-in-line package is 100° C/W, junction to ambient.

Note 2: The inputs are shunted with back-to-back diodes for overlvoltage protection. Therefore, excessive current will flow if a differential input voltage in excess of 1V is applied between the inputs unless some limiting resistance is used.

Note 3: For supply voltages less than ±15V, the absolute maximum input voltage is equal to the supply voltage.

Note 4: These specifications apply for $±5V \leqslant VS \leqslant ±20V$ and $−55°C \leqslant TA \leqslant 125°C$, unless otherwise specified. With the LM208, however, all temperature specifications are limited to $−25°C \leqslant TA \leqslant 85°C$.

Note 5: The LM108A has a guaranteed offset voltage less than 0.5 mV at 25°C and 1.0 mV for $−55°C \leqslant TA \leqslant 125°C$ and VS $=±15V$. The average temperature coefficient of input offset voltage is quaranteed to be less than 5 μV/°C for these same conditions.

ABSOLUTE MAXIMUM RATINGS

Supply Voltage	±20V
Power Dissipation (Note 1)	500 mW
Differential Input Current (Note 2)	±10mA
Input Voltage (Note 3)	±15V
Output Short-Circuit Duration	Indefinite
Operating Temperature Range LM108	−55°C to 125°C
LM208	−25°C to 85°C
Storage Temperature Range	−65°C to 150°C
Lead Temperature (Soldering, 60 sec)	300°C

INPUT RESISTANCE: The ratio of the change in input voltage to the change in input current on either input with the other grounded.

SUPPLY CURRENT: The current required from the power supply to operate the amplifier with no load and the output at zero.

OUTPUT VOLTAGE SWING: The peak output voltage swing, referred to zero, that can be obtained without clipping.

LARGE-SIGNAL VOLTAGE GAIN: The ratio of the output voltage swing to the change in input voltage required to drive the output from zero to this voltage.

POWER SUPPLY REJECTION: The ratio of the change in input offset voltage to the change in power supply voltages producing it.

Appendix D
MC1741/MC1741C
Operational Amplifiers

INTERNALLY COMPENSATED, HIGH
PERFORMANCE MONOLITHIC OPERATIONAL AMPLIFIER

...designed for use as a summing amplifier, integrator, or amplifier with operating characteristics as a function of the external feedback components.

☐ No Frequency Compensation Required
☐ Short-Circuit Protection
☐ Offset Voltage Null Capability
☐ Wide Common-Mode and Differential Voltage Ranges
☐ Low-Power Consumption
☐ No Latch Up
☐ Same Pin Configuration as the MC1709

Table D-1. Maximum Ratings. (TA = +25°C Unless Otherwise Noted).

Rating	Symbol	MC1741C	MC1741	Unit
Power Supply Voltage	V_{CC}	+18	+22	Vdc
	V_{EE}	-18	-22	Vdc
Input Differential Voltage	V_{ID}	±30		Volts
Input Common Mode Voltage (Note 1)	V_{ICM}	±15		Volts
Output Short Circuit Duration (Note 2)	t_S	Continuous		
Operating Ambient Temperature Range	T_A	0 to +70	-55 to +125	°C
Storage Temperature Range	T_{stg}			°C
Metal, Flat and Ceramic Packages		-65 to +150		
Plastic Packages		-55 to +125		
Junction Temperature Range	T_J			°C
Metal and Ceramic Packages		175		
Plastic Packages		150		

Note 1.   For supply voltages less than ± 15 V, the absolute maximum input voltage is equal to the supply voltage.

Note 2.   Supply voltage equal to or less than 15 V.

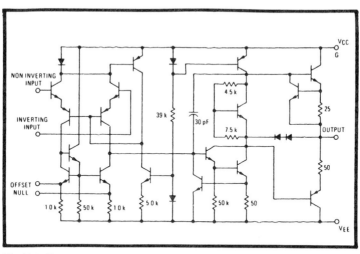

Fig. D-1. Equivalent circuit schematic.

Table D-2. Thermal Information (continued on page 269).

The maximum power consumption an integrated circuit can tolerate at a given operating ambient temperature, can be found from the equation:

$$PD_{(TA)} = \frac{T_{J(max)} - T_A}{R_{\theta JA}(Typ)}$$

Where: $PD_{(TA)}$ = Power Dissipation allowable at a given operating ambient temperature. This must be greater than the sum of the products of the supply voltages and supply currents at the worst case operating condition.

$T_{J(max)}$ = Maximum Operating Junction Temperature as listed in the Maximum Ratings Section

T_A = Maximum Desired Operating Ambient Temperature

$R_{\theta JA}(Typ)$ = Typical Thermal Resistance Junction to Ambient

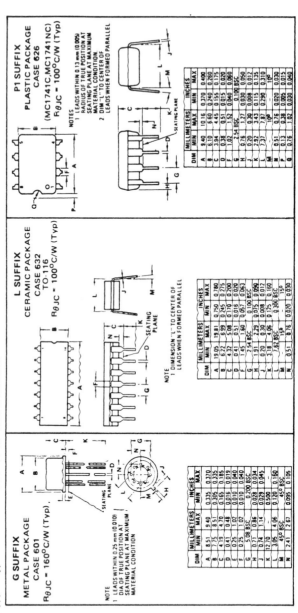

Table D-2. Thermal Information (continued from page 268).

P2 SUFFIX
PLASTIC PACKAGE
CASE 646
(MC1741C, MC1741NC)
$R_{\theta JC} = 100°C/W$ (Typ)

NOTES:
1. LEADS WITHIN 0.13 mm (0.005) RADIUS OF TRUE POSITION AT SEATING PLANE AT MAXIMUM MATERIAL CONDITION
2. DIMENSION "L" TO CENTER OF LEADS WHEN FORMED PARALLEL

DIM	MILLIMETERS MIN	MILLIMETERS MAX	INCHES MIN	INCHES MAX
A	18.16	18.80	0.715	0.740
B	6.10	6.60	0.240	0.260
C	4.06	4.57	0.160	0.180
D	0.38	0.51	0.015	0.020
F	1.02	1.52	0.040	0.060
G	2.54 BSC		0.100 BSC	
H	1.32	1.83	0.052	0.072
J	0.20	0.30	0.008	0.012
K	2.92	3.43	0.115	0.135
L	7.37	7.87	0.290	0.310
M	—	10°	—	10°
N	0.51	1.02	0.020	0.040
P	0.13	0.38	0.005	0.015
Q	0.51	0.76	0.020	0.030

F SUFFIX
CERAMIC PACKAGE
CASE 606-04
TO-91
$R_{\theta JC} = 100°C/W$ (Typ)

NOTE:
1. LEADS WITHIN 0.25 mm (0.010) TOTAL OF TRUE POSITION AT MAXIMUM MATERIAL CONDITION (AT BODY)

All JEDEC dimensions and notes apply

DIM	MILLIMETERS MIN	MILLIMETERS MAX	INCHES MIN	INCHES MAX
A	6.10	7.36	0.240	0.290
B	6.10	6.60	0.240	0.260
C	0.762	1.77	0.030	0.070
D	0.254	0.482	0.010	0.019
F	0.077	0.152	0.003	0.006
G	1.15	1.39	0.045	0.055
H	0.127	0.889	0.005	0.035
K	1.78	—	0.070	—
R	—	0.381	—	0.015

U SUFFIX
CERAMIC PACKAGE
CASE 693
$R_{\theta JC} = 100°C/W$ (Typ)

NOTES:
1. LEADS WITHIN 0.13 mm (0.005) RAD OF TRUE POSITION AT SEATING PLANE AT MAXIMUM MATERIAL CONDITION
2. DIMENSION "L" TO CENTER OF LEADS WHEN FORMED PARALLEL.

DIM	MILLIMETERS MIN	MILLIMETERS MAX	INCHES MIN	INCHES MAX
A	9.91	10.92	0.390	0.430
B	6.22	6.99	0.245	0.275
C	4.32	5.08	0.170	0.200
D	0.41	0.51	0.016	0.020
F	1.40	1.65	0.055	0.065
G	2.54 BSC		0.100 BSC	
H	1.14	1.65	0.045	0.065
J	0.20	0.30	0.008	0.012
K	3.18	4.06	0.125	0.160
L	7.37	7.87	0.290	0.310
M	—	15°	—	15°
N	0.51	1.02	0.020	0.040

269

Table D-3. Electrical Characteristics.

$(V_{CC} = +15\ V,\ V_{EE} = -15\ V,\ T_A = 25°C$ unless otherwise noted)

Characteristic	Symbol	MC1741			MC1741C			Unit
		Min	Typ	Max	Min	Typ	Max	
Input Offset Voltage ($R_S \leqslant 10\ k$)	V_{IO}	–	1.0	5.0	–	2.0	6.0	mV
Input Offset Current	I_{IO}	–	20	200	–	20	200	nA
Input Bias Current	I_{IB}	–	80	500	–	80	500	nA
Input Resistance	r_i	0.3	2.0	–	0.3	2.0	–	MΩ
Input Capacitance	C_i	–	1.4	–	–	1.4	–	pF
Offset Voltage Adjustment Range	V_{IOR}	–	±15	–	–	±15	–	mV
Common Mode Input Voltage Range	V_{ICR}	±12	±13	–	±12	±13	–	V
Large Signal Voltage Gain ($V_O = \pm10\ V,\ R_L \geqslant 2.0\ k$)	A_v	50	200	–	20	200	–	V/mV
Output Resistance	r_o	–	75	–	–	75	–	Ω
Common Mode Rejection Ratio ($R_S \leqslant 10\ k$)	CMRR	70	90	–	70	90	–	dB
Supply Voltage Rejection Ratio ($R_S \leqslant 10\ k$)	PSRR	–	30	150	–	30	150	μV/V
Output Voltage Swing	V_O							V
($R_L \geqslant 10\ k$)		±12	±14	–	±12	±14	–	
($R_L \geqslant 2\ k$)		±10	±13	–	±10	±13	–	
Output Short-Circuit Current	I_{os}	–	20	–	–	20	–	mA
Supply Current	I_D	–	1.7	2.8	–	1.7	2.8	mA
Power Consumption	P_C	–	50	85	–	50	85	mW
Transient Response (Unity Gain — Non-Inverting)								
($V_I = 20\ mV,\ R_L \geqslant 2\ k,\ C_L \leqslant 100\ pF$) Rise Time	t_{TLH}	–	0.3	–	–	0.3	–	μs
($V_I = 20\ mV,\ R_L \geqslant 2\ k,\ C_L \leqslant 100\ pF$) Overshoot	os	–	15	–	–	15	–	%
($V_I = 10\ V,\ R_L \geqslant 2\ k,\ C_L \leqslant 100\ pF$) Slew Rate	SR	–	0.5	–	–	0.5	–	V/μs

Table D-4. Electrical Characteristics.

(V$_{CC}$ = +15 V, V$_{EE}$ = –15 V, T$_A$ = *T$_{high}$ to T$_{low}$ unless otherwise noted)

Characteristic	Symbol	MC1741			MC1741C			Unit
		Min	Typ	Max	Min	Typ	Max	
Input Offset Voltage (R$_S$ ≤ 10 kΩ)	V$_{IO}$	–	1.0	6.0	–	–	7.5	mV
Input Offset Current (T$_A$ = 125°C) (T$_A$ = –55°C) (T$_A$ = 0°C to +70°C)	I$_{IO}$	– – –	7.0 85 –	200 500 –	– – –	– – –	– – 300	nA
Input Bias Current (T$_A$ = 125°C) (T$_A$ = –55°C) (T$_A$ = 0°C to +70°C)	I$_{IB}$	– – –	30 300 –	500 1500 –	– – –	– – –	– – 800	nA
Common Mode Input Voltage Range	V$_{ICR}$	±12	±13	–	–	–	–	V
Common Mode Rejection Ratio (R$_S$ ≤ 10 k)	CMRR	70	90	–	–	–	–	dB
Supply Voltage Rejection Ratio (R$_S$ ≤ 10 k)	PSRR	–	30	150	–	–	–	µV/V
Output Voltage Swing (R$_L$ ≥ 10 k) (R$_L$ ≥ 2 k)	V$_O$	±12 ±10	±14 ±13	– –	±10 –	±13 –	– –	V
Large Signal Voltage Gain (R$_L$ ≥ 2 k, V$_{out}$ = ±10 V)	A$_v$	25	–	–	15	–	–	V/mV
Supply Currents (T$_A$ = +125°C) (T$_A$ = –55°C)	I$_D$	– –	1.5 2.0	2.5 3.3	– –	– –	– –	mA
Power Consumption (T$_A$ = +125°C) (T$_A$ = –55°C)	P$_C$	– –	45 60	75 100	– –	– –	– –	mW

*T$_{high}$ = 125°C for MC1741 and 70°C for MC1741C
T$_{low}$ = –55°C for MC1741 and 0°C for MC1741C

Table D-5. Noise Characteristics (continued on page 273).

(Applies for MC1741N and MC1741NC only, $V_{CC} = +15$ V, $V_{EE} = -15$ V, $T_A = +25°C$)

Characteristic	Symbol	MC1741N			MC1741NC			Unit
		Min	Typ	Max	Min	Typ	Max	
Burst Noise (Popcorn Noise) (BW = 1.0 Hz to 1.0 kHz, t = 10 s, $R_S = 100$ k) (Input Referenced)	E_n	—	—	20	—	—	20	μ V/peak

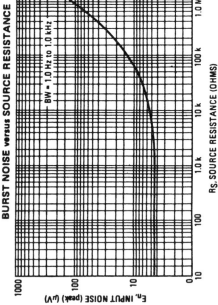

RMS NOISE versus SOURCE RESISTANCE

BURST NOISE versus SOURCE RESISTANCE

Table D-5. Noise Characteristics (continued from page 272).

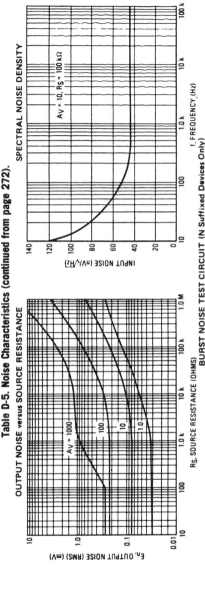

OUTPUT NOISE versus SOURCE RESISTANCE

SPECTRAL NOISE DENSITY

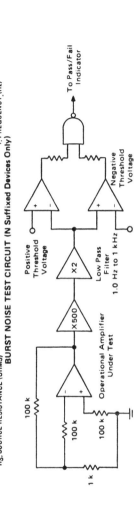

BURST NOISE TEST CIRCUIT (N Suffixed Devices Only)

For applications where low noise performance is essential, selected devices denoted by an N suffix are offered. These units have been 100% tested for burst noise pulses on a special noise test system. Unlike conventional peak reading or RMS meters, this system was especially designed to provide the quick response time essential to burst (popcorn) noise testing.

The test time employed is 10 seconds and the 20 μV peak limit refers to the operational amplifier input thus eliminating errors in the closed-loop gain factor of the operational amplifier under test.

273

Table D-6. Typical Characteristics (continued on page 275).

(V_{CC} = +15 Vdc, V_{EE} = -15 Vdc, T_A ± +25°C unless otherwise noted).

POWER BANDWIDTH
(LARGE SIGNAL SWING versus FREQUENCY)

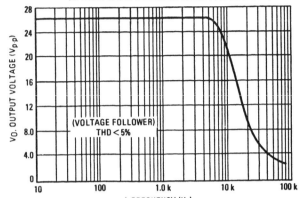

POSITIVE OUTPUT VOLTAGE SWING
versus LOAD RESISTANCE

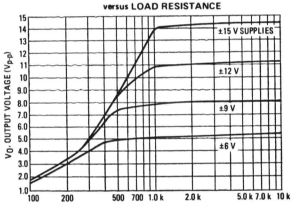

OUTPUT VOLTAGE SWING versus
LOAD RESISTANCE (Single Supply Operation)

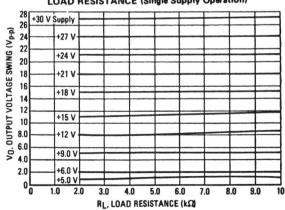

OPEN LOOP FREQUENCY RESPONSE

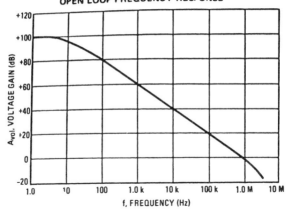

NEGATIVE OUTPUT VOLTAGE SWING
versus LOAD RESISTANCE

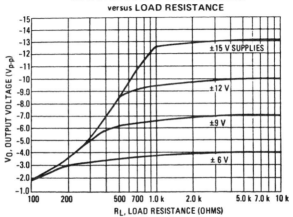

SINGLE SUPPLY INVERTING AMPLIFIER

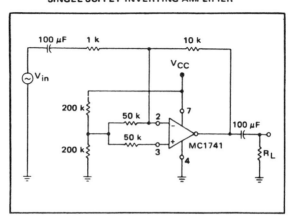

Table D-6. Typical characteristics (continued from page 275).

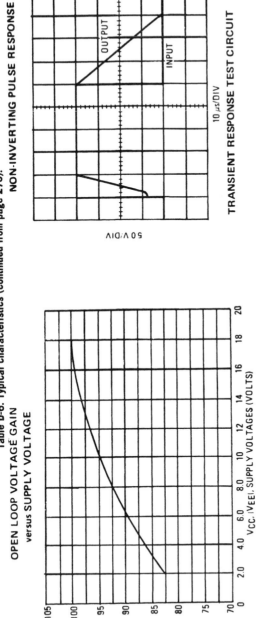

NON-INVERTING PULSE RESPONSE

OUTPUT

INPUT

50 V/DIV

10 μs/DIV

TRANSIENT RESPONSE TEST CIRCUIT

To Scope (Input)

To Scope (Output)

C_L

R_L

OPEN LOOP VOLTAGE GAIN versus SUPPLY VOLTAGE

A_V, VOLTAGE GAIN (dB)

$V_{CC}, |V_{EE}|$, SUPPLY VOLTAGES (VOLTS)

Circuit diagrams utilizing Motorola products are included as a means of illustrating typical semiconductor applications; consequently, complete information sufficient for construction purposes is not necessarily given. The information has been carefully checked and is believed to be entirely reliable. However, no responsibility is assumed for inaccuracies. Furthermore, such information does not convey to the purchaser of the semiconductor devices described any license under the patent rights of Motorola Inc. or others.

276

Additional Reading

LINEAR CIRCUITS DISCRETE AND INTEGRATED *by Rodney Faber; Merrill.*

INTRODUCTION TO NETWORK ANALYSIS *by Ben Zeines; Prentice Hall.*

TRANSIENTS IN ELECTRIC CIRCUITS *by Lago and Waidelich; Ronald Press.*

INTRODUCTION TO AUTOMATIC CONTROL SYSTEMS *by Robert Clark; John Wiley and Sons.*

ACTIVE FILTERS: LUMPED, DISTRIBUTED, INTEGRATED, DIGITAL, AND PARAMETRIC *by Lawrence Huelsman; McGraw-Hill.*

ACTIVE FILTER COOKBOOK *by Don Lancaster; Sams.*

HANDBOOK OF INTEGRATED CIRCUIT OPERATIONAL AMPLIFIERS *by George Rutkowski; Prentice Hall.*

APPLICATION OF LINEAR INTEGRATED CIRCUITS *by Eugene Hnatek; John Wiley and Sons.*

INTRODUCTION TO OPERATIONAL AMPLIFIER THEORYANDAPPLICATIONS*by Wait,Huelsman,and Korn; McGraw-Hill.*

INTEGRATED CIRCUITS AND SEMICONDUCTOR DEVICES: THEORY AND APPLICATIONS *by Deboo and Burrous; McGraw-Hill.*

DIGITAL INTEGRATED CIRCUITS AND OPERATIONAL AMPLIFIER AND OPTOELECTRONIC CIRCUIT DESIGN *by Texas Instruments Incorporated; McGraw-Hill.*

INTRODUCTION TO FILTER THEORY *by David Johnson; Prentice Hall.*

MANUAL OF ACTIVE FILTER DESIGN *by Hilburn and Johnson; McGraw-Hill.*

ACTIVE FILTER DESIGN *by Arthur B. Williams; Artech House, Inc.*

THE DESIGN OF ACTIVE FILTERS, WITH EXPERIMENTS *by Howard M. Berlin; Bugbook, E & L Instruments*

AUDIO HANDBOOK *by National Semiconductor Corporation; National Semiconductor.*

Index